JEWISH L...
CRACOW
1918–1939

JEWISH LIFE IN CRACOW
1918-1939

Sean Martin

FOREWORD
Antony Polonsky
Brandeis University, Waltham, MA

VALLENTINE MITCHELL
LONDON • PORTLAND, OR

First published in 2004 in Great Britain by
VALLENTINE MITCHELL
Suite 314, Premier House
112–114 Station Road,
Edgware, Middlesex MA8 7BJ

and in the United States of America by
FRANK CASS PUBLISHERS
c/o ISBS, 5804 58th Avenue, Suite 300
Portland, Oregon, 97213-3786

Website: www.vmbooks.com

British Library Cataloguing in Publication Data

Martin, Sean
  Jewish life in Cracow, 1918–1939
  1. Jews – Poland – Krakow – Ethnic identity 2. Jews – Poland – Krakow – Social life
  and customs – 20th century 3. Jews – Poland – Krakow – Social conditions –
  20th century 4. Jews – Poland – Krakow – History– 20th century 5. Jews – Cultural
  assimilation– Poland – Krakow 6. Nationalism – Poland – History – 20th century
  7. Krakow (Poland) – Ethnic relations 8. Poland – social life and customs – 1918–1945
  I. Title
  305.8'924'04386

ISBN 0-85303-507-5 (cloth)
ISBN 0-85303-510-5 (paper)

Library of Congress Cataloging in Publication Data

Martin, Sean
  Jewish life in Cracow, 1918–1939/Sean Martin
    p. cm.
  Includes bibliographical references (p.) and index.
  ISBN 0-85303-507-5 (cloth) (invalid) 0-85303-510-5 (pbk)
    1. Jews – Poland – Krakow – Identity. 2. Jews – Poland – Civilization – 20th century.
  3. Krâkaw (Poland)–Ethnic relations. I. Title.

  DS135.P62K68364 2003
  305.892'4043862'09042–dc22

                                                                    2003057608

Typeset in 11/13pt Palatino by FiSH Books, London WC1
Printed in Great Britain by
MPG Books Ltd, Bodmin, Cornwall

For Jarosław R. Romaniuk
and
in memory of my parents, Richard and Rose Marie Martin

Contents

List of Plates

(between pages 142 and 143)

1. Flag bearers of the Hebrew High School on a school march in Cracow, Poland, 1938 (Beth Hatefutsoth Photo Archive, Tel Aviv)
2. Members of the YMCA, Cracovia and Makkabi swimming teams, winter tournament in Cracow, 1937 (Muzeum m. Krakowa)
3. Ping-pong players of the Ha-Gibor sports club, 1936 (Muzeum m. Krakowa)
4. The principal of the Hebrew gymnasium, Hirsch Scherer, receiving the school flag from the gymnasium director, Dr Chaim Hilfstein, Cracow, 1929 (Beth Hatefutsoth Photo Archive, courtesy of Natan Gross, Israel)
5. Teachers at the Hebrew gymnasium, Cracow, around 1935. From right to left: Waldman, N. Mifelew, Mordecai Gebirtig, Sperber (Beth Hatefutsoth Photo Archive, Tel Aviv, courtesy of Nahum Manor, Israel)
6. Hanukkah play performed at the Hebrew gymnasium, Cracow, 1930 (Beth Hatefutsoth Photo Archive, Tel Aviv, courtesy of Natan Gross, Israel)
7. Members of the Hebrew school orchestra during the Lag Ba'Omer celebrations in the Makkabi playing field, Cracow, 1935 (Beth Hatefutsoth Photo Archive, Tel Aviv, courtesy of Natan Gross, Israel)
8. Graduation photo of students of Dr Chaim Hilfstein, Hebrew gymnasium, Cracow, 1936/37 (Beth Hatefutsoth Photo Archive, Tel Aviv, courtesy of Natan Gross, Israel)
9. The Temple synagogue, Miodowa Street, around 1925 (Muzeum m. Krakowa)
10. The Temple synagogue, Miodowa Street, around 1925 (Muzeum m. Krakowa)
11. The Old Synagogue/Alta Shul/Stara Synagoga, interior, 1925 (Muzeum m. Krakowa)

Foreword

THE OLD SYNAGOGUE

Quiet
Empty
A gold chandelier glitters
Like the eye of a fox

An invisible rabbi
Sings without a care
His song ascends slowly
Like smoke

A youth with peyes
Courageous and unbowed
Smiles from a picture
He wipes the drops of blood from his forehead

My grandfathers
Nod to me from the bimah
They don't yet know that the crown
Will fall on their heads

Covered by a talles
With a silver crown on my lips
I cry out
I call
But no-one hears me

Szeroka Street1
Is ever narrower

You won't ever be able to squeeze in there

Julian Kornhauser

---

1. Literally 'Broad Street', the street on which the Old Synagogue is located
   and the heart of Jewish Cracow.

This book deals with an important and somewhat neglected subject. Cracow was one of the six largest Jewish communities in Poland in the inter-war years (the others were Warsaw, Vilna, Łódź, Białystok and Lwów). It had a Jewish population of around 60,000, which made up just over a quarter of the population of the town, and the relations of this community to the majority took a different form from that in the other major urban centres. The community was much more polonized than those in the towns of the former Tsarist Empire (Warsaw, Vilna, Łódź, Białystok) and the Polish–Jewish interaction was less inflamed than in Lwów, which was the scene of a serious outbreak of anti-Jewish violence in late 1918 provoked by the Jews' attempt to remain neutral in the Polish–Ukrainian conflict over the former eastern part of Galicia. Although old-style assimilation, as advocated by people such as Adolf Gross and his Klub Niezawisłych Ędów (Party of Independent Jews) declined in importance in inter-war Cracow, the community leadership tried to achieve a synthesis between a modern Jewish national or ethnic identity and loyalty to the Polish state. There are few studies of the unique place that Cracow filled in the history of inter-war Polish Jewry, and Sean Martin's book thus fills an important gap.

He explores in detail the specific features of Jewish life in Cracow. Among these was the existence of a daily Polish-language newspaper intended for Jews, a consequence of the tense relations between Poles and Jews that developed when Poland was emerging as an independent state. Many acculturated Jews felt that Polish society did not respond adequately to manifestations of anti-Jewish violence and anti-Semitism. It was anti-Semitic incidents in Cracow that led to the establishment of *Nowy Dziennik* in 1918, and Martin describes well the special role this newspaper, like *Chwila* in Lwów and *Nasz Przeglàd* in Warsaw, played in Cracow Jewish life. It was non-party Zionist but also committed to finding an appropriate place for Jews in Polish society, and saw its role as a double one: that of satisfying its nationally conscious Polish-speaking Jewish audience and of interpreting Jewish society to the Poles.

Other chapters describe the response of the more religious and less acculturated sections of the community to the growing acculturation and Polonization of Cracow Jewry and of those circles that wanted to establish a modern Yiddish-based culture here. Much attention is paid to young people. One chapter describes how Jewish young people in Cracow (pre-teens to late adolescents), even those educated in the state educational system, developed a strongly Jewish, often Zionist identity, which was, however, expressed, above all, in the Polish language, a pattern that would probably have been duplicated in Poland as a whole had the war not cut short the process of Polonization that was proceeding elsewhere though at a slower pace. This identity was combined with a sense of the need to foster conditions that would favour the coexistence of the different ethnic groups in the new Poland. Another examines the extensive network of private Jewish schools in Cracow. Although the great majority of Jewish primary schoolchildren were educated in the state system, the majority of those in secondary education attended Jewish private schools, whether Zionist, Orthodox or secular. Martin's analysis of the functioning of these schools is based on memoir material and the reports of the Polish school inspectorate, and his conclusion contrasts with other more, pessimistic, assessments of the situation of the Jews in inter-war Poland. In his words:

> ...none of these schools, not even the most traditional, was immune to the influence of the larger Polish community. Each school confronted this influence in its own way... They provided a number of ways Jews could participate in a larger Jewish community. None of these, from sports clubs to theatre societies, was isolated from participation in the majority culture around them. (pp. 189–90)

A final chapter describes the large number of Jewish cultural organizations – academic, professional, theatrical, social and sporting – that the community produced.

The book thus provides a detailed and nuanced picture of a Jewish community whose evolution was rather different from that of those in other large Polish towns. That vibrant and creative community was often deeply divided and riven by controversy, as Martin demonstrates. But beyond these divisions, there was a sense of higher purpose. This is well articulated by one of the most distinguished surviving Cracow Jews, Rafael Scharf:

The community was fragmented and torn by internal strife, but there was also a sense of sharing a common fate that transcended social and political differences. There was a marked spirituality even among the non-religious, a response to what was felt to be the Jewish ethos, a deeply ingrained universal conviction that beyond the daily sweat and strife, men had to aspire to higher things.[2]

Cracow Jewry no longer exists. A small group of Jews is valiantly trying to preserve the remnants of Jewish life in the city. Much has also been done to preserve the monuments of the Jewish past and to study its history. The annual Festival of Jewish Culture organized by the redoubtable (and non-Jewish) Makuch brothers attracts large audiences. And yet one cannot help feel a certain sadness at reading of the achievements of the 60,000 Jews of Cracow, the overwhelming majority of whom were murdered in the genocide carried out by the Nazis. This sadness is well articulated in the poem 'Cracow Autumn', by another Cracow Jewish survivor, Natan Gross:

At this time of year chestnuts fall from the trees in Cracow.
But no one any longer hangs them in a *sukkah*.
Wawel stands as it always has. But at the dragon's cave
There are no Jewish children.

The leaves cover the ground with a thick blanket
Near the University, as always a favourite meeting place for lovers.
But today the student corporations are not to be seen
And no-one cries 'Beat the Jews', because there are no Jews.

The tower of the Virgin's Church still stands, so does the Sukiennice
And Mickiewicz still looks out over the Rynek.
The same houses, shops, churches and streets.
Only on Orzeszkowa you won't find *Nowy Dziennik* . . .

There is no more *Dziennik*, there are no more Jews
In Kazimierz the ghosts of the past still walk.
The Old Synagogue is falling down from age
And perhaps from sadness and shame . . .

We gather like the chestnuts on the Planty of Cracow
We thread a chain of memory longer than slavery;
Our idyllic Cracow Jewish childhood,
Days of struggle and exaltation, days youth and pranks,
Days of love, days of happiness, days of disaster, days of sadness.
Who knows as well as you , you Cracow streets,
What once pained us, what still pains us –
Our Jewish fate.

At this season, the chestnut trees are wet from the rain in Cracow
It is already autumn on the Planty and winter in our hearts
Darkness falls. It is time to return. The gates are closing.
It is slipping away, my unforgettable Cracow,
That Cracow which is no more.

Antony Polonsky
2004

Acknowledgements

Researching the Jewish history of Cracow and writing this book fulfils personal and professional goals, and I am very grateful to all those who have helped me finish the project. Michael Berkowitz first suggested that I examine the Jewish history of Cracow, and I am thankful for that suggestion and all his later advice. Irina Livezeanu, Katherine David-Fox and Eve Levin read and commented thoroughly on an earlier version of the text, and their support and advice have long been vital to my continuing efforts to learn more about the history of Eastern Europe.

Most of the research for this work was completed in Cracow and Warsaw, where Polish scholars of Judaic studies generously offered advice in navigating Polish archives and provided me with many opportunities to discuss my work. Annamaria Orla-Bukowska has always acted as a wonderful guide to Cracow and to Polish academia. Adam Kaźmierczyk and Michał Galas always gave me a warm welcome in Cracow. Anna Ciałowicz introduced me to the Jewish community in Poland and remains an admirable example of dedication to the study of Jewish culture. Mirosława Bułat and Krystyna Samsonowska graciously shared their studies on the Jewish history of Cracow and so made my initial research much easier. Joanna Wiszniewicz and Andrzej Żbikowski introduced me to the rich collections of the Jewish Historical Institute in Warsaw. Czesław Brzoza's bibliographical work on the Jewish press of Cracow was an immense help in this study. His works are a basic starting point for any research on Jewish Cracow, and they made my work in Polish libraries considerably lighter. Joachim Russek was kind enough to allow me to present an aspect of my work at the Center for Jewish Culture in Cracow, where I had the privilege of meeting many Jews from Cracow and learning much more about the Jews in Poland. Conversations about the Jewish history of Cracow with Henryk Hałkowski, Paweł Vogler, William Brand, Mary McCune, Shaul Stampfer, Michael Steinlauf and Hanna Kozińska-Witt often helped me to clarify my course of research and encouraged me to challenge my assumptions and conclusions. Zbigniew Leś gave me a memorable tour of Kamierz and Podgórze that literally enabled me to see Cracow from a different perspective. Marek Glogier arranged for me to speak on the Jewish press of Cracow at the Polish Academy of Sciences and introduced me to a number of people who provided insightful suggestions and helped me to realize the importance of the study of the press. Sian Mills at Vallentine Mitchell made the process of publication much easier; I am grateful to her for always patiently answering my questions.

The Jagiellonian University staff, who provided me with the most important materials for this study and who so often photocopied or microfilmed them as well, deserve special thanks for their patience and hard work. Others who made this study possible were the librarians and archivists of the Jewish Historical Institute and National Library in Warsaw, the Central Archives for the History of the Jewish People and the Central Zionist Archives in Jerusalem and the YIVO Institute for Jewish Research in New York. I am also grateful for access to excellent resources in libraries in the United States, particularly at Ohio State University, Kent State University, Case Western Reserve University, the Siegal College of Judaic Studies and the Cleveland Public Library.

During the course of this research, I sought material from public elementary schools in Kazimierz that served Jewish students before World War II. The administrations of Stanisław Konarski Elementary School Nr. 9 (Szkola Podstawowa 9), Jozef Dietl Elementary School Nr. 11 (Szkoła Podstawowa 11), and Jan Śniadecki Elementary School Nr. 16 (Szkoła Podstawowa 16) generously shared what remains of their records from before the war. Teresa Anderle-Bilińska at the Jan Śniadecki Elementary School Nr. 16 spoke with me at great length about the history of Jewish schoolchildren and explained significant material that suggested the complexity of relations between Jews and Poles.

The resources located in the branch of the Museum of the City of Cracow in the city's Old Synagogue proved especially helpful. I am grateful to Eugeniusz Duda, Anna Jodłowiec and Beata Łabno for their invaluable assistance in pointing me to the unpublished work of Zofia Wordliczek and in locating photographs of inter-war Cracow. Józef Lorski and Aleksandra Jaklińska assisted me in obtaining the rights to reproduce some of these photographs here. Zippi Rosenne and Pazit Shani-Schwartz of the Visual Documentation Center at Beth Hatefutsoth, the Nahum Goldmann Museum of the Jewish Diaspora in Tel Aviv, provided additional photographs.

Funding for this project came primarily from grants provided by the US Fulbright Commission of the Council for the International Exchange of Scholars, the American Council on Learned Societies, Ohio State University and the American Historical Association. The Jagiellonian University Research Center on Jewish History and Culture in Poland, now the Department of Judaic Studies, assisted me during my extended stays in Cracow, and Krzysztof Link-Lenczowski and Edward Dąbrowa provided needed encouragement. Without such institutional support, I simply would not have been able to undertake this project.

I owe a special debt to those individuals who generously shared with me their experiences as children or young adults in inter-war Cracow. These include Miriam Akavia, Natan Gross, Felicja Haberfeld, Bernhard Kempler, Emilia Lajbel, Ryszard Löw, Emanuel Melzer, Halina Nelken, Henryk Vogler, Leopold Page and Rafael F. Scharf. It is these individuals to whom I feel most responsible as a historian. As so many of them have told their own stories in memoirs or fiction, it is perhaps immodest even to suggest that I might have anything to add. I hope they can forgive the shortcomings of this study and that readers will be encouraged to turn to the memoirs to learn more about the Jewish history of Cracow and its legacy.

I am most appreciative that Antony Polonsky agreed to write the Forword. His encouragement has often made it easier to continue in such a difficult and challenging field.

A note on spelling and transliteration: I have chosen Cracow over Kraków or Kracow, except where a different spelling was used in the title of another work. Throughout the text, I have maintained the spelling of groups and organizations as it was in the original sources. This means that some Hebrew terms appear in Polish transliteration. An example is Makkabi, the name of the Jewish sports organization. For the names of well-known individuals I have chosen the most common spelling in English. I have tried to follow the standard YIVO system of transliteration for names and terms from Yiddish and, in all cases, I have provided English translations of the names and organizations alongside the Yiddish, Polish, or Hebrew original.

Without the unfailing support and patience of Jarosław R. Romaniuk, this book would have been much more difficult to finish. In thanks for his constant encouragement of my efforts, I dedicate this book to him.

Introduction

In May 1939, a short article highlighting how Jews fought for their own nation and for Poles appeared in a Polish-language magazine for Jewish children published in Cracow. The author, Anna Nichthauser, often wrote brief articles focusing on aspects of Jewish and Polish history for young readers. In 'For Your Freedom and Ours', she outlined some important events in Jewish and Polish history.[1] She told of the Jewish uprising against the Romans led by Bar Kokhba in 131, the signing of Poland's Constitution on 3 May 1791, and the assistance given by the Jewish Colonel Berek Joselewicz to Tadeusz Kościuszko during the 1794 uprising against the Russians. Nichthauser concluded with an anecdote about adults and children standing in a long line to donate money to the Polish National Defence Fund in 1939. Facing a long line of individuals waiting to donate money, a civil servant gruffly asked a young boy what he was doing there. The child replied that he wanted to give something, too, and he pointed to his father standing with him, a solemn-looking, bearded Jew. A woman in line asked the child how much money he had to donate. A young blonde girl, with a father who looked like a worker, interrupted and said that she had over two zlotys. The girl added, explaining her boastful attitude and an apparent need to compete with the boy, 'We live on the same street, so we know each other ...' Another man in line patted the children on the head and, as if on cue, everyone standing in line heard the sound of aeroplanes and looked up in the sky to see Poland's mighty air force, confident that without exception all of Poland's citizens were ready to contribute to the country's defence. The children Nichthauser describes lived on the same street. They were members of the same community. They were both ready to make sacrifices to defend that community.

This picture of Jewish aid to the Polish nation was an idealization of the relationships between the two peoples.[2] In part, it merely reflects the desperate situation in which Polish Jews found themselves in early 1939. But neither of those explanations accounts for the publication of the Jewish children's magazine in Polish or the focus on both Jewish and Polish history in the magazine's pages from its inception in 1937. This magazine, *Okienko na Świat* [*Window to the World*], was not simply a political tactic. It was a successful attempt to introduce Jewish youth to Jewish and Polish history and culture in the Polish language.

This attempt to mediate the Jewish experience through Polish was certainly not innovative. It simply continued a trend that had begun in Cracow already before the end of the First World War, with the publication of the first Polish-language Jewish daily newspaper, *Nowy Dziennik* [*New Daily*].[3] As Poles and Jews emerged from the chaos of war to find themselves in an independent Polish state, Jewish community leaders worked to build their community and improve the economic, political, cultural and social prospects for Jews, both as individuals and as a distinct national group.[4] They did so by founding newspapers, periodicals, schools, and social and cultural organizations that reflected their needs as a community. During the inter-war period, the Jews of inter-war Cracow developed distinctly modern forms of Jewish national identity that denied neither Jewish heritage nor Polish citizenship. In their efforts to assert both Jewish and Polish identities, the Jewish leaders of Cracow represented varying subcultures within the Jewish community. The development of Polish patriotism among the leading Jews of Cracow paradoxically allowed for the formation of separate Jewish national identities. The institutions of Jewish civil society existed as individual entities and did not usually result from unified efforts of the entire Jewish community. In their varied goals and programmes, they reflected the goals of Jewish nationalists and a growing involvement with Polish life and Polish national culture.

The independence of Poland after 1918 signalled significant change for the ethnic and national minority groups within the country, including Jews, Ukrainians, Germans and Byelorussians.[5] In Polish, this period is often referred to as a 'rebirth', echoing the rhetoric of East European intellectuals who led 'national awakenings' all over the region. Such rhetoric is not entirely unjustified. Only during the inter-war period were Poles, along with the country's national minorities, developing their own modern educational systems, a highly diversified press, and cultural organizations that supported all manner of professional activities and leisure interests, making up a complex network of urban institutions we can recognize today as a developing civil society. The unprecedented freedom of a nominally democratic Poland presented all ethnic groups within the country with the opportunity to grow politically, socially, educationally and economically. The private and public institutions these groups developed – the schools, the political organizations, the libraries, the reading rooms, the sports clubs, the theatre societies – made evident the nation's multi-ethnic character.

This work is a local study of how one national minority community in Eastern Europe fostered and supported distinct forms of ethnic identity while attempting to integrate into the larger community. The history of Jewish organizational life in Cracow points to a continuing support of basic Jewish needs and the cultural aspirations of the community towards the development of Polish, Yiddish and Hebrew culture. The book focuses on both larger institutions, such as Jewish schools and newspapers, and smaller groups, such as community theatres and sports teams, in order to understand how these cultural institutions defined and promoted national identity. This survey reveals the different ways Jews identified as Jews as well as how participation in Polish culture affected the Jewish community's development. The Jews of inter-war Cracow, just like Jews elsewhere in the Diaspora, tied themselves to the majority culture in which they lived while at the same time working towards Jewish national aims. Out of necessity, many leaders of Cracow Jewry accepted a broad definition of Jewish identity inclusive of many ideologically diverse Jewish groups along with a practical, administrative definition of Polish identity. Jewish nationalists in Cracow fought against the politically active Jewish assimilationism of the late nineteenth and early twentieth centuries, but they did so in a way that was calculated to aid the Cracow Jewish community in adapting to the goals and needs of the Polish state. Understanding the commitment to a Jewish identification alongside the process of acculturation helps us to recognize the ways in which both Polish Jews and Polish society were changing during the inter-war period.

How the state regulated the emerging civil society necessarily conditioned the nature of the relations between majority and minority and the extent of acculturation or assimilation. As Ezra Mendelsohn has asked so succinctly, were conditions in inter-war Poland good for the Jews, or bad for the Jews? Mendelsohn concluded that Polish society may have been both hospitable and hostile, writing 'The experience of Polish Jews between the wars was a combination of suffering, some of which was caused by anti-Semitism, and of achievement, made possible by Polish freedom, pluralism, and tolerance.'[6] But how did anti-Semitism affect that achievement and what did that achievement mean for Polish Jews? The task is to understand how the Jewish community's freedom to participate in a fledgling democratic society affected Jews and Poles and to identify the factors that limited that freedom.

All of the institutions discussed in this study set out to improve the Jewish community in some way, whether through providing news, an education, or a cultural experience to enlighten or entertain. While certainly not free of political ties, these institutions were not the work of radical revolutionaries. Rather, they were the culmination of the efforts of writers, teachers, doctors, lawyers and workers of all kinds, who came together in pursuit of common goals. All of them faced various restrictions on their freedoms, whether this took the form of the confiscation of a daily newspaper, police harassment, or the denial of adequate financial support from city authorities. Jews in Poland simply had to 'build their own home', to establish the political, educational, social and cultural institutions that would defend and support their community. To house their community, the Jewish leaders of inter-war Cracow built a network of private organizations where Jews could express their hopes and fears for their own community and serve their own material, educational, social and cultural interests. These organizations, often explicitly nationalist in character, promoted the ideals of Jewish nationalism and an attachment to the larger Polish society.

CONTINUING THE ENCOUNTER WITH MODERNITY

The development of a modern Polish nation-state necessarily conditioned the course of Polish Jewish history. This was but one more step in the Jewish encounter with modernity that had begun during the Enlightenment. Much of the historiography of the Jewish experience concerns just this encounter between Jews and political states that held out the promise of civil rights and full participation in the life of the nation.[7] Changing definitions of the meaning of Jewish identity accompanied the process of emancipation as Jews struggled for complete civil and political equality. The development of modern Jewish nationalism by the end of the nineteenth century transformed the hopes and dreams of individual Jews, who joined nationalist groups with the aim of liberating Jewish workers from economic oppression or of realizing a Jewish state in Palestine. Modern Jewish nationalism offered Jews living in hostile communities clear options for improving their immediate material conditions. Varying forms of Jewish nationalism, such as Zionism, Bundism or Diaspora Nationalism, were defined in the decades before the end of the First World War and offered Jews alternative solutions to the 'Jewish question'.[8] These innovative solutions sought to maintain Jews' integrity as members of the Jewish nation and as subjects or citizens of the empires and nations where they lived.[9] This study shows how Jewish leaders in one city, both nationalists and others who worked to promote specifically Jewish cultural values, continued the process of finding a place for their minority community within the majority society. Legally, Polish Jews were Polish citizens. Polish nationalists, especially from the right, challenged that citizenship, but it none the less represented a change in political order to which the Jews had little choice but to become accustomed.[10] Like Jews elsewhere, and at different points in history, the Jews of Poland began to determine how Jews could remain Jewish within a new, and rapidly changing, political environment.

Like Polish nationalism, Jewish nationalism was well developed before the inter-war period presented Jews with the opportunity to develop modern political and educational systems. Nationalization and national mobilization occurred in this case before the development of modern education and without the benefit of industry tied to one ethnic group.[11] Nationalism was the impetus for the founding of separate Jewish schools, for example, not the result of educating Jewish children in exclusively Jewish schools. Moreover, nationalism for the Jews in Poland was the expression of a distinctive ethnic identity that existed prior to the economic modernization of inter-war Poland and of the Jewish community.

The peace of 1918 allowed for the development of independent states in Eastern Europe and unleashed new discussions of the place of national character in national ideology, a phenomenon that took place in the Jewish community as well. Unlike most other developing nations in inter-war Eastern Europe, the Jews developed without the benefit of a political state apparatus or even any kind of official government support. The absence of Jews from surveys that focus on the many different countries of the region is unfortunate, because the Jewish experience of cultural nationalism in the region highlights what stateless East European ethnic communities had to do to become at first cultural, and only then political, nations.[12] Like the East European peoples who had achieved independence as successor states after 1918, Jews, too, sought ways to realize the ideal of self-determination, whether in Palestine or as members of the newly formed nations of Eastern Europe.

While many Jews were optimistic that the goals of a Jewish political nationalism could be achieved, others recognized that both Jews and non-Jews would more easily accept a nationalism that focused on the improvement of the material conditions of Jewish culture and society in the Diaspora. Political and cultural nationalism may only be different aspects of the same phenomenon, but the distinction for the Jewish community is crucial. Thus, Jewish leaders worked towards developing a Jewish nation in much the same way as nineteenth-century non-Jewish East European intellectuals had done for their own nations: by writing and discussing the ideals of a cultural nation separate from the nation in political control. Their explicitly national ethnic identity was expressed culturally and politically, but it was the cultural goals that could be achieved more easily for a stateless group in the Diaspora. With the secure establishment of the Polish state, the Jews could now look after their own needs and work towards goals of Jewish national autonomy, or at least towards Jewish cultural development. As a writer for *Nowy Dziennik* pointed out, Jews supported the cause of Polish nationalism by declaring themselves as Poles in the Austrian census of 1910, recognizing the need for an independent Poland and the role such a state could play in the achievement of their own goals. By the census of 1921, the time had come to identify themselves as Jews.[13]

Jewish national goals were, to an extent, dependent on the success of the goals of Polish nationalism, a success that allowed Jewish groups to develop and assert their own forms of ethnic and national distinctiveness. The many Jewish political parties in inter-war Poland were the practical expressions of these different alternatives. They worked on behalf of the Jewish community in the *Sejm*, the Polish parliament, and on city councils and within the *kehillot*, the self-governing Jewish community organizations. Though these political parties were often actively involved in promoting Jewish cultural activity, other institutions and organizations, which may or may not have maintained ties to a specific political party, became increasingly important proponents of Jewish culture in local communities. During the inter-war period, Jewish leaders continued to find new ways in which individuals could be a part of a larger Jewish community. In addition, individual Jews could, of course, still express their separate identity through membership in a synagogue or a specifically religious or charitable organization. The institutions and voluntary associations Jews formed were often, but not always, nationalist in character. This newly developing civil society, which reached both the religious and the secular, carried on the work of promoting Jewish cultural nationalism within a multinational state.

Jewish community leaders in Cracow before the Second World War were trying to achieve goals that can loosely be defined as cultural rather than political. These goals included, among others, a rapprochement with the Poles through a Polish-language Jewish press, the development of a thriving school system, and the establishment of a permanent residential Yiddish theatre troupe in the city. The freedom that allowed for the establishment of these organizations was one of the undoubtedly positive benefits of Polish independence for the Jews. The growth of so many different institutions and

voluntary associations, however, only provided more
opportunities for Jews to identify as Jews and thereby promoted
the diversity of the Jewish community. Those who worked to
unite the Jewish community behind a nationalist or religious
ideal now faced even greater challenges from within their own
community as well as from increasingly aggressive Polish
nationalists. Thus, in highlighting how Jewish community
leaders encouraged the expression of varying forms of Jewish
national identity and attempted to integrate into Polish society,
this study illustrates how Jewish nationalists and cultural
leaders presented themselves as a national group and aimed to
bring together the diverse elements of their community.

THE GROWTH OF JEWISH CIVIL SOCIETY

The institutions discussed in this study were clearly part of a
modern infrastructure, part of a developing society that we can
recognize as similar to our own and similar to the non-Jewish
societies among whom the Jews lived. The evidence for a change
in Jewish nationalism in Cracow comes from the institutions of
civil society that the Jews developed as they attempted to find
room for their nation within a multinational state, to become
both Jews and Polish citizens. The growth of separate
institutions helps to shape separate identities, in much the same
way as political boundaries divide states.[14] Separate institutions
may serve as a bureaucratic framework for an ethnic community
if a government does not. That Jews are a minority makes the
study of their civil society in a multinational state that much
more complicated. If civil society plays a role in the
development of citizens, as scholars of European history have
suggested, then what are the effects of the growth of civil society
among a population that, though citizens, could never be a part
of the nation-state in the same way as others?[15]

Jewish initiatives to found newspapers, establish schools,
present Yiddish plays, or to teach Hebrew ensured a high level
of Jewish ethnic cohesiveness. The need to provide opportunities for Jewish children, to ensure their material survival and
future in Poland no less than the future of the Jewish community
itself, led many Jewish leaders to encourage separate Jewish

education even as they publicly advocated Jewish integration into the Polish community. That Jewish leaders managed such apparently conflicting goals in the face of their own diversity and ever present anti-Semitism only attests to the sincerity of their efforts and the skills they brought to the task of building the institutions that would house their community. As Polish politics drifted towards the right, especially after the death of Józef Piłsudski in 1935, the need to unite as a community and to integrate into the Polish state was even greater.[16] The process, however, had begun even before the declaration of Polish independence on 11 November 1918.

This study of Jewish civil society is limited to institutions and voluntary associations with explicitly cultural goals for two reasons. First, nationalist groups have long used cultural groups such as those discussed here to transmit ideas of national identity to their communities. Scholars have long recognized culture as the way in which groups imagine their communities and nations.[17] Second, the number of private Jewish organizations in Cracow alone – over 300 during the inter-war period for a community of fewer than 60,000 – necessitated the exclusion of other groups, such as political parties, trade guilds or social welfare organizations, themselves topics worthy of separate, extended treatment.[18]

Many of the institutions and organizations discussed here were very small; others had hundreds of members. Some of these groups, even some of the smaller ones, lasted for several years throughout the inter-war period. Others were very short-lived. Similarly, many titles of the Jewish press in Cracow appeared for only a few issues. Only a few titles lasted well over a year.[19] Most of the private Jewish schools discussed here were successful enterprises, with at least a couple of hundred students. But others, such as those founded in the late 1930s, were significantly smaller. This study looks at both smaller and larger institutions in order to portray the range of opinion within the Jewish community. The largest, seemingly most influential Jewish institutions of the city, such as *Nowy Dziennik* or the Hebrew gymnasium, are usually associated with a middle-class Polish-speaking population inclined towards, and usually openly supportive of, Zionism. Important as they are as indicators of the positions of the city's Jewish leadership, they cannot be taken to represent all of the city's Jews. For example, Jewish leaders founded other groups to promote Yiddish culture or established Yiddish newspapers specifically for an Orthodox audience. These expressions of Jewish cultural identity are discussed here in order to present as comprehensive a picture of Jewish community life in Cracow as possible.

All of these institutions assisted the Jews in meeting the goal of a liberal society, to 'give the lower class people the security to reach their possibilities, even though cultural bonds may be stretched and broken in the process'.[20] Both Poles and Jews were interested in reaching their possibilities, in improving their war-torn circumstances and making better lives for themselves. Cultural bonds were indeed stretched and broken during the inter-war period; the modernization of the Polish Jewish community entailed a certain identification with the Polish government and Polish culture as well as an assertion of a unique ethnic identity. It required Jews to move from the communal isolation of the *kehillah* to greater involvement in the local school and city council. The establishment of a modern state and competitive economy also required Poles to view Jews as Poles, if not ethnically, at least as Polish citizens with an equal stake in the consequences of state policy. This is precisely why the ethnic homogeneity of post-war Poland is so tragic. Efforts such as those of the Jews of Cracow to forge identities compatible with life in a multicultural society suggest that both Jewish and Polish societies were developing in ways that now can never be realized.

ASSIMILATION, ACCULTURATION AND THE FORMATION OF IDENTITIES

In an article for his newspaper *Di post* [*The Post*] in 1937, the Yiddish editor Moyshe Blekher wrote that, unlike in Vilnius, in Cracow it was possible to observe the contrast of 'a Jew with a beard and *peyes*, a tallis and *shtrayml*, who was thoroughly assimilated toward Polish, speaking Polish at home and on the street, reading and supporting the Polish press'.[21] At the same time, Blekher continued, this Jew from Cracow viewed his own cultural heritage with indifference and contempt. Clearly, the

Jews of Cracow had taken assimilation too far. Blekher's newspaper was an effort to check that progress.

Blekher's description of a typical Jew from Cracow may be exaggerated but it conforms with the general picture of Cracow as a Jewish community with close ties to Polish culture. This study, focusing on questions of cultural allegiance and national identity rather than political developments or economic structure, has developed from questions raised by historians writing local studies of Jewish communities outside of Poland. These questions, not fully addressed in the Polish context, involve the encounter with modernity, the nature of assimilation and acculturation, and the role of the Jewish intelligentsia in developing Jewish nationalism. Just as Marsha Rozenblit re-evaluated Jewish assimilation and Jews' ties to traditional Jewish culture in her important work on the Jews of Vienna, so this study explains how Jews in Cracow accommodated Polish culture as they continued to live Jewish lives.[22] Though this study focuses on the history of a minority population, this history cannot be told without an evaluation of the influence of the majority community on the minority culture.

The term 'assimilated Jews' in the context of inter-war Poland is usually used to describe those Jews who really had truly assimilated, exchanging an identification with the Jewish community for a home among Poles and in Polish. This group would include, to take better-known examples, the Polish writers Julian Tuwim, Bolesław Leśmian and Aleksander Wat. The cultural identity of Polish Jews like Tuwim, Leśmian and Wat has long been a topic of interest for scholars of Polish literature. Assimilation was not limited to the literary sphere. The president (or mayor) of Cracow in the late 1930s, Mieczysław Kaplicki, and the city's garrison commander, Bernard Mond, are local, Cracow examples. The Cracow native Rafael Scharf recalls that 'Cracovians were used to seeing, on state occasions, an odd trinity: Archbishop Sapieha supported by the two Jews – Kaplicki and Mond.'[23] Assimilated Jews like Kaplicki and Mond, however, placed themselves outside of the Jewish community and thus do not come under consideration in this work.

The social theorist Milton Gordon distinguished between different types of assimilation. While individual Jews like Tuwim or Kaplicki may appropriately be described as assimilated, the Jewish community certainly never went through any process of structural assimilation, which Gordon describes as the 'large-scale entrance into cliques, clubs, and institutions of the host society'.[24] As Theodore R. Weeks has pointed out, assimilation of the Jews into Polish society was no longer an option in the early twentieth century.[25] The development of nationalisms within both the Polish and Jewish communities rendered such a solution to the 'Jewish question' unworkable. After the high point of Polish–Jewish co-operation during the 1863 uprising, at least one strain of Polish nationalism had begun to hate, in the words of one historian,[26] and Jewish nationalism, whether in the form of Zionism or Bundism, had matured, offering Jews new ways to improve their lives and define their community.

Some Jewish political leaders did lead efforts to integrate the Jewish community into Polish society. Most representative of these efforts at integration is Adolf Gross. The party Gross founded in 1900, known as the Party of Independent Jews, 'opposed both the complete assimilation of the Jews and their medieval-style segregation in ghettos'.[27] But the linguistic and cultural assimilation many Jews in Cracow had already undergone in the nineteenth century had not stemmed anti-Semitism or resulted in any kind of real rapprochement between the Poles and Jews of the city. The violence against Jews immediately following the First World War was a stark reminder of the difficulties that lay ahead for those wishing to forge better relationships between Jews and Poles.

The anti-Semitism present in all levels of Polish society always conditioned the course of Jewish development. Indeed, anti-Semitism often provided the most important motivation for the formation of separate Jewish institutions. Nationalist groups made several attempts to challenge Jewish citizenship from the very inception of the state.[28] Constitutional guarantees of the Polish state did not overturn previously existing laws that often placed restrictions on the Jews, including restrictions regarding the use of Yiddish and Hebrew in public life. These challenges accompanied efforts to introduce a *numerus clausus* (a restriction on the number of Jews allowed to be educated in the universities) in the early 1920s. As elsewhere in Central and Eastern Europe, proposals for anti-Semitic legislation increased in the late 1930s.[29] The ghetto benches of the universities, attacks on Jewish students, and legislative initiatives forbidding ritual slaughter caused many Polish Jews to question their place within the still relatively young multicultural republic. The climate Polish nationalist students and political leaders created threatened the Jewish community as never before.[30] As a result, new Jewish institutions were founded even into the late 1930s, as Jews continued the process of defining and defending their nation and, with varying degrees of hope, of integrating into the majority culture.

The Jews of inter-war Cracow were continuing what the sociologist Milton Gordon would have termed cultural assimilation, or acculturation, that is, adapting to the cultural patterns of another group.[31] This process continued throughout the inter-war period. Cultural assimilation went along with a process of increasing Jewish national identification. By examining the efforts of the Polish state to develop a uniform society and how the Jews of Cracow remained Jews in the face of anti-Semitism and linguistic assimilation, this study illustrates how one community courageously acknowledged its difference while refusing to settle for the second-class position in which the majority culture often placed it. For minority groups, multiple identities are possible, and perhaps preferable, when the minority confronts systemic changes, such as those after the First World War. More importantly, separate minority conceptions of national identity are not necessarily destabilizing for the majority government or society. Jews in the Diaspora had always possessed more than one identity by definition, being able to consider themselves, for example, as both Jews and as imperial subjects or citizens of the country in which they lived. Jewish nationalists, as demonstrated in the context of inter-war Cracow, supported the Polish state and were intensely patriotic, if not Polish nationalists. This was in part a response to the anti-Semitism of Polish society and, because of the Zionists' own linguistic and cultural assimilation, a natural development of Jewish nationalism in Cracow immediately after the war. Searching for ways to achieve equality of opportunity in political, social, economic and cultural life, Jewish community leaders established organizations to meet their needs and to educate Jews for lives as Jews and as Polish citizens. Becoming both Polish and Jewish was perhaps unavoidable, even desirable, in spite of an often hostile environment. The most important contribution of this work is to reveal how Jews in Cracow attempted to integrate into Polish society yet remained Jews at the same time.

The need to develop Jewish society after the war was taken as a given by the editors of *Nowy Dziennik*, Cracow's only daily Jewish newspaper, Zionist in political orientation. A reading of Cracow's *Nowy Dziennik* indicates that Jewish leaders in the city distinguished themselves from Jews in the West. This is not especially surprising, given the particularities of the Jewish situation in Poland, including the Jews' greater numbers, reliance on Yiddish, and greater commitment to traditional Judaism. Polish Jews recognized that they were different from the more assimilated West European Jewry. One writer stated unequivocally that, 'we do not want to assimilate on the Western model'.[32] There was an awareness that East European Jewry did not follow the same pattern of development as West European Jewry, even if they too acculturated. This writer does not mention the assimilated nature of the Jewish communities in Prague or Budapest or explain which of these Jewish communities is 'Eastern' or 'Western'. Jewish leaders in inter-war Cracow had no desire to preside over the assimilation of their community. In stating that they did not wish to emulate Western Jewish leaders, they were demonstrating their wish to develop a new form of Jewish identity that allowed for participation in both majority and minority cultures. While common religious and cultural traditions continued to bind the Jews together in one national group (in spite of their many differences), their use of the Polish language bound them to another group as well, a tie Jewish nationalists expressed as loyalty to an administrative state they hoped would provide the conditions necessary for Jewish national development. Language remained 'a mediator of authentic national experience', tying acculturated Polish Jews to Poland while the common cultural traditions reinforced a separate national identity as Jews.[33] The 'linguistic promiscuity' of the Jews did not act as a hindrance to Jewish identity, nor was it always a step on the road to complete assimilation.[34] Rather, it was a tool to be employed in the making of Jewish nationalists and, in this case, Polish citizens.

The Jewish community of Cracow adopted the Polish language and Polish culture at least partly in a concerted effort to reach out to and identify with the Polish community. For example, Jewish students celebrated Polish national holidays in Jewish schools, and Jewish teachers assigned homework about Polish bishops to Jewish students. For many of the Jews writing in Polish or attending Polish schools or plays, it was possible to be both Jewish and Polish at the same time. The Jewish culture lost during the Holocaust was often one that Jews expressed in Polish.

Neither solely a study of assimilation nor of Jewish intellectuals, this study invites comparisons of the Cracow Jewish community with Jewish communities elsewhere in Central Europe. Such efforts among Jews to integrate into the larger, non-Jewish society were not unknown in inter-war Eastern Europe. Emil Dorian describes his attempt to bridge the gap between Romanian and Jewish societies in his diary, *The Quality of Witness*. Similarly, Raphael Patai shows in his memoir how his father, the well-known Zionist Joszef Patai, continually laboured to introduce Hungarians to Jewish culture and was comfortable as both a Magyar and a Jew.[35] Thus, asserting a separate cultural identity, even a separate national identity, did not preclude efforts to integrate into the majority culture.

Echoing the earlier work of Calvin Goldscheider and Alan Zuckerman, Pierre Birnbaum and Ira Katznelson have insisted on the importance of the Jewish tie to the non-Jewish community.[36] In their edited volume on emancipation, Birnbaum and Katznelson assert that the process of emancipation illustrates that there were many different ways in which Jews could demonstrate their Jewishness. This study underscores the multiplicity of ways that Jews could be Jews in inter-war Poland. Assimilation into Polish culture or the Polish nation after 1918 was certainly not inevitable; indeed, it was not even an option. Jews remained Jews in spite of their attachment to Polish culture. Social and economic modernization does not necessarily lead to assimilation. What remains to be studied are the ways in which Jews and Poles accommodated the culture of the other group as they both proceeded to build their national communities. Addressing these issues, at least in part, is one goal of this study.

WHY CRACOW?

Like other Polish cities, Cracow was a town where different cultures conflicted and coexisted. The proportion of Jews in the city's population remained steady throughout the inter-war period, at 25 per cent. In 1924, 46,197 of Cracow's 184,415 inhabitants were Jews. In 1939, 64,958 of the city's 251,451 residents were Jewish.[37] Jews made up an even greater proportion of the urban populations of Warsaw, Łódź, Lwów, and Vilnius. Vilnius, with 55,006 Jews in 1931 making up 28.2 per cent of the city's population, is the city with the most comparable Jewish population in size. In that same year, 99,595 Jews lived in Lwów (31.9 per cent of the total city population); 202, 497 in Łódź (33.5 per cent of the total number of residents); and 352,659 Jews lived in Warsaw (30.1 per cent of the population).[38] Cracow was, certainly, a small big city. Its reputation as a cultural centre was well deserved but out of proportion to its size and status within inter-war Poland.

Each of Poland's cities is justly celebrated in both Polish and Jewish history for the various accomplishments of its residents, and each is deserving of more thorough scholarly examination.[39] Warsaw's role as the country's largest city and administrative capital of the country grew only during the inter-war period. Lwów had been the administrative capital of Galicia and, as such, had closer ties to Vienna and a status as a regional capital that was greater then Cracow's. Yiddish culture and Jewish nationalism flourished in Vilnius, the home of the founding of the Bund in 1897 and of YIVO after its transfer from Berlin in 1925. Łódź, the young Polish city developed as an industrial centre during the 1800s, hosted a larger Jewish population than Vilnius, Cracow or Lwów; and it quickly outstripped Cracow or Lwów as a centre of Yiddish art and literary culture.[40] In addition, Łódź offers an opportunity for the study of the relationships between Jews, Poles and Germans. Similarly, Lwów offers the same opportunity for those interested in ties between Jews, Poles and Ukrainians.

The choice of Cracow as the topic of this study is not meant to suggest that the city is somehow representative of the history of Polish Jews. Cracow's Jewish community was not necessarily more conservative or innovative than Poland's other Jewish communities, but its unique history during the early modern period as a centre of government and culture for the Poles and a centre of religious learning for the Jews makes Cracow of lasting, perhaps even central, importance for both national groups. Just as Poles look to Cracow as their country's royal and cultural capital (at least until the early twentieth century), so many Jews return to Cracow regularly to visit the grave of one of Polish Jewry's most important rabbinical leaders, Rabbi Moses Isserles, whose work *Mapah* helped to codify Jewish law.[41] Because both Poles and Jews regard the city of Cracow as of unique historical importance, it is especially worthy of an investigation focusing on questions of Jewish national and cultural identity in multinational Poland.

The Jewish community itself singled out Warsaw, Cracow and Vilnius for special recognition. Colloquially, Warsaw was known as the Jerusalem of Poland, Vilnius as the Jerusalem of Lithuania, and Cracow as the Jerusalem of Galicia.[42] These cities were important regional centres for East European Jewry. Given the differences between all of these communities, none can claim to be truly representative of the diverse experiences of Polish Jews.[43] By outlining the characteristics of one specific community and suggesting points of comparison with other Jewish communities, this study draws attention to the lasting regional differences within inter-war Poland, differences that a unified Polish state could not efface in the mere twenty years of the inter-war period. In doing so, it can point the way towards further research that will help historians reach broader conclusions about both Polish Jews and the Polish state, thereby restoring the experience of minority communities to the historiography of Poland.

The increased attention paid to Polish-Jewish studies in the West in the last decade has provided the foundation for new studies in East European Jewish history. This includes much work on local Jewish communities in Poland that has been done by Polish scholars, work that has documented the experiences of the Jews of many different communities throughout Poland. The two most important works on inter-war Polish Jewish communities have been written by Gabriela Zalewska, on Warsaw, and Wacław Wierzbieniec, on Przemyśl.[44] Both works are serious attempts to determine the structure of the Jewish communities by an examination of statistical data and the role of the Jews in the local economy. Zalewska and Wierzbieniec succeed in presenting a picture of the economic position in which the Jews found themselves. Their work leaves open questions of Jewish cultural life or national identity and makes apparent the lack of such studies on other Polish Jewish communities, such as Cracow, Lwów, Vilnius, Łódź, and Białystok.

Local studies focusing on Jewish communities throughout Central and Eastern Europe in the inter-war period may well challenge historians to reconsider common notions of the characteristics of Western and Eastern European Jewries. In his work on the Jews of East Central Europe between the wars, Mendelsohn describes East European Jews as more traditionally religious than West European Jews, much more accepting of Jewish nationalist ideas, and representative of 'the relative weakness of acculturation and assimilation'.[45] In contrast, West European-type Jewish communities in Eastern Europe were more assimilated, less nationalistic, and more involved with the political activities of the host state.

Mendelsohn explains well the exceptions to this useful typology, but he does not challenge it directly. He writes,

> In modern Jewish history in the Western world, the classical pattern has been progression from nonacculturation and nonassimilation to acculturation and efforts to assimilate, from the physical and spiritual ghetto to integration, of one sort or another, into the broader society. In inter-war East Europe, this pattern is not in evidence. The East European-type communities, despite a certain, and sometimes even an impressive, degree of acculturation during the 1920s and 1930s, remained basically Yiddish-speaking, lower middle class and proletarian, and strongly influenced both by religious Orthodoxy and by modern separatist Jewish nationalism.[46]

Cracow's Jews certainly illustrate the impressive degree of acculturation Mendelsohn mentions. I contend they integrated into Polish society extensively enough during the inter-war period that they cannot easily be classified as either 'Eastern' or

'Western'. These labels point to very general trends within the pre-1939 European Jewish community, but they do not help us to understand how the Jewish communities met the challenges they faced as a result of anti-Semitic restrictions or how Jews developed a vibrant culture in inter-war Eastern Europe. Given the relative lack of attention to the Jews of inter-war Poland, Europe's largest Jewish community before the Second World War, definitive conclusions about Jewish acculturation and assimilation and the urban history of Poland, before the development of a historiography that considers the growth of Jewish civil society *vis-à-vis* the Polish state, may be premature.

The official Jewish community leadership and the Jewish intellectuals of Cracow developed a Jewish cultural identity that was neither Western nor Eastern, but rather Jewish and Polish. By examining how Jews began literally to build their own national home in Cracow while accepting Polish patriotism and the more inclusive form of Polish nationalism stemming from the noble tradition of the Polish-Lithuanian Commonwealth, this study challenges the accepted typology of Jewish communities in Eastern Europe. Local studies of Jewish communities in Eastern Europe focusing on Jewish culture as well as politics are likely to continue to challenge this typology. While the similarities Mendelsohn points out lead to understandable generalizations, historians need local studies illustrating the uniqueness of European Jewish communities to confirm or deny broad conclusions. Cracow was perhaps more acculturated than other Polish Jewish communities, but it was also the fifth largest Jewish community in the country. The Jewish nationalism expressed in Cracow, the types of organizations founded there, the Polish-language Jewish press, and the need to integrate into Polish society were present in other Polish cities as well. By focusing on one community, we can better understand how Jews experienced their Jewish identity in their daily lives, in the schools, in the theatres, or at the soccer games. Studies such as this one on Cracow will aid in the development of a comparative Jewish historiography that will clarify trends in European Jewish cultural, political, economic and social development.

The most important sources for a study of Cracow's Jews are archival information about Jewish organizational life, the Jewish press and the memoir literature of the Jews from Cracow who survived the Holocaust. Remarkably, the records of the official Jewish community of Cracow survived the war and can be accessed at the Jewish Historical Institute in Warsaw.[47] These records reflect the concerns of the official organization of the Jewish community and are in that respect limited. The *kehillah* of a Polish Jewish community focused on very local concerns, such as the regulations for the ritual slaughterhouses and baths, the collection of community dues, relief of the poor, disputes between synagogues, and the religious education of the community's Jewish children. As a result, these records are primarily useful when considering views of religious life. Andrzej Żbikowski mined these sources for his study and I have used them extensively in mine, though they are much less useful for questions of cultural life and identity. The involvement of the Cracow kehillah in cultural life was minimal, though it occasionally subsidized cultural institutions such as the Yiddish theatre (a subsidy won after quite a long fight) and provided small scholarships for Jewish students. Of equal importance for this study are the materials in the Polish state archives in Cracow and Warsaw. These include police reports on Jewish organizations, the registration of Jewish organizations with the city, and official inspection reports of private Jewish schools. These documents occasionally reflect the biases of the majority community, as can be seen in the concern with Jewish political organizations of the left.

The memorial books of Cracow, *Sefer kroke* and the Memorial Book of the New Cracow Friendship Society, provide the most detailed information of Jewish life in the city, along with memoirs published in Polish and Hebrew.[48] The memoir literature of Jews from Cracow who survived the Holocaust or who had emigrated before the Second World War offers the most detailed picture of individual Jewish lives.[49] These memoirs have been written, however, primarily by well-educated members of the community, inclined during the inter-war period towards either Jewish national ideals or Polish cultural life. More problematic, many of them focus primarily on the Holocaust and not on the inter-war period. Some exceptions include the excellent ghetto diary and memoir of Halina Nelken, which, while an account of the author's life in the Cracow ghetto, nevertheless also details her life before the war. The memoirs of the literary critic Henryk Vogler, the journalist and film historian Natan Gross, Irena Bronner and Henryk Ritterman-Abir are also notable exceptions.

These sources have been examined for information related to three different categories of cultural institutions: the press, schools and voluntary associations with specifically cultural goals, whether the development of Yiddish theatre in Cracow, the promotion of Jewish literature or the playing of soccer or chess. Chapter 1, 'From Habsburg Rule to Independent Poland', addresses the development of Jewish history and civil society until 1918. While some of the institutions founded during this period grew into important cultural centres for Jews, such as the Hebrew gymnasium, the First World War represents a real break in the development of Cracow Jewish life. This is so not only because of the establishment of the Polish state, but because of the cultural developments within the Jewish community during and after the war. Most important among these was the founding of *Nowy Dziennik* and the founding of the Yiddish theatre society, new institutions that represent the efforts of Jewish leaders to educate other Jews and improve their community.

Chapters 2 and 3, ' "Building Our Own Home": The Jewish Press of Inter-war Cracow', and 'The Yiddishist Reaction to Assimilation: Religious and Cultural Responses', concern the factors that led to the development of the Jewish press in Cracow in both Yiddish and Polish and the response of the press to the phenomenon of assimilation. Given the influence of the Polish-language Jewish press in Cracow, it is the Polish-speaking Jewish intelligentsia for whom we have the most reliable source of information. Writing in Polish, the editors of Cracow's *Nowy Dziennik* defined themselves very clearly as both Polish patriots and Jewish nationalists. *Nowy Dziennik* provides the perspective of an educated, Zionist Jewish elite. Other views of the Jewish community can be found in the Yiddish press, which was addressed either to a significantly more traditional audience, in the case of *Dos yidishe vort* [*The Jewish Word*], or to an audience of secular Yiddishist intellectuals, as in the case of *Di post* [*The Post*]. Dismissing the Zionists writing in Polish as assimilationists and working towards the development of a strong secular Jewish culture, *Di post* focused much more on issues of high Yiddish culture.

Significantly, the community was not able to sustain a Hebrew periodical of any kind during the inter-war period.

Standard theories of nationalism justify a focus on the educational institutions of the Jews of Cracow, the subject of Chapters 4 and 5, 'Making Jews Polish: The Education of Jewish Children in Polish Schools' and 'Maintaining Community: Jewish Participation in Private Jewish Schools'.[50] These chapters examine both the public and private schools attended by Jewish children. Whether public or private, educational institutions conditioned Jewish children to enter the larger society, both Jewish and Polish. Examining how the community educated its children can tell us more about the Polish and Jewish cultures to which they were exposed as well as the effects of this exposure. The overwhelming majority of Jewish children attended Polish public schools. Private Jewish schools promoted distinct forms of national or ethnic identity, but they also helped to integrate Jewish children into Poland. School registers and attendance records, from the state archives in Cracow, have helped in determining how many Jews attended Polish schools where the primary language of instruction was Polish. The curriculum offered by the schools to Jewish students can be evaluated from the publications of the schools themselves, the records of the Jewish community, and the Jewish press.[51] The establishment of private schools may be seen as the first step towards a kind of cultural autonomy. Significantly, however, the schools also represent the attempt to integrate both Jewish and Polish experiences into the lives of Jewish children.

The establishment of other Jewish cultural institutions provided different ways for Jews to express their Jewishness. While an examination of the schools will indicate the direction of Jewish education in the inter-war period, Chapter 6, 'Voluntary Associations and the Varieties of Cultural Life', aims to show the contemporary scope of Jewish cultural activity. Jewish academic, professional, theatrical, social and sports organizations arose alongside more traditional Jewish religious organizations, resulting in a more secular and diversified Jewish community. These organizations did not, however, serve to divide the Jewish community from the Polish population. At times, they even promoted Polish patriotism and a Jewish affiliation with Polish culture. For example, the Cracow Yiddish Theatre Society premièred the plays of Stanisław Wyspiański in Yiddish, and the Jewish Amateur Scene Club specifically encouraged its members to learn and improve their Polish. This chapter is based on police reports of the activities of these organizations. These reports reveal the activities of the groups and their political orientation, if any. In some cases, the reports of the organizations themselves are available. This is especially important in the case of the reading rooms, as they detail the readings and lectures the organizations sponsored. In addition, the Jewish press included accounts of the cultural activities in the city, announcing meetings and publishing reports of the groups' activities. The Zionist youth organizations published accounts of their activities in regular journals published in co-operation with Zionist youth groups in other Polish cities. Organizations of Jewish artists in Cracow also published journals devoted to literature and the visual arts. This chapter includes an evaluation of the position of the Yiddish Theatre Society in Cracow based on the sources in both Polish and Yiddish. A study of the Yiddish theatre in Cracow, along with an examination of the other institutions discussed above, suggests that the Jews of Cracow began to develop unique subcultures during the inter-war period, distinguishable from traditional Jewish culture as well as from Polish culture.

Poland's minorities did not enjoy any official approbation of national autonomy, but the many separate organizations Jews developed did grant Jews some control over their material conditions and educational and cultural development. If national autonomy is defined in terms of culture rather than politics, the experience of Cracow's Jews shows that an ethnic community may be able to develop, and even flourish, while adapting to the majority community at the same time. As Poland became increasingly authoritarian after Piłsudski's death, more ethnically based conceptions of Polish nationalism came to the fore and there was little place for the Jews within the Polish nation. Still, many Jews had already adopted the Polish language and graduated from Polish schools. They faced discrimination in education and limitations on their professional careers. Any hopes that the Polish government would act benevolently towards its minority communities in hopes of achieving a stable state had long since disappeared. But many Jews retained their commitment to the Polish state and nation. Reporting on the 1937 Polish Independence Day celebration, the *kehillah* publication *Gazeta Gminna* [*Community Gazette*] described the activities sponsored by the Jewish community for the Polish national holiday.[52] The celebration in the progressive Tempel included a choir singing the Polish national hymn *Boże coś Polskę* [*God Bless Poland*]. In the *Alte Shul* [Old Synagogue], a stronghold of the Orthodox, the Polish tune was also sung, but with Hebrew lyrics. Whether progressive or Orthodox, the Jews of Cracow adjusted to their Polish surroundings.

NOTES

1. Anna Nichthauser, 'For Your Freedom and Ours', *Okienko na Świat*, 4 May 1939, 2.
2. For the most extended treatment of this relationship as reflected in both Polish and Jewish literature, see Magdalena Opalski and Israel Bartal, *Poles and Jews: A Failed Brotherhood* (Hanover, NH: University of New England Press, 1992). See also Theodore R. Weeks, 'Poles, Jews, and Russians, 1863–1914: The Death of the Ideal of Assimilation in the Kingdom of Poland', in *Polin, Jewry, Focusing on Galicia: Jews, Poles, and Ukrainians 1772–1918*, 12 (1999), 242–56.
3. On the phenomenon of the Jewish press in Polish, see Michael Steinlauf, 'The Polish-Jewish Daily Press,' *Polin*, 2 (1987), 219–45 and Czesław Brzoza, 'The Jewish Press in Kraków (1918–1939)', *Polin*, 7 (1992), 133–46. The Polish scholar Eugenia Prokop-Janiec has reviewed the phenomenon of Jewish writers writing in Polish at length in her important work, *Międzywojenna literatura polsko-żydowska jako zjawisko kulturowe i artystyczne* (Kraków: Universitas, 1992).
4. On the general development of the Jewish community in inter-war Poland, see Volume 8 of *Polin: Jews in Independent Poland, 1918–1939*, eds Antony Polonsky, Ezra Mendelsohn, and Jerzy Tomaszewski (London: Littman Library of Jewish Civilization, 1994); the survey of Ezra Mendelsohn in *The Jews of East Central Europe Between the Wars* (Bloomington: Indiana University Press, 1983); Joseph Marcus, *Social and Political History of the Jews in Poland, 1918–1939* (The Hague: Mouton, 1983); Celia S. Heller, *On the Edge of Destruction: Jews of Poland Between the Two World Wars* (Detroit, MI: Wayne State University Press, 1977, 1994); and the essays in the volume edited by Joshua A. Fishman, *Studies on Polish Jewry: 1919–1939* (New York: YIVO Institute for Jewish Research, 1974).
5. On the status of other minorities in inter-war Poland, see Jerzy Tomaszewski, *Mniejszości narodowe w Polsce w XX wieku* (Warsaw: Editions Spotkania, 1991).
6. Ezra Mendelsohn, 'Inter-war Poland: Good for the Jews or Bad for the Jews', *The Jews in Poland*, eds Chimen Abramsky, Maciej Jachimczyk and Antony Polonsky (Oxford: Blackwell, 1986), 130–9.
7. The encounter has been examined in various contexts. Some examples include Lois Dubin, *The Port Jews of Habsburg Trieste: Absolutist Politics and Enlightenment Culture* (Stanford, CA: Stanford University Press, 1999); Steven Zipperstein, *The Jews of Odessa: A Cultural History, 1794–1881* (Stanford, CA: Stanford University Press,

1985); Todd Endelman, *The Jews of Georgian England, 1714–1830: Tradition and Change in a Liberal Society* (Philadelphia, PA: Jewish Publication Society of America, 1979); Paula Hyman, *The Emancipation of the Jews of Alsace: Acculturation and Tradition in the Nineteenth Century* (New Haven, CT: Yale University Press, 1991); Jacob Katz, ed., *Toward Modernity: The European Jewish Model* (New Brunswick, NJ: Transaction Books, 1987); Artur Eisenbach, *The Emancipation of the Jews of Poland, 1780–1870*, trans. Janina Dorosz (Oxford: Blackwell, 1991); Benjamin Nathans, *Beyond the Pale: The Jewish Encounter with Late Imperial Russia* (Berkeley: University of California Press, 2002); and Michael Brenner, *The Renaissance of Jewish Culture in Weimar Germany* (New Haven, CT: Yale University Press, 1996).

8. The most succinct overview of political movements Jews regarded as options for their community is Ezra Mendelsohn's *On Modern Jewish Politics* (New York: Oxford University Press, 1993). Other works examining these movements extensively include Jonathan Frankel, *Prophecy and Politics: Socialism, Nationalism, and the Russian Jews, 1862–1917* (Cambridge: Cambridge University Press, 1981) and David Vital, *The Origins of Zionism* (Oxford: Clarendon Press, 1985).

9. Marsha Rozenblit has written about the ways Jews divided their loyalties in Habsburg Austria. For her conception of a tripartite Jewish identity in Galicia under Habsburg rule, see her *Reconstructing National Identity: The Jews of Habsburg Austria During World War I* (Oxford: Oxford University Press, 2001) and 'Jewish Ethnicity in a New Nation-State: The Crisis of Identity in the Austrian Republic', in *In Search of Jewish Community: Jewish Identities in Germany and Austria, 1918–1933*, eds Michael Brenner and Derek Penslar (Bloomington: Indiana University Press, 1998). Her earlier work also addresses issues of assimilation and identity: *The Jews of Vienna, 1867–1914: Assimilation and Identity* (Albany: State University of New York Press, 1983).

10. See Paweł Korzec, 'Antisemitism in Poland as an Intellectual, Social and Political Movement', in *Studies on Polish Jewry, 1919–1939*, 12–104; for the later period, see Emanuel Melzer, *No Way Out: The Politics of Polish Jewry, 1935–1939* (Cincinnati, OH: Hebrew Union College Press, 1997).

11. See Liah Greenfeld, *Nationalism: Five Roads to Modernity* (Cambridge, MA: Harvard University Press, 1992); Ernest Gellner, *Nations and Nationalism* (Oxford: Basil Blackwell, 1983) and 'The Dramatis Personae of History', *East European Politics and Societies*, 4, no. 1 (Winter 1990): 117–33. For a perspective from another part of Eastern Europe, see the work of Irina Livezeanu, *Cultural Politics in Greater Romania: Regionalism, Nation Building, and Ethnic Struggle, 1918–1930* (Ithaca, NY: Cornell University Press, 1995).

12. See the standard survey of articles edited by Ivo Lederer and Peter Sugar, *Nationalism in Eastern Europe* (Seattle: University of Washington Press, 1969) and a more recent collection of articles edited by Ivo Banac and Katherine Verdery, *National Character and National Ideology in Inter-war Eastern Europe* (New Haven, CT: Yale Center for International and Area Studies, 1995).

13. 'Narodowość i język ojczysty', *Nowy Dziennik*, 24 August 1921, 1–2.

14. For more on this observation, see Jeff Spinner, *The Boundaries of Citizenship: Race, Ethnicity, and Nationality in the Liberal State* (Baltimore, MD: Johns Hopkins University Press, 1994), 168–72 and John Keane, *Civil Society and the State: New European Perspectives* (London and New York: Verso, 1988).

15. In the Russian and East European context, see Joseph Bradley, 'Subjects into Citizens: Societies, Civil Society, and Autocracy in Tsarist Russia', *American Historical Review*, 107 (4), October 2002, 1094–123 and Keely Stauter-Halsted, *The Nation in the Village: The Genesis of Peasant National Identity in Austrian Poland, 1848–1914* (Ithaca, NY: Cornell University Press, 2001).

16. On the increase of the right in Polish politics after Piłsudski's death, see Edward Wynot, _Polish Politics in Transition: The Camp of National Unity and the Struggle for Power, 1935–1939_ (Athens: University of Georgia Press, 1974). Irina Livezeanu has described the narrow options of secular Jewish intellectuals as young ethnic Polish members of the intelligentsia stepped up their efforts to remove Jews from the universities and limit their chances for professional advancement in 'Inter-war Poland and Romania: The Nationalization of Elites, the Vanishing Middle, and the Problem of Intellectuals', in _Cultures and Nations of Central and Eastern Europe_, eds Zvi Gitelman et al. (Cambridge, MA: Ukrainian Research Institute, Harvard University, 2000).

17. Benedict Anderson, _Imagined Communities: Reflections on the Origins and Spread of Nationalism_ (London: Verson, 1983).

18. The unpublished material of Zofia Wordliczek in the archives of the Cracow city museum provides an idea of the range of the separate institutions that were founded during the inter-war period. Her work is the most helpful starting point for any research into the Jewish history of the city. Separate institutions, such as the Jewish clubs listed by Wordliczek, the Yiddish theatre, or the Jewish student organizations at the university provided the private spaces where ethnic identity could flourish. Zofia Wordliczek, 'Wystawa' and 'Szkolnictwo żydowskie na terenie miasta Krakowa w okresie II Rzeczypospolitej Polskiej', unpublished material in the library of the Muzeum m. Krakowa, Stara Synagoga. The local archives of Cracow, the Wojewódzkie Archiwum Państwowe w Krakowie (State Archives in Cracow, hereafter, WAPKr), holds files related to the official registration of these organizations and, in many cases, their activities.

19. Czesław Brzoza, 'Jewish Periodicals in Krakow (1918–1939)' in _Bibliographies of Polish Judaica. International Symposium Cracow 5th–7th July 1988 (Proceedings)_ (Cracow: Research Center of Jewish History and Culture in Poland, 1993). Brzoza's complete bibliography, detailing publication information for each title, is the starting point for any research into the city's Jewish press.

20. Spinner, _The Boundaries of Citizenship_, 171, 187.

21. Moyshe Blekher, 'Vilne un Kroke – Tsvey veltn', _Di post_, 3 September 1937, 6. Blekher's role in the development of the Cracow Yiddish press is discussed further below and at length in Chapter 3.

22. Rozenblit, _The Jews of Vienna, 1867–1914: Assimilation and Identity_.

23. Rafael F. Scharf, _Poland, What Have I to Do with Thee: Essays without Prejudice_ (London: Vallentine Mitchell, 1998), 69.

24. Milton M. Gordon, _Assimilation in American Life: The Role of Race, Religion, and National Origins_ (New York: Oxford University Press, 1964), 71.

25. Weeks, 'Poles, Jews, and Russians, 1863–1914: The Death of the Ideal of Assimilation in the Kingdom of Poland', 242.

26. The phrase is Brian Porter's, from his _When Nationalism Began to Hate: Imagining Modern Politics in Nineteenth-Century Poland_ (New York: Oxford University Press, 2000).

27. Józef Buszko, 'The Consequences of Galician Autonomy after 1867', _Polin: Focusing on Galicia: Jews, Poles, and Ukrainians 1772–1918_, 12 (1999), 94.

28. On the immediate post-First World War violence in Cracow, see Shlomo Leser, _The Polish–Jewish Relations in Cracow and Vicinity, on the background of the events and the frictions in the area, in the years 1918–1925. Part I, The anti-Jewish events, the Jewish self-defense, the frictions and the attempts at reaching understanding in 1918–1920_ (Haifa: Preliminary Edition, Vaadat Hahantsakha shel Yotsey Krakov b'haifa, 1992).

29. These are discussed at length in the work of Emanuel Meltzer, _No Way Out: The Politics of Polish Jewry, 1935–1939_.

30. For an extended discussion of the attempts to limit the number of Jewish students in the universities, see Szymon Rudnicki, 'From "Numerus Clausus" to "Numerus Nullus"', in *From Shtetl to Socialism, Studies from Polin*, ed. Antony Polonsky (London: Littman Library of Jewish Civilization, 1993), 359–85.

31. Milton Gordon, *Assimilation in American Life*, 71.

32. 'O szkołę żydowską', *Nowy Dziennik*, 24 July 1919, 1.

33. Joshua Fishman, 'Ethnicity as Being, Doing, and Living,' in *Ethnicity*, eds John Hutchinson and Anthony Smith (Oxford: Oxford University Press, 1996), 68.

34. The phrase is Roman Szporluk's, quoted by Zvi Gitelman, 'A Centenary of Jewish Politics in Eastern Europe: The Legacy of the Bund and the Zionist Movements', *East European Politics and Societies*, 11, no. 3 (Fall 1997): 548.

35. Emil Dorian, *The Quality of Witness: A Romanian Diary, 1937–1944*, trans. Mara Soceanu Vamos (Philadelphia, PA: Jewish Publication Society of America, 1982) and Raphael Patai, *Apprentice in Budapest: Memories of a World that is No More* (Salt Lake City: University of Utah Press, 1988).

36. Calvin Goldscheider and Alan Zuckerman, *The Transformation of the Jews* (Chicago, IL: University of Chicago Press, 1984); Pierre Birnbaum and Ira Katznelson, 'Emancipation and the Liberal Offer', in *Paths of Emancipation: Jews, States, and Citizenship*, eds Birnbaum and Katznelson (Princeton, NJ: Princeton University Press, 1995): 3–37.

37. These figures come from the reports of the city's statistics office, the Biuro Statystyczne Miasta Krakowa, and are cited by Stanisław Piech in his *W cieniu kościołów i synagog: Życie religijne międzywojennego Krakowa 1918–1939* (Cracow: Secesja, 1999), 22. This source, *Sprawozdania statystyczne z lat 1924–1939*, cites 54,233 Jews in Cracow in 1931; 56,515 is the number of Jews in Cracow cited by Jacob Lestchinsky in his 1943 article on the urban population of Poland, 'Yidn in gresere shet fun poyln 1921–1931', *YIVO bleter* (January–February 1943) 22 (1), 25. The problem of the censuses of 1921 and 1931 in relation to the city's Jewish press is discussed further in Chapter 2.

38. These numbers are taken from Ezra Mendelsohn, *The Jews of East Central Europe Between the World Wars*, 23. Mendelsohn quotes Rafael Mahler, *Yehude polin ben shte milhamot ha-olam* (Tel Aviv, 1968), 35.

39. The most important account of Cracow's early Jewish history is the two-volume *Historja Żydów w Krakowie i na Kazimierzu 1304–1868* (Cracow: 'Nadzieja' Towarzystwo ku wspieraniu chorej młodzieży żydowskiej szkół średnich i wyższych w Krakowie, 1931; reprinted in Cracow by Krajowa Agencja Wydawnicza, 1991), the work of the eminent Polish-Jewish historian Majer Bałaban. Andrzej Żbikowski has written a major and impressive work, *Żydzi krakowscy i ich gmina 1867–1918* (Warsaw: Żydowski Instytut Historyczny, 1994). An important addition to the history of *fin-de-siècle* Cracow, *Żydzi krakowscy* is meant intentionally to address the lack of attention to Jewish issues in other, more general studies. Two important collections of articles in Hebrew are *Ha-yehudim b'krakov: khayah v'khurbanah shel kehila etika* (Haifa: Vaadat Hahantsakha shel Yotsey Krakov b'haifa, 1981), ed. Shlomo Leser and *Kroka-Kaz'imiyez'-Krakov: mekharim be-toldot Yehude Krakov*, ed. Elhanan Reiner (Tel-Aviv: ha-Merkaz le-heker toldot ha-Yehudim be-Polin u-morashtam, ha Makhon le-heker ha-tefutsot, Universitat Tel Aviv, 2001). An increasingly popular tourist destination, Cracow is the subject of many guidebooks and brief works for popular audiences, but scholarly material in English is limited to survey articles of the period before the First World War and the inter-war period. The survey articles by Jan Małecki, 'Cracow Jews in the 19th Century: Leaving the Ghetto', *Acta Poloniae Historica*, LXXVI (1997): 85–97; Francis W. Carter, 'Ethnic Groups in Cracow', in *Ethnic Identity in Urban Europe*, ed. Max Engman (New York:

New York University Press, 1992): 241–67; and Lawrence Orton, 'The Formation of Modern Cracow (1866–1914)', *Austrian History Yearbook*, XIX–XX, Part I, 105–19 provide the best introduction in English to the history of Cracow and its ethnic minorities. Also see the long *Encyclopedia Judaica* entry 'Cracow' by A. Cygielman and 'Krakov', *Pinkas Hakehillot, Polin*, V. 3, eds A. Wein and A. Weiss (Jerusalem: Yad Vashem, 1984), 1–43. At least one scholarly article in Yiddish has been written on inter-war Cracow. Kalman Shtayn examines the relationship between the Jews and the city government from his own perspective as a participant in 'Di yidn in krokever shtotrat, 1918–1939', *Yorbukh* (Buenos Aires: World Federation of Polish Jews, 1970). Other secondary work concentrates on specific aspects of the Cracow Jewish community, such as Jews within Cracow's Jagiellonian University, religious life, or the Yiddish theatre. These works include Mariusz Kułczykowski, *Żydzi-studenci Uniwersytetu Jagiellcońskiego w dobie autonomicznej Galicji (1867–1918)* (Kraków: Instytut Historii Uniwersytetu Jagiellcońskiego, 1995); Stanisław Piech, *W cieniu kosciołów i synagog: Życie religijne międzywojennego Krakowa 1918–1939* (Kraków: Wydawnictwo i Drukarnia 'Secesja', 1999); Jan Michalik and Eugenia Prokop-Janiec, eds, *Teatr żydowski w Krakowie* (Kraków: Uniwersytet Jagiełłonski, Międzywydziałowy Zakład Historii i Kultury Żydów w Polsce, 1995) and Mirosława Bułat, 'Historia teatru żydowskiego w Krakowie: rekonesans badawczy', in *Żydzi i Judaizm w współczesnych badaniach polskich*, ed. K. Pilarczyk (Krakow: Księgarnia Akademicka, 1997), 413–28. Bułat's groundbreaking study of the Yiddish theatre in Cracow is vital to understanding how Yiddish culture developed among a polonized Jewish community. On other Jewish communities in Poland, see Gabriela Zalewska, *Ludność żydowska w Warszawie w okresie międzywojennym* (Warsaw: Państwowe Wydawnictwo Naukowe, 1996); Wacław Wierzbieniec, *Społeczność żydowska Przemyśla w latach 1918–1939* (Rzeszów: Wydawnictwo wyższej szkoły pedagogicznej, 1996); Konrad Zieliński, *W cieniu synagogi: Obraz życia kulturalnego społeczności żydowskiej Lublina w latach okupacji austro-węgierskiej* (Lublin: Wydawnictwo Uniwersytetu Marii Curie-Skłodowskiej, 1998); Aleksander Pakentreger, *Żydzi w Kaliszu w latach 1918–1939* (Warsaw: Państwowe Wydawnictwo Naukowe, 1988); Hanna Domańska, *Żydzi znad Gdańskiej Zatoki* (Warsaw: Agencja Wydawnicza TU, 1997); and the anthology, *Żydowskie gminy wyznaniowe* (Wrocław: Towarzystwo Przyjaciół Polonistyki Wrocławskie, 1995).

40. Cracow was still something of a competitor, though. Fears that Cracow was overtaking Lwów as a centre for regional trade were expressed in the Yiddish press of Lwów. See 'Lemberg's tsukunft', *Togblat*, 13 November 1920, 1.

41. Israel Bartal and Antony Polonsky, 'Introduction: The Jews of Galicia Under the Habsburgs', *Polin: Focusing on Galicia: Jews, Poles, and Ukrainians 1772–1918*, Vol. 12 (1999), 7.

42. Contemporaries used these appellations and debated their applications to specific cities. See, for example, 'Fraye tribune', *Di post*, 17 September 1937, 7.

43. On the current trend in Jewish historiography to focus on the multiple dimensions of the Jewish experience in various settings, see Robert Seltzer, 'Jewish History After the End of Ideology', Hunter College Jewish Social Studies Program, Occasional Papers in Jewish History and Thought, No. 9, New York, 2000.

44. See note 39.

45. Mendelsohn, *The Jews of East Central Europe Between the Wars*, 6.

46. Ibid., 8.

47. Gmina Wyznania Żydowskiego Krakowa, Żydowski Instytut Historyczny.

48. Aryeh Bauminger et al., eds, *Sefer kroke* (Jerusalem: Mosad ha-Rav Kuk, 1958); *New Cracow Friendship Society Silver Anniversary, 1965–1990* (New York: New Cracow Friendship Society, 1990).

49. See especially Miriam Akavia, *Moja Winnica* (Warsaw: Państwowy Instytut Wydawniczy, 1990) and *Jesień młodości* (Cracow: Wydawnictwo Literackie, 1989); Michał Borwicz, *Ludzie, Książki, Spory* (Paris: Księgarnia Polska w Paryżu, 1980); Irena Bronner, *Cykady nad Wisłą i Jordanem* (Kraków: Wydawnictwo Literackie, 1991); Natan Gross, *Kim pan jest, panie Grymek?* (Kraków: Wydawnictwo Literackie, 1991); Halina Nelken, *Pamiętnik z getta w Krakowie* (Toronto: Polski Fundusz Wydawniczy w Kanadzie, 1987) [published in English as *And Yet, I am Here!* (Amherst: University of Massachusetts Press, 1999)]; Henryk Ritterman-Abir, *Nie od razu Kraków zapomniano* (Tel Aviv: Związek Żydów Krakowian w Izraelu, 1984); Rafael F. Scharf, *Poland, What Have I to Do with Thee?*; Bronisław Szatyn, *Na aryskich papierach* (Kraków: Wydawnictwo Literackie, 1983); Henryk Vogler, *Autoportret z pamięći* (Kraków: Wydawnictwo Literackie, 1978) and *Wyznanie mojżeszowe* (Warsaw: Państwowy Instytut Wydawniczy, 1994). See also the long article by Manuel Rympel, 'Słowo o Żydach krakowskich w okresie międzywojennym (1918–1939)', in *Kopiec wspomnień*, ed. Jan Gintel (Cracow: Wydawnictwo Literackie, 1964), 555–88.

50. Ernest Gellner has asserted that education confers citizenship and 'an educational system must operate in some medium, some language … and the language it employs will stamp its products'. Ernest Gellner, *Thought and Change* (Chicago, IL: University of Chicago Press, 1965), 159.

51. Records relating to private Jewish organizations and public institutions in which Jews participated can be found in Cracow's city and regional archives, Wojewódzkie Państwowe Archiwum w Krakowie.

52. *Gazeta Gminna*, 25 November 1937, 1.

1
From Habsburg Rule to Independent Poland

*I suddenly have the desire to write about my native Kroke –
I don't mean, God forbid, goyish Cracow with its noble
palaces, its gardens and its hundred monasteries, but simply
old Jewish Kroke with its main streets and its alleyways, its
synagogues, prayerhouses,* minyans *and* khevres, *its
Hasidic* shtiblekh, *and its 'Reform Temple'.*

Gershom Bader, *Mayne zikhroynes*
(Buenos Aires: Tsentral-farband fun
poylishe yidn in argentine, 1953), 9

Jews have been present in Cracow since 1176. They lived on the
narrow streets of the old city, near the city centre, on the same
streets where the university would be built in 1364 and on
which acculturated Jewish students would be attacked in the
late 1930s. Their physical location in the city centre at such an
early date suggests that they were never far from Poles and
Polish culture. But the history of the Jews of Cracow is
primarily the history of the Jews of Kazimierz, the
neighbouring city in which Jews lived after various regulations
excluded them from Cracow, and the area where the Jewish
journalist and writer Gershom Bader grew up in the late
nineteenth century.

The population of Cracow during the inter-war period grew
from nearly 184,000 in 1921 to over 245,000 in 1935. Jews
consistently made up about 25 per cent of that total, over 28 per
cent in 1935. Most of these Jews, 56.9 per cent, lived in
Kazimierz and Stradom, the neighbouring district.[1] In these two
districts, Jews made up 71.2 per cent of the total population.
The next largest Jewish neighbourhood was Podgórze, directly
across the river from Kazimierz. While Francis W. Carter points

out the importance of residential segregation for the maintenance of ethnic ties among the Jewish community, he also notes that the more upwardly mobile Jews of Cracow had begun to move to other districts, notably Śródmieście, the centre of the city, by 1910.[2] But there was still no need to establish a synagogue outside of Kazimierz until the 1930s.

Kazimierz, immortalized in film in the 1930s and the 1990s, has long reminded visitors to Cracow of a typical Jewish neighbourhood, such as the one Bader describes in his memoir depicting Jewish life in the city in the late nineteenth century. The neighbourhood served as the setting of the Molly Picon Yiddish film classic *Yidl mitn Fidl* and as the wartime ghetto of Cracow for Spielberg's *Schindler's List*, even though the real ghetto had been located across the river in Podgórze. Kazimierz was initially separated from the royal capital of Cracow by decree. In the modern period, Cracow Jewish history is at least in part the story of how Jews returned to the city centre, physically, politically, socially and culturally.

Settlement of Jews in Kazimierz occurred only gradually until the late fifteenth century. The area of Kazimierz, just outside of Cracow's old town and a short walk from the Planty, the ring of trees surrounding the city centre, was not founded as a separate settlement until 1335, when the Polish King Kazimierz Wielki [Casimir the Great] established the town as a commercial rival to Cracow.[3] Jews settled in Kazimierz shortly after its founding; the two cities were originally separated only by the city walls. In the late fourteenth century, Jews living on the streets where the university was to be built were forced to give up their homes and move to another nearby location (today's Plac Szczepański). The visit of the Franciscan preacher Juan Capistrano in 1454 resulted in riots against the Jews. Two fires in the last twenty-five years of the fifteenth century exacerbated the already tense relations between the town's Jews and non-Jews, and in 1495, King Jan Olbracht expelled the Jews from Cracow.[4] They went to Kazimierz, which was thereafter known as a *miasto żydowskie* [Jewish city].

The Alte Shul [Old Synagogue] was built in Kazimierz in the middle of the fifteenth century. In time, the Jewish community established other synagogues and cemeteries, and Kazimierz became one of the most important intellectual centres of Polish

Jewry. The most notable Jewish leader to emerge from Kazimierz in the sixteenth century was Rabbi Moses Isserles (1520–72), the codifier of Jewish religious law known widely as the 'Remu' or 'Remah'. His work *Mapah* [tablecloth] accompanied Joseph Karo's *Shulhan Arukh* [the set table], a set of legal codes applied to daily life. Isserles's legacy enriched the Jewish community of Cracow greatly, giving it a reputation that reached far beyond the city's borders.

Later Jewish leaders have emphasized Isserles's friendly relations with the non-Jewish community. The social scientist Feliks Gross has written that conditions for the Jews were 'favorable' in the fifteenth and sixteenth centuries.[5] Comparing the situation of the Jews in Cracow to that of the Jews in Germany, Isserles wrote to a friend: 'I believe it is better to eat dark bread in our countries ... because in our lands we do not feel hatred, as you feel in Germany.'[6] Ber Meisels, the chief rabbi of Cracow in the mid-nineteenth century, remarked that Isserles 'indicated to us that we should love the Polish nation above all other nations, for the Poles have been our brothers for centuries'.[7] In his study of the spiritual legacy of Polish Jews, Byron Sherwin notes the conflict between Cracow's Rabbi Isserles and Isaac Luria.[8] Luria argued that the study of non-Jewish sources by Jewish scholars could damage the Jewish tradition. In contrast, Isserles employed the works of Aristotle in his analyses of Jewish law. The use of non-Jewish culture by Jewish leaders in the inter-war period echoes Isserles's unorthodox approach to the study of Jewish tradition. Even during the medieval period, Jewish leaders in Cracow looked to outside sources to assist in the organizing of their own community. Isserles's grave still stands in the city's old Jewish cemetery, near what is known today as the Remuh synagogue. Cracow remains a place of pilgrimage for religious Jews from all over the world because of the work of Isserles.

At the time of Isserles's death, in 1572, the population of Cracow numbered just over 2,000. Immigrants from Bohemia and Moravia, Germany, Italy, Portugal and Spain added to the community, increasing economic competition between Jews and non-Jews and making it necessary to expand the areas in which Jews could own property and live. After their settlement in Kazimierz, the Jews continually fought for rights to trade and work in Cracow. Restrictions placed on the Jews' ability to trade in Cracow were occasionally overturned, only to be put in place again later. In spite of the economic anti-Semitism, the Jewish community of the city continued to grow. Though they were affected by the general economic decline of the region after the violence and pogroms of 1648, Jews expanded their role in local trade, worked as goldsmiths, and participated in the arenda system of the leasing of estates.[9] The tension between the Jews of Kazimierz and the citizens of Cracow over the right of Jews to trade in Cracow continued throughout the eighteenth century.

The boundary changes of the late eighteenth and early nineteenth centuries left permanent marks on the populations of Cracow and Kazimierz. The partitions of 1772–76 divided Kazimierz, which found itself under Austrian rule, from Cracow, which still belonged to Poland. Kazimierz was returned to Poland in 1776, but the prohibition on Jewish commerce in Cracow continued. Although some wealthy Jews left Cracow for other cities, this prohibition led to the development of Kazimierz as many Jews transferred their businesses there.

Further political changes prevented any stable development. In 1795 Kazimierz came under Austrian rule, but in 1809 Cracow was made a part of the Grand Duchy of Warsaw. In 1815 the Congress of Vienna formed the Republic of Cracow, which lasted until 1846. This period allowed the Poles of Cracow at least some degree of self-rule, and this historic memory of relative freedom became important as Poland continued under the rule of the partitioning powers. It is at least partly this historic memory that made visiting Poles to Cracow, such as Stefan Żeromski, marvel at the Polishness of the city.[10] The Republic distinguished the city from other areas in Poland and at least partly accounts for Cracow's reputation as 'the most Polish of Polish cities'. During the period of the Republic, there were slightly over ten thousand Jews living in Cracow, making up over a quarter of the city's population.[11] Cracow's subsequent development within Austrian Galicia, combined with trends from within the Jewish community, would help to transform the community over the next century.

TOWARDS REFORMING THE COMMUNITY

In the early to mid-nineteenth century the Jews of Cracow were primarily oriented towards German culture. By the end of the century, the non-Jewish culture the Jews aspired to adopt had switched to Polish. Religious reforms accepted by Jewish elites in Western Europe had their counterparts in the largest Jewish communities of Eastern Europe, and Cracow was no exception. Moves towards integration and greater participation in the non-Jewish majority culture accompanied religious reform, and, in Cracow, where Polish national identity was so strong, led to an affiliation with Polish culture that later generations maintained even as they returned to Yiddish and Hebrew.

The ideas of the Haskalah, or Jewish Enlightenment, reached Cracow in the early nineteenth century. A group of *maskilim*, or Jewish enlighteners, established in 1844 what came to be known colloquially as the 'Tempel', or the Reform Temple or Progressive Synagogue.[12] The synagogue arose through the efforts of the Association of Progressive Israelites (*Stowarzyszenie Izraelitów Postępowych*). Services in this architecturally impressive synagogue in the Moorish Renaissance style were first conducted in German, highlighting the influence of the Haskalah on the *maskilim* of Cracow and their differentiation from less assimilated, more Orthodox Jews.

Cracow's Jews were active in the 1848 revolutionary fighting in Cracow and Rabbi Dov Berush Meisels was elected to the Reichsrat in Vienna in the 1848 elections. Though some Jewish leaders continued to fight for emancipation and for integration into Polish society, the hopes of 1848 were not realized until further political developments in the Habsburg Empire brought significant changes. The high point of co-operation between Polish Jews and Polish romantic nationalists came during the 1863 uprising against the Russian Empire, which Rabbi Meisels supported.[13] As Feliks Gross has written about the Jews in Poland, and specifically Cracow, during the nineteenth century, ' ... a tie between Polish patriotic insurrectionists and Polish Jews was established and a foundation laid for future integration and unity'.[14]

Greater cultural autonomy in Galicia after 1867 allowed for the development of Polish cultural institutions in Cracow.[15]

Cracow has come to be known colloquially as the 'Polish Athens', due largely to its royal heritage and its role in *fin-de-siècle* Polish culture. In addition, the influence of German culture in Cracow remained minimal, as Lwów was the administrative capital of Galicia and thus had more direct contact with the Austrians.[16] As Lwów had the greater tie to Vienna, Cracow was left free to become a centre of Polish culture; indeed, the *fin-de-siècle* artistic movement Young Poland (*Młoda Polska*) assured Cracow's status as the spiritual centre of the divided Polish nation. In Cracow, a city of primarily Poles and Jews, Jews could identify with the West through a Polish culture that acted as a mediator for Vienna.[17]

Widely regarded as a bastion of Polishness during the period of the partitions, Cracow nevertheless was home to a significant minority population, and political developments within the Austrian Empire always affected the Jews. Greater cultural autonomy for the Poles in 1867/1868 was accompanied by the emancipation of the Jews.[18] The more liberal conditions of the Austrians in the mid-nineteenth century, combined with internal trends of the Jewish community such as the Haskalah, made it possible for the Jews of Cracow to acculturate towards Polish culture in the late nineteenth century, thus transforming Jewish national identity.

COMPETING TRENDS: ORTHODOXY, INTEGRATION AND ZIONISM

Perhaps partly due to the moderate political climate, political movements of different persuasions found a home in Cracow. By the beginning of the twentieth century, Jewish nationalists, both Zionists and Bundists, complicated a Jewish political scene that already included Orthodox and progressive leaders. The Jews, too, were able to find a place within city government as early as the last years of the nineteenth century. As Jews began to move increasingly towards Polish culture at the turn of the century, a group of politically active Jews served at various times on the Cracow city council.[19] Jewish participation in the city government at this point was not a specific assertion of Jewish ethnic identity but rather the result of individual Jews' efforts to integrate into Polish society. Indicating that this integration was not quite total assimilation, Józef Sare was the first city council member not to renounce his Jewish religious identity.[20] While some Jewish leaders became involved in city government, others continued to work specifically within the Jewish community and to develop political parties that would eventually wield local, regional and national influence.

The *kehillah* (*kehillah* in Hebrew, *kahal* in Yiddish, and *gmina* in Polish) was the mostly autonomous Jewish community organization governing the most important questions of Jewish religious life and acting as the formal representative of the community in interactions with first Polish and then Austrian authorities. Throughout the nineteenth century, control of the *kehillah* was the focus of constant struggle between the progressives gathered around the Tempel, often termed assimilationists, and the city's Orthodox community.[21] The progressives and Orthodox clashed over important issues in the late nineteenth century, most notably over Jewish religious education in the public schools.[22] As might be expected, the progressives favoured a gradual polonization of the Jewish community while the Orthodox fought for the instruction of Hebrew and continued to establish and maintain the traditional schools, called heders, for the religious education of Jewish boys, even after a sharp wave of criticism of the heders in the 1870s.[23] Nevertheless, the Polish-language education of Jewish children begun by the city's progressives had its effect. Just as Jews were developing education for Jews in Polish, so too were Poles beginning the process of polonizing the Galician school system. Józef Buszko attributes the Jews' pro-Polish stance to these changes in the Galician schools in the 1860s.[24]

The progressives and Orthodox controlled the *kehillah* in Cracow for decades before the inter-war period, having come to the workable political accommodation that the Jewish progressive leaders would act as a liaison with the Polish community while the Orthodox would manage religious matters such as the rabbinate, *mikvah* (ritual bath) and ritual slaughter. But the last decades of the nineteenth century would see the emergence of a new trend that would completely transform the Jewish community during the inter-war period.

Writing in the Jewish Polish-language weekly *Nasza Opinja*

[*Our Opinion*] in 1936, the Cracow Zionist leader Dawid Bulwa noted that in the 1880s there was no Jewish social work or political life in Cracow, but that the situation changed with the advent of Zionist activity in the 1890s. While Bulwa's statement is an exaggeration, the development of a new group within Jewish civil society began in that decade. Early Zionist organizations in Cracow inclined towards the political Zionism of Theodor Herzl included Sfas Emes and Libanon. Przedświt-Haszachar, a Zionist organization for Jewish youth, was founded in 1897 by a group of Jewish leaders that included Chaim Hilfstein, later the director of the Hebrew gymnasium during the inter-war period. Przedświt-Haszachar remained active throughout the inter-war period. During the early years of the organization, members organized special events for Hanukkah and Makkabi evenings. Other organizations began to develop as well, such as Achdut, an association of small traders, Ruth, a women's organization, and Beys Israel, a religious group. The appearance in the 1880s of the Hebrew newspaper *Hamagid*, edited by Samuel Fuchs and then Simeon Menahem Lazar, is also an important indication of the national awakening taking place within the Jewish leadership of the city.

The arrival of Ozjasz Thon in Cracow in 1897 as rabbi of the Tempel can serve as the beginning of the transformation of part of the Jewish community of Cracow into Jewish nationalists. Thon's arrival spurred Zionist activity. Born in Lwów, Thon was without doubt the most significant Jewish political leader to come out of Cracow; his influence on the Zionist politics of Western Galicia is unparalleled, while his contributions to the betterment of the position of the Jews in Cracow should not be underestimated.[25] After his arrival in the city, Thon taught the Jewish religious classes in the public schools. He was later instrumental in founding the Hebrew gymnasium. Although he was a delegate to the *Sejm*, the Polish parliament, during the inter-war period, Thon remained connected to his community through his daily work. He wrote often for *Nowy Dziennik* and presided over the Hebrew gymnasium's *matura* examinations (university entrance examinations) for Hebrew language and literature.

The first steps toward greater involvement in Polish society were taken well before 1918. By the time Thon became rabbi at the Tempel, services were held in Polish and the Tempel served as the spiritual centre of Cracow's acculturated Jewish leadership. This Reform synagogue built in the 1840s with German as the language of prayer was clearly assimilationist but, not unlike the Great Synagogue in Warsaw, became increasingly Zionist at the turn of the century.[26] The emergence of Polish as the language of Reform Judaism in Cracow, however, is at the same time evidence of a tendency towards greater involvement in aspects of the majority culture. Thon, who led the Tempel as well as the Zionists of Cracow and the region of Małopolska until his death in 1936, was instrumental in the effort to maintain a Jewish identity within a Polish environment. Thon's tireless efforts for the Zionist cause and for the improvement of living conditions for Jews in Poland exemplify the tendency of Cracow Jewry to live their lives in both the Jewish and Polish communities.

In addition to the Zionists and the progressive and Orthodox leaders of the *kehillah*, a new political force emerged. Though the Zionists often receive greater attention in the history of Jewish politics in light of their organizational activities and subsequent events, the integrationists have been called the strongest political force in Cracow Jewish politics in the early twentieth century.[27] Represented by Adolf Gross, who formed the Party of Independent Jews in 1900, this group 'opposed both the complete assimilation of the Jews and their medieval-style segregation in ghettos'.[28] Sare, also an advocate of integration, was elected deputy mayor of Cracow in 1905. The journal *Tygodnik* [*Weekly*] served as the voice of these Jewish democrats when it first appeared in 1905. According to the Zionist leader Dawid Bulwa, the Zionists regarded the integrationists as a reactionary force 'darkening' national consciousness.

The appearance of the Bund in Cracow in 1902, along with the activities of the Polish Socialist Party, also offered the Zionists competition. Both the Bund and the Polish Socialist Party criticized the Zionists, declaring Zionism a reactionary movement. Since Jewish votes were needed for a socialist mandate in local elections, Zionists had to work harder to attract supporters. Other organizations were founded in the first decade of the twentieth century as well. These included two political groups that would provide the toughest competition for the Bund, the Mizrakhi group of religious Zionists and Poale Zion, the group of labour Zionists, the latter being one of the more politically significant Jewish groups in Cracow. Both groups would later be active throughout the inter-war period.

The increase in political activity led to cultural development as well. Jewish nationalists began to establish their own organizations in the city, including a reading room and lending library and organizations the purpose of which was to establish private Jewish education in the city. Fighting the fight on both political and cultural fronts, as elsewhere in Eastern Europe, Cracow's Jews laid the foundation for political ideas and institutions that would characterize their community during the inter-war period.

COMMUNAL TRANSFORMATION AND COMMUNAL AUTHORITY

The Zionists began to win over larger and larger segments of the Jewish community after the First World War. Bulwa described the war as a real break in the development of the Jewish community. According to Bulwa, Cracow Jews turned to Zionism after the war as the result of the immediate post-war anti-Jewish violence and as a response to the new spirit of self-determination in Europe. Jewish leaders in Cracow who espoused integration into the majority population as a solution to the Jewish question now faced even greater challenges from a renewed Zionist community following the First World War.

The last years of the war saw the appearance of the Polish-language Jewish daily *Nowy Dziennik* [*New Daily*], which grew to have international significance within the Jewish community and became the most important newspaper of Cracow Jewry. *Nowy Dziennik* was founded amid the turmoil of war and at least partly in response to the violent anti-Semitic outbreaks of 1918. The pogrom in Cracow of 16–21 April 1918, in which one Jewish man was killed, was said to be the 'revenge of the Poles for Chełmszczyzna', the territory in the east occupied by the Red Army after the establishment of the Central Ukrainian Council in February 1918.[29] A recent increase in the price of flour may also have been a significant factor in the civil unrest.[30] The pogrom intensified the fear of the Jewish community and suggested that relations between

Poles and Jews would change for the worse after the period of independence. The importance of the pogroms in Poland at the end of the First World War, in late 1918 and early 1919, cannot be overestimated in the development of Jewish national consciousness in Poland, and particularly in Cracow.[31] The anti-Semitic violence coincided with the reorganization of the Polish state, and Jewish nationalists responded to this in various ways, depending on where they lived. Western Galicia was more clearly on the side of Polish independence than the other regions of Poland, because of Cracow's unique position under Habsburg rule. Yet the need for self-defence among Jews in Cracow is clear.

In response to the pogrom atmosphere in Cracow, the editors of *Nowy Dziennik* called for the formation of a Jewish National Council (*Żydowska Rada Narodowa*), a self-defence organization.[32] The Jewish National Council originally included the general Zionists, the labour Zionists and the Jewish socialists. The socialists bowed out of the council in December of 1918, to be replaced by the Mizrakhi, the religious Zionists, making the Jewish self-defence organization much less an organization representing Cracow Jewry and more of a Zionist instrument to protect and defend the Jewish community.

Like the formation of the Jewish National Council, the establishment of *Nowy Dziennik* in July of 1918 signalled a new level of activity for the Jewish nationalists. The editors of *Nowy Dziennik* made urgent pleas in its first issues for the cause of Jewish self-defence, while at the same time expressing genuine enthusiasm for the establishment of an independent Poland, recognizing this as part of the solution to the terrible conditions in which the Polish Jews found themselves. Thus the history of Jewish national development in Cracow cannot be separated from the history of anti-Semitism or the history of independent Poland.

In spite of Jewish support for an independent Poland, tensions between Poles and Jews increased in 1919 when a trivial incident in the Sukiennice (Cracow's Cloth Hall, the dominant feature of the market square) erupted into a full-scale pogrom.[33] The incident involved an altercation between a Jewish merchant and two soldiers from the division of the Polish legionnaire General Józef Haller. Some in the Polish press termed the subsequent looting of Jewish stores the result of 'Jewish–German–Ukrainian' provocateurs. Others called on the 'good' elements among the Jews to continue their fight against the Jewish nationalists. Haller's commanding officers denied that any of their soldiers had participated in what the socialist journal *Naprzód* unhesitatingly termed a pogrom.[34]

While the leaders Adolf Gross and Józef Sare still advocated their integrationist stance and began working with the Union of Poles of the Jewish Faith based in Warsaw, the Zionists who had founded the Jewish National Council spoke out against ethnic violence and positioned themselves to take over the leading position in Cracow Jewry. Although it took them ten years to win any electoral victories in the *kehillah*, the Zionists succeeded in establishing a network of ethnically based organizations that addressed many important needs of the Jewish community, including the care of Jewish children orphaned during wartime. Indicating the tensions between the different Jewish groups, an important article in *Nowy Dziennik* called the *kehillah* the 'foundation of nation building' and asserted that assimilationists should not be allowed within the *kehillah*.[35] Andrzej Żbikowski also points out that the establishment of the Hebrew gymnasium in 1918, the culmination of the efforts of a Jewish educational society that had been founded in 1902, added to the increasing influence of the Zionists at this time.

Jewish integrationists such as Gross and Sare, also often termed assimilationists, were increasingly weakened as a result of the Zionist political activity in Cracow during and after the last years of the war. While Cracow's Zionists did not demand a Jewish political state within Poland, the recent success of Polish nationalism, the establishment of an independent Poland, inspired Jewish nationalists to work harder to achieve their goals. Furthermore, the Zionists had not abandoned the goal of the integrationist leaders to work towards coexistence between Poles and Jews. They had simply recognized that assimilationist tactics had not worked.[36] Throughout the inter-war period, Zionist leaders would reiterate that part of their goals as Jewish nationalists was to work towards the rapprochement of Jews and Poles through the founding of separate Jewish institutions. The wisdom of adopting this tactic is not readily apparent, but the activities of Cracow's Zionist leaders make a strong case for the argument that private minority institutions can often impart cultural values of the majority community as well.

The issue of which groups represented the Jewish community is a particularly difficult one. The different Jewish political groups in Cracow included the Zionists (themselves divided into several factions), Agudes yisroel (the newly formed political party of the Orthodox), groups of independent Jewish leaders who advocated assimilation towards Polish culture, and the Bund (the nationalist party of the Jewish working class). Within the community, political power was centred in the local governing bodies of the Polish Jewish communities or in the growing Jewish press that expressed definite political opinions. Thus, in Cracow, progressive leaders governed the official community, but the Zionists were quickly establishing the institutions of civil society, such as newspapers, schools and cultural organizations, that would transform Jewish communal life within a relatively short period.

In 1918, the Zionists were poised to take over the political and cultural leadership of the community. The arrangement between the Orthodox and progressives did not work after the First World War, when Jewish nationalists and Zionists increasingly began to argue for the democratization, nationalization and secularization of the *kehillah*.[37] The Zionists wished to transform the *kehillah* from an organization based on religious ideals into a communal institution that encompassed all the varying groups within the Jewish community, both religious and secular. This desire alone challenged the traditional structure of the community. As one scholar has noted, the democratization of Poland begun in 1918 seemed to some to be a chance for the democratization of the Jewish community.[38] Polish Zionists lobbied for the democratization of the *kehillah* before the *Sejm*. Eventually, new regulations governing the *kehillah* adopted by the state in 1927 led to greater democratization of the *kehillah* by allowing for more political parties to participate in the *kehillah* elections. The two inter-war elections for the governing board of the *kehillah* in Cracow, in 1924 and 1929, demonstrate the effects of these regulations.[39] The Zionists conducted intensive election campaigns before each election. Their opponents were a coalition of the progressive assimilationist leaders, led by Rafał Landau, the president of the *kehillah*, and the Orthodox, the so-called *kahalnicy*. The coalition, unlike the Zionists, stressed the *kehillah*'s religious functions. In 1924, the Zionists attained only one seat on the governing board out of twenty-five, but in 1929 they were more successful, winning nine seats.[40] The *kahalnicy* still had more seats, having won eleven, but the Zionists of Cracow had finally achieved some success in their long struggle to wrest control of the city's official Jewish community from the alliance of the city's Orthodox and 'assimilated' Jews.[41] This victory signalled an end to one chapter of the city's Jewish history and reflected the increasingly visible profile of Jewish nationalism in inter-war Poland.

Still, Rafał Landau remained president of the *kehillah* throughout the inter-war period. Assimilation as a viable political option for the Jewish community had clearly died by 1918, but its advocates did not necessarily become Jewish nationalists. Rather, they continued to work within the Jewish community, giving way as necessary to the emerging Zionists. While the Tempel never lost its influence within the Jewish community, the more assimilationist Jewish leaders did lose influence as Cracow's Zionists became more active. The threat of Jewish nationalism encouraged the assimilationist leaders and the Orthodox to close ranks in an alliance against Jewish nationalist influence within the *kehillah*. This unlikely political partnership led the official community until 1939.

While the Zionists had yet to win over the entire Jewish community, their focus on practical political solutions made them a formidable presence in the Jewish political arena. Even such a relatively acculturated city as Cracow could not escape the influence of the Zionists. The emergence of a Jewish nationalist politics that worked concretely and openly for goals of Jewish national autonomy transformed the Jewish community. Ezra Mendelsohn chronicles how the Zionists set out consciously to 'take over' Jewish politics in Poland and how they succeeded in this task, due in no small measure to the able efforts of Zionist leaders such as Yitzhak Grunbaum, Leon Reich and Ozjasz Thon.[42]

The growth of Jewish nationalism, like linguistic and cultural acculturation, was an important sign that the Cracow Jewish community was changing in some important ways during the inter-war period, most notably in the functioning of the *kehillah* and in the development of an increasingly visible civil society. While no institution or organization should be taken as representative of such a diverse community, taken together, the institutions and organizations Jews founded in inter-war Cracow can provide a picture of a community during a period of turbulent political development and economic distress. While the portents of war were obvious for many in the 1930s, the two decades under discussion here began with the hope that new national communities could develop and even coexist in an independent Poland. This hope was best expressed in the pages of *Nowy Dziennik*, a newspaper founded for the explicit purpose of improving the relationship between Poles and Jews.

NOTES

1. Piech, *W cieniu kościołów i synagog*, 23. See also *Drugi powszechny spis ludności z dn. 9 XII 1931 r. Miasto Kraków. Statystyka Polska*, Seria C, zeszyt 64, tab. 10–11.
2. Francis W. Carter, 'Ethnic Groups in Cracow', in *Ethnic Identity in Urban Europe*, ed. Max Engman (New York: New York University Press, 1992), 241–67.
3. Much of this background information is taken from three sources: the *Encyclopedia Judaica* article, 'Cracow', by A. Cygielman; Israel Bartal and Antony Polonsky, 'Introduction: The Jews of Galicia Under the Habsburgs', in *Polin: Focusing on Galicia: Jews, Poles, and Ukrainians, 1772–1918* ; and the classic study on the Jews in Cracow and Kazimierz, Majer Bałaban's *Historia Żydów w Krakowie i na Kazimierzu, 1304–1368*, Vols 1–2.
4. For a detailed examination of the politics surrounding the move of the Jews of Cracow to Kazimierz in 1495, see Bożena Wyrozumska, 'Did King Jan Olbracht Expel the Jews of Cracow in 1495?', in *The Jews in Poland*, Vol. 1, ed. Andrzej Paluch (Cracow: Jagiellonian University, Research Center on Jewish History and Culture in Poland, 1992).
5. Feliks Gross, *World Politics and Tension Areas* (New York: New York University Press, 1966), 134.
6. *Responsa of Moses Isserles*, No. 95 (Hebrew edition, Hanau, 1710), quoted in Gross, *World Politics and Tension Areas*, 135.
7. Meisels is quoted by Stanisław Krajewski in '"The Jewish Problem" as a Polish Problem', *Więź, Under One Heaven: Poles and Jews*, 1998: 75.
8. Byron Sherwin, *Sparks Amidst the Ashes: The Spiritual Legacy of Polish Jewry* (New York: Oxford University Press, 1997).
9. Israel Bartal and Antony Polonsky, 'Introduction: The Jews of Galicia Under the Habsburgs', 8.
10. Lawrence D. Orton, 'The Formation of Modern Cracow (1866–1914)', *Austrian History Yearbook*, XIX–XX (1983–84): Part I, 111.
11. A. Cygielman, 'Cracow', *Encyclopedia Judaica*, 1034.
12. The best full-length study of this synagogue covers a later time period but provides much information on the context of nineteenth-century Jewish history in Cracow. See Hanna Kozińska-Witt, *Die Krakauer Juedische Reformgemeinde 1864–1874*

(Frankfurt am Main: Peter Lang, 1999).

13. See Israel Bartal and Magdalena Opalski, *Poles and Jews: A Failed Brotherhood*.

14. Feliks Gross, *World Politics and Tension Areas*, 136.

15. On the process of emancipation and modernization among the Jews of Cracow, see Józef Buszko, 'The Consequences of Galician Autonomy After 1867' and Jerzy Holzer, 'Enlightenment, Assimilation, and Modern Identity: The Jewish Elite in Galicia', both in *Polin*, 12, *Focusing on Galicia: Jews, Poles, and Ukrainians, 1772–1918*.

16. Orton, 'The Formation of Modern Cracow', 107.

17. Unlike the city of Lwów, Cracow did not have a sizeable Ukrainian population.

18. For an extended study on Jewish emancipation in Poland, see Artur Eisenbach, *The Emancipation of the Jews of Poland, 1780–1870*, trans. Janina Dorosz (Oxford: Blackwell, 1991).

19. Małecki, 'Cracow Jews in the 19th Century', 93; AndrzejŻbikowski,*Żydzi krakowscy*, 135–57.

20. Małecki, 'Cracow Jews in the 19th Century', 93.

21. Assimilationists was the term used to describe this faction of Jewish leaders within the *kehillah*. It is important to remember, though, that those Jewish leaders who were called assimilationists, first by the Orthodox and then by the city's Zionists, were still active within the Jewish community.

22. Żbikowski, *Żydzi krakowscy*, 242.

23. Ibid., 247.

24. Józef Buszko, 'The Consequences of Galician Autonomy After 1867', 90.

25. For more on the biography of Thon, see the memoir of his daughter, Nella Thon Rost Hollander, *Jehoshua Thon: Preacher, Thinker, Politician* (Buenos Aires, 1966). Hollander published this memoir initially in English and then in Yiddish. Much of the material was originally published in Polish in the Jewish news weekly, *Nasza Opinja*.

26. Alexander Guterman, *Kehilat varshah ben shete milhamot ha-'olam: otonomyah le'umit be-khivle ha-hok veha-metsi'ut, 1917–1939* (Tel-Aviv: Universitat Tel-Aviv, 1997).

27. Bartal and Polonsky, 'Introduction: The Jews of Galicia Under the Habsburgs', 20.

28. Buszko, 'The Consequences of Galician Autonomy After 1867', 94.

29. Żbikowski, *Żydzi krakowscy*, 304–5.

30. Ibid., 304. For a recent re-evaluation of the pogrom, see Jan M. Małecki, 'Zamieszki w Krakowie w kwietniu 1918 r. Pogrom czy rozruchy głodowe?' in *The Jews in Poland*, Vol. 1, ed. Andrzej K. Paluch (Cracow: Jagiellonian University, 1992).

31. For a detailed account of the post-war events see Shlomo Leser, *The Polish-Jewish Relations in Cracow and Vicinity, on the Background of the Events and the Frictions in the Area, in the Years 1918–1925. Part I: The Anti-Jewish Events, the Jewish Self-defense, the Frictions and the Attempts at Reaching Understanding in 1918–1920* (Haifa: Vaadat Hahantsackha shel Yotsey Krakov b'haifa, April 1992, preliminary edition). In English and Hebrew.

32. Żbikowski, *Żydzi krakowscy*, 306.

33. Ibid., 307-8.

34. Ibid., 308.

35. Ibid., 309.

36. 'U schyłku asymilacji żydowskiej', *Chwila*, 19 March 1919, 1.

37. Samsonowska, *Zarys funkcjonowania żydowskiej gminy wyznaniowej w Krakowie w latach 1918–1939*, 40–3.

38. Ibid., 41.

39. Jewish males over the age of twenty-five who were permanent residents in Cracow were eligible to vote. Samsonowska, *Zarys funkcjonowania żydowskiej gminy wyznaniowej w Krakowie*, 30–1.

40. Ibid., 43–60.

41. Scheduled elections for 1936 were indefinitely postponed, at least partly because of the fear that the Bund, the party of the Jewish working class, would participate and take advantage of increasing influence within Poland due to a significant increase in Polish anti-Semitism. Bundist influence within the *kehillah* would have been rejected by Zionists, Orthodox, and assimilationists alike.
42. For a thorough study of the role of each of these Zionist leaders, see Ezra Mendelsohn, *Zionism in Poland: The Formative Years, 1915–1926* (New Haven, CT: Yale University Press, 1981).

2

'Building Our Own Home':
The Jewish Press of Inter-war Cracow

*During the bombings in Cracow, the Endek press behaved
like the resident of a home who refuses to help his neighbour
during a fire, because the fire did not start in his apartment,
but in his neighbour's. The Endeks do not see that this is one
home. The Endeks always segregate Polish and Jewish and, in
their incomprehensible blindness, forget that each home
standing in the lands of Poland – is Polish, that every part of
the home is Polish, though in it may live Jews, Ukrainians, or
others.*

'Wobec zamachów warszawskich',
Nowy Dziennik, 27 May 1923

Whether expressed in Polish, Yiddish or Hebrew, the aspirations
of Cracow's Jewish community leaders were to unite a diverse
community within a particular conception of Jewish identity,
and, for some, to integrate this community into the larger
society. The divisions within the community did not help the
Jews (in Cracow, as elsewhere in Poland) in their struggle to
improve material conditions, to build a homeland in Palestine,
or to gain the support of other communities and nations, but
they did ensure that individual Jews had the opportunity to
affiliate with the Jewish community in different ways. The forms
of Jewish identity present in Cracow included various versions
of Zionism, Yiddish cultural politics and traditional religious
Orthodoxy. Jewish leaders could not easily reconcile such
different conceptions of religious and secular identity. The
history of the Jewish press in inter-war Cracow often reflects the
tension between the proponents of these conflicting identities.

Jewish national identity prospered in Cracow in spite of what
the Yiddish press termed an 'assimilationist plague' in the city.

All of the Jewish newspapers published in inter-war Cracow revealed a level of unease with the state of the contemporary Jewish community. For most of the Jewish newspapers that emerged in Cracow during the inter-war period, the publication of the newspaper itself was to be a part of the solution to the Jews' political, social, cultural and religious problems. Examining how the publishers, editors and writers behind the growing Jewish press of Cracow attempted to shape the discussion of Jewish national identity helps us to identify different groups within the city's Jewish intellectual community, to distinguish their varied goals, and to begin to determine their influence within Cracow as well as within the larger Jewish community. A survey of the Jewish press shows that the Jews of Cracow attempted to maintain their own ethnic identity in spite of internal divisions and in the face of growing pressures to assimilate to Polish society.

Like all Polish Jewish communities, Cracow Jewry was trilingual, oriented towards Yiddish, Hebrew and Polish cultures. The Polish-language Jewish press throughout the country indicates that linguistic assimilation was not limited to Cracow and Western Galicia. In an article on the tricultural orientation of Polish Jews, Chone Shmeruk called for research on the Jewish press in Polish that would compare it to the Jewish press in non-Jewish languages in other countries.[1] Unfortunately, the secondary literature on the Jewish press of inter-war Poland is rather limited and still far from addressing comparative concerns. Examining how the Polish-language Jewish press in one major city attempted to integrate Jews into Polish culture while insisting on a separate Jewish national identity, this chapter lays the groundwork for future studies comparing Nowy Dziennik to Jewish dailies elsewhere in Poland and in other languages. It also describes the type of Jewish national identity promoted by Cracow's Zionists, who because of their increased activities during the inter-war period emerged as the most influential Jewish group in the city.

Frustratingly, there are no exact data regarding the number of Jewish speakers of Polish, Yiddish or Hebrew in inter-war Cracow. Statistics from the Polish censuses of 1921 and 1931 are problematic, given the ambiguity of the questions asked and the involvement of the press in successfully attempting to influence the results for political ends. According to the census of 1921, there were 45,229 people in Cracow who identified as of the Jewish faith.[2] Of this total, 18,058, or just less than 40 per cent, identified themselves as being of Polish nationality.[3] The rest, with some exceptions for other nationalities, presumably identified as Jews by nationality. The total number of Jews by religion in 1931 was 56,515.[4] In 1931, declaring a Jewish language was the only way to express Jewish nationality. The 1931 census did not ask specifically about nationality, and so it is difficult to make direct comparisons. The 1931 census did include a question about language, however. According to the Jewish historian and demographer Jacob Lestchinsky, 41.3 per cent declared Yiddish as their native language and 39.8 per cent declared Hebrew.[5]

An examination of the inter-war census results shows us how the editors of *Nowy Dziennik* identified with the goals of Jewish nationalism, even at the newspaper's own expense, and artificially inflated the number of native Hebrew speakers in the city. Calling for the Jews of Cracow to identify their native language as Hebrew or Yiddish, rather than Polish, *Nowy Dziennik* (and other Jewish newspapers throughout Poland as well) encouraged the affirmation of a separate, national identity for a minority within a multi-ethnic state. At the same time, this campaign diminished the number of Jews who should more truthfully have declared Polish their native language.[6] While *Dos yidishe vort* merely noted that the census of 1931 had been taken (remarking that Jews in Cracow, as elsewhere throughout Poland, declared Yiddish their native language),[7] *Nowy Dziennik* wrote extensively on the subject in the days before the census. The editors of *Nowy Dziennik* regretted that the census, unlike in 1921, did not include any explicit question about nationality.[8] They feared that the situation of the Jews would return to what it was before the war, when they were regarded as simply a religious community and not as a nation. To ensure that Jews would be regarded as a separate nationality, they instructed their readers to declare Yiddish or Hebrew their native language, making a clear distinction between native language and language of daily use. As the numbers just cited make clear, the newspaper was successful in its campaign.

Jacob Lestchinsky, in his article on the native language of the

Jews in independent Poland, describes such results as completely unrealistic; Jewish nationalists had succeeded in increasing Jewish nationalist consciousness but had distorted the statistics. Lestchinsky, comparing the 1931 census to previous census results, concluded that such high numbers for Cracow and other cities can be accepted only if we absurdly assume that ten years of Polish statehood and political domination put an end to linguistic assimilation.[9] Significantly, the appeal of the Jewish nationalists in Cracow was made in Polish, demonstrating by this as well how Jews in inter-war Cracow developed their own separate national identity using the Polish language. Polish remains an important language for Jews from Cracow. Rafael Scharf, a Jewish native of the city, has written that for him, the Polish language is 'the furniture without which the inner space would be empty'.[10]

The census figures also show that Cracow was linguistically different from other large Polish cities such as Warsaw or Lwów. While 41.3 per cent of the Jewish population in Cracow declared Yiddish as their native language, 88.9 per cent of Jews in Warsaw and 67.8 per cent of Jews in Lwów did so.[11] But only 5.6 per cent of Warsaw's Jews declared Hebrew, and only 7.8 per cent declared Hebrew in Lwów. The 39.8 per cent of Jews in Cracow who declared Hebrew their native language were answering *Nowy Dziennik*'s call to identify themselves as Jews by nationality, even though they most likely spoke Polish, rather than Yiddish or Hebrew, in their daily lives. The census figures point to the success of the post-1867 polonization efforts and the acculturated nature of Jewish life in Cracow.

While the numbers cited above depict Cracow as a city of the linguistically assimilated, the German Jewish author Alfred Döblin noted the phenomenon of linguistic assimilation in other cities during his 1925 journey to Poland. After some time in Lwów, Döblin wrote of the Jewish community there, 'Why do they speak Polish and not Yiddish? Why is the Jewish newspaper published in Polish?' He remarked further, 'Jews are very Polish here. They start learning Polish as infants. They don't believe in the cultural significance of Yiddish. Hebrew is not spoken. That's why Polish is the language of the Jewish intelligentsia and upper classes.'[12] Visiting a Hebrew newspaper in Vilnius, Döblin wrote, 'Most of the Hebraists are bourgeois, assimilated Jews concealing their assimilation. When they're off duty, they speak Polish.'[13]

Döblin's remarks highlight the changing linguistic abilities of Polish Jews. These abilities went along with calls for a new form of Jewish identity, an identity predicated on Jews' existence as both Jews and Poles. By calling for Jews in 1931 to identify themselves as Jews by language when not offered the alternative of identifying by nationality, *Nowy Dziennik* demonstrated its commitment to a separate Jewish national identity in spite of an ongoing process of linguistic assimilation. This identity did not preclude participation in the Polish state or Polish cultural life, but it did require an acknowledgement of belonging to an overtly national community. The Jewish press of inter-war Cracow is an example of how the Jewish community was changing after the First World War. Neither solely an expression of national separatism nor a capitulation to pressures to assimilate, the editors of the Jewish press fostered particular visions of national identity even as they worked to strengthen the Jewish community.

THE JEWISH PRESS AND LINGUISTIC ASSIMILATION

Questions regarding language within the Jewish community were certainly not new in the inter-war period. They had been raised well before the Yiddish language conference in Czernowitz in 1908. There, Jewish leaders discussed whether Yiddish or Hebrew should be the national language of the Jews, and Yiddish was declared *a* national Jewish language. While the Yiddish intellectuals gathered there stopped short of declaring it *the* national language, the conference achieved some official recognition for what was commonly called a jargon. One linguist has written, 'During the inter-war period Yiddish became the true cultural and national language of Ashkenazic Jewry.'[14] None of the three languages used by the Jews in Poland, however, can objectively claim to be 'the true cultural and national language of Ashkenazic Jewry.' Since Polish, Yiddish and Hebrew were all used in different contexts, such claims are somewhat exaggerated, unless some larger value system is taken into consideration (such as claiming Hebrew as the true national language because of its specifically religious uses). Research into the Jewish press of Cracow suggests that generalizations are not useful in describing the complex ways in which Jews expressed their Jewish identity.

The work of Czesław Brzoza shows that, if one takes the Jewish press as a guide to the linguistic identification of a community, Polish was by far the most important language of Cracow's Jews, while Yiddish and Hebrew played lesser roles.[15] By the 1920s, Cracow's Jews had been polonized to a greater extent than those in other Polish Jewish communities because of Galicia's unique experience under Habsburg rule, which had allowed for a great degree of Polish political and cultural autonomy. Brzoza has concluded that, while Jews made up 25 per cent of the city's population, the titles of the Jewish press comprised only 10 per cent of all the titles published in the city. Brzoza attributes this disparity to the fact that Jews read Jewish newspapers from other cities as well as the non-Jewish Polish-language press.[16]

The Polish-language *Nowy Dziennik* was the city's only Jewish daily newspaper during the inter-war period. Titles such as *Rzut* [*Look*] and *Sztuka i Życie Współczesne* [*Art and Contemporary Life*] addressed literature and art, respectively. *Przegląd Kupiecki* [*Merchant Review*] and *Rzemiosło i Przemysł* [*Trade and Industry*] were concerned primarily with economic issues and published for Jews involved in commerce. In general, these trade publications had a greater circulation than the most successful Yiddish titles, *Dos yidishe vort* [*The Jewish Word*] and *Di post* [*The Post*].[17] In Cracow, even the Bund, the Yiddishist Jewish labour organization, published in Polish. Its theoretical journal published in Cracow was titled *Walka* [*Struggle*]. A group of Jewish women edited and published the Polish-language *Okienko na Świat* [*Window on the World*] from 1937 to 1939. *Okienko na Świat* featured stories, poems and puzzles about Jewish holidays and Jewish and Polish leaders such as Ahad Ha-Am and Ignacy Mościcki. And, perhaps most significantly, the *kehillah* published its official publication, *Gazeta Gminna* [*Community Gazette*], not in Yiddish or Hebrew, but in Polish. In addition, *Dos yidishe vort* added a Polish section, beginning with one or two pages in the mid-1930s and increasing in later years. Further, the publications of the Zionist youth organizations, such as *Diwrej Akiba* [*The Sayings of Akiba*, Hebrew, in Polish transliteration] and *Ceirim* [*Youth*, Hebrew, in Polish transliteration] were initially published in Polish as well, though they sometimes included short sections in Hebrew, sections that increased in the late 1930s.[18] That the Bund with its Yiddishist politics and devotion to the education of the Jewish worker should publish in Polish indicates the uniqueness of Cracow's Jewish community. Moreover, the simple lack of a more extensive Yiddish or Hebrew press in Cracow demonstrates the extent to which linguistic assimilation had already taken place.

Significantly, the Jewish community did not support a Hebrew periodical throughout the inter-war period, attesting to the weakness of Hebrew as a daily language in Cracow.[19] The most important Hebrew periodical in Cracow was *Hamitzpeh* [*The Watchtower*], which began publication in 1904 but ceased in 1921. *Hamagid*, a Hebrew paper published in various locations from the time of its first publication in the Russian shtetl of Lik in 1865, was taken over by Gershom Bader and published in Cracow after 1886.[20] Yakov Shmuel Fuks, who co-operated with Bader in the editing of *Hamagid*, began *Hamitzpeh* in 1904, after Bader left for a teaching position in Lwów in 1903. The intent of *Hamitzpeh* was to be a broad, general newspaper in Hebrew. Since it was published outside the Russian border in Cracow, its editor, Menakhem Lazer, was comparatively freer to report the news and express his Zionist views.

Nation building in Galicia was, however, not simply connected to the development of Hebrew, and the Hebrew press faced an ongoing struggle. Jewish leaders inclined towards assimilation rejected the nationalist position of *Hamitzpeh*. Neither did Lazer win the support of Zionist leaders, who failed to consider *Hamitzpeh* an official representative of their cause. Fuks and Lazer also met with competition from Jewish intellectuals sympathetic towards Polish culture. The attempt of *Hamitzpeh* to integrate nationalist views and religious ideals, though considered by Lazer to be his greatest achievement as an educator, may also have created some difficulties. For *maskilim*, *Hamitzp'h* was too religiously conservative, while Hasidim regarded the paper as heretical.

Perhaps more important, though, was the opportunity the

paper provided for young, promising writers to publish their work. The paper eventually concentrated around a group of Hebrew writers in Galicia whom the editor encouraged. One of these writers was the young Shmuel Yosef Agnon from Buchach. Lazer criticized Agnon's early work and provided suggestions for improvement. *Hamitzpeh* proved an important venue for young Hebrew writers from Galicia interested in joining the literary elite.

No Hebrew periodical during the inter-war period emerged seriously to promote the cause of Hebrew as a daily language of Polish Jews. Shmuel J. Imber, the well-known Yiddish writer, published a short-lived weekly in Hebrew, *Shavuon* [*Weekly*], Zionist in orientation like *Hamitzpeh*. Imber achieved greater success as a publicist with his writings in Polish.[21] The goal of *Shavuon* was to be read from Shabat to Shabat. Each issue was to conclude with a special pedagogical section that would teach the next generation about Palestine and encourage its younger readers to confront the negative characteristics of Jewish life in the Diaspora. At the same time, Imber took a practical approach to the Jewish future, stating clearly that Jewish children should be sent to public schools, so that they would be prepared to advance in the secular world. Jewish children needed both the Torah and a future, a future that only education in secular studies could secure.

Later efforts to establish some kind of Hebrew periodical in the city failed. In an article remembering the well-liked Hebrew teacher Nakhman Mifelew, Chaim Löw recalled the time when Mifelew came to him with the idea of establishing a Hebrew weekly.[22] Löw himself was sceptical, but he encouraged Mifelew to organize a meeting. Löw explained that if the meeting did not provide enough motivation to establish the Hebrew weekly, it was through no fault of Mifelew, who was 'the soul behind the idea'.[23] Among those who promoted the cause of Hebrew in Cracow were the writers of *Nowy Dziennik* or, like Mifelew and Löw, the teachers in the Hebrew gymnasium. Mifelew's attempt to establish a Hebrew newspaper was a grassroots effort to advance the profile of Hebrew within a Jewish community that was at best indifferent, if not overtly hostile, to the cause. Those who wished to promote a separate Jewish culture in Cracow simply had to do so in either Polish or Yiddish.

Though Cracow was never a centre of Yiddish culture comparable to Warsaw or Vilna, Yiddish remained an important Jewish language in the city, despite polonization. Jews from Cracow relate that Yiddish was the daily language of Kazimierz, which was also home to the most beloved Yiddish folk poet and composer, Mordecai Gebirtig. The Yiddish newspapers that did appear in Cracow came out on an irregular basis. *Dos yidishe vort*, the most important of these, appeared weekly from 1925 to 1932, but only irregularly from 1932 to 1939. Politically, the newspaper was religious Zionist in orientation and so was published with an Orthodox audience in mind. Another Yiddish title, *Dos likht* [*The Light*], served the needs of those in the Orthodox community who did not identify with Zionism. It appeared only for a year in 1931. Other Yiddish titles included *Der reflektor* [*The Reflector*, or *Mirror*], published in the mid-1930s and a forerunner of *Di post*, published from 1937 to 1939. Both focused primarily on issues of Yiddish cultural life and published many interviews with international Yiddish writers as well as original prose and poetry. *Der reflektor* and *Di post* aspired to a higher level of journalism than did *Dos yidishe vort* and aimed to attract a larger, more international audience. A separate Yiddish cultural scene was reflected in the specifically culture-oriented publications *Der reflektor* and *Di post* and, to a lesser extent, in *Dos yidishe vort* and *Dos likht*. *Dos yidishe vort* and *Dos likht* assumed and attracted an audience that was more religious and not as politically active. *Di post* published without interruption during the two years of its publication. Though its run was cut short, it was a successful Yiddish title.

While the Polish-language Jewish press was nearly exclusively Zionist and dominated by one title, it is a mistake to speak of 'the Yiddish press' as any kind of unified entity. The various Yiddish titles, discussed at length in the next chapter, contributed to the discussion regarding Jewish national identity by expressing views at times widely divergent from those put forth in *Nowy Dziennik* and from one another. Political parties or other political organizations published many titles of Cracow's inter-war Jewish press, a phenomenon seen among Yiddish and Polish publications as well. Most of these Yiddish titles were single-issue publications and socialist Zionist in political orientation. Some were meant to continue but failed to appear after the first issue.

Cracow's Jewish newspapers, in both Polish and Yiddish, most probably circulated informally among many readers. But circulation numbers for *Nowy Dziennik* and other Polish-language periodicals confirm that Polish was the dominant language of the Jewish press in Cracow. *Nowy Dziennik*, by far the most influential Jewish newspaper in the city, had a circulation that, according to state and police registers, ranged from 4,000 to 18,000 copies.[24] The longest-running Yiddish publication, *Dos yidishe vort*, had a circulation ranging from 500 to 700 copies. Thus, even if one accepts the lower estimate for *Nowy Dziennik*, it is clear that the Polish-language Jewish publication enjoyed a much larger readership.

Nowy Dziennik provides the best example of Jewish leaders and intellectuals in Cracow fighting both for Jewish separateness and uniqueness as well as for integration into the larger community. As such, this Polish-language Jewish newspaper deserves special consideration. While its pages include some of the most detailed information about Jewish life in the city and articles written by Cracow's most prominent Jewish leaders, including the respected rabbi, Zionist politician and delegate to the Polish parliament, Ozjasz Thon, international and national news often took precedence over stories of local interest. *Nowy Dziennik* appeared throughout the entire inter-war period, the only Jewish newspaper in Cracow able to sustain itself for such a long time. There is even some indication that the Hasidim of Cracow read *Nowy Dziennik*.[25]

That *Nowy Dziennik* could attract Hasidic readers serves as an indication of the newspaper's unique approach to the language question among Jews in Poland. The language battle, between Yiddish and Hebrew, but also among Yiddish, Hebrew and Polish, was surprisingly absent from the pages of the inter-war Cracow Jewish press. The editors of *Nowy Dziennik* did not have an official policy regarding language. Perhaps this was because it was so clear that Polish was the language of communication chosen by most of the community. But *Nowy Dziennik* also included many translations of Yiddish and Hebrew literature and enthusiastically encouraged the study of Hebrew, as part of the Zionist programme. Contributors to *Nowy Dziennik* also included Isaac Deutscher, a young yeshiva student from the nearby town of Chrzanów and the future biographer of Leon

Trotsky. According to David Lazer, Deutscher used to appear in a long *kapote* at the paper's offices immediately after morning prayer with new translations of Hebrew poetry into Polish.[26] In addition, while Nowy Dziennik might not have encouraged the instruction of Yiddish specifically, it did support the cause of the Yiddish theatre.[27] Clearly, *Nowy Dziennik* was interested in all expressions of Jewish national identity, in any language.

Wilhelm Berkelhammer, the editor of *Nowy Dziennik*, described the language question among Polish Jews as a problem rather than a struggle. Treating the issue of language as a real struggle only gave anti-Semites an excuse to dismiss Jews' basic claims. Rather, Berkelhammer argued, the language question should be viewed as a problem that is simply the result of certain historical phenomena. He argued that agitating against Hebrew neither helped Yiddish nor hurt Hebrew. He lamented that the development of the language question in American Jewish society was worrisome, recognizing that Yiddish schools in the United States could not stop the spread of English. The debate between Hebrew and Yiddish was not simply a matter of language, but rather a larger problem of the future in Jewish culture. Berkelhammer wrote,

> Our language problem determines the development of Jewish life and will be solved as life determines the actual language of reality, which means that each party should work on the altar of Jewish culture according to its own principles and convictions, and not considering the principles and convictions of another party as a betrayal of Jewishness and the Jewish people.[28]

Berkelhammer's position was fairly moderate in a minority community often damaged by its own divisiveness. It was perhaps the only defensible position he could take as the editor of a Polish-language Jewish newspaper. The attitude of tolerance, and even support, for Yiddish and Hebrew was absolutely necessary, as *Nowy Dziennik* was prone to accusations of assimilationism because of its use of Polish.

Berkelhammer wrote in 1925, when the language issue for Jews in Poland was far from settled. Fears of the linguistic assimilation that was taking place at an ever greater rate fuelled the language debate for proponents of Yiddish and Hebrew. But, for the editor of *Nowy Dziennik*, the priority was clearly *Jewish* culture, not a specific Polish, Yiddish or Hebrew culture. Language learning was important for the Jewish community and the Zionists of *Nowy Dziennik*, but it did not determine Jewish national identity. They encouraged those Jews who did not know Polish to learn it and hoped all Jews would learn Hebrew. They also tirelessly promoted Yiddish culture. Unqualified support of Hebrew and Yiddish was perhaps the only way the editors of *Nowy Dziennik* could make up for their calculated decision to publish in Polish.

Nowy Dziennik supported the Hebrew-language movement generously and enthusiastically. Chaim Bialik is said to have taken note of the paper's support for Hebrew, commenting during a visit to the paper's office, 'Here at last one can speak Hebrew!'[29] *Nowy Dziennik* often included articles about specific Hebrew cultural events, such as the Days of Hebrew, an event designed to spread knowledge of Hebrew language and literature among Jewish youth, which took place in June 1927. *Nowy Dziennik* freely admitted the necessity of such an event, since Jewish youth simply did not know modern Hebrew and were not acquainted with its literature. The Days of Hebrew were not an indication of the strength of a flourishing culture in Hebrew; rather, they were the initial steps by which proponents of Hebrew hoped to overcome the 'apathy' of Jewish youth.[30] The programme even aimed to increase knowledge of Hebrew among young Jewish women, with a lecture on the 'Hebrew woman'. Benzion Katz, who published often in *Nowy Dziennik*, described the need of Jewish youth to be acquainted with Hebrew literature in terms that judged rather harshly both the Hebrew writers and their potential readers. Katz wrote, somewhat surprisingly, that the Jewish student was a significant internal enemy of Jewish national development. The student might have 'a shekel in the pocket, but in the heart – emptiness and Satan'.[31] In other words, Jewish students may have supported the movement for Hebrew in some concrete, material way, but they failed to give it their full spiritual support. Katz's criticism of 'Satan' within the hearts of students suggests his disregard for young Jews who did not share his views. Katz also criticized the Hebrew writers of the 1920s, asserting that they paled in comparison to the great earlier Hebrew writers Moshe Leib Lilienblum, Chaim Bialik and Yosef Chaim Brenner. He leaves the reader wondering how a knowledge of contemporary Hebrew literature would have aided the rapidly assimilating Jewish population, illustrating, perhaps, one of the reasons Jewish youth simply were not interested. *Nowy Dziennik's* support of the Days of Hebrew is noteworthy; it is an indication of the paper's devotion to issues of Hebrew literature and culture. Yet Katz's remarks, a call for the strengthening of Hebrew culture, are also a sign of the challenges Hebrew cultural activists faced and the relative strength of Polish within the Jewish community of Cracow.

Even more surprising is the attitude of *Dos yidishe vort* towards Hebrew. While one might expect that a Yiddish newspaper would take a different line, *Dos yidishe vort* often encouraged the study of Polish and Hebrew, recognizing the importance of Polish for its audience as well as the growing role of Hebrew within the Zionist community. Further, the paper reported on a *kehillah* meeting where it was recognized that the city of Cracow was unique in not having to cope with different camps on the language position.[32] In this way, Cracow was positively differentiated from Warsaw and Łódź, where disputes among proponents of Polish, Yiddish and Hebrew often interrupted the business of the community, preventing it from taking action on a number of projects. Only in Cracow, according to the article, could speakers at the *kehillah* meeting speak in the language of their choice without fear of reprisal. In addition, a writer for *Dos yidishe vort* declared in 1929 that the language battle between Hebrew and Yiddish only hurt Jews in assuring that Jewish schools would receive less support than German, Ukrainian and Byelorussian schools because of the internal Jewish dissent.[33] The writer implied that respect for all the languages the Jews of Cracow spoke, including Polish, would help Jews to win more state support for Jewish education. Altogether, *Dos yidishe vort* was not an unqualified champion of the cause of Yiddish; rather, it sought to serve the community by pointing out how difficult questions regarding language could be solved to the greater benefit of the community.

Moyshe Blekher was the most prominent Yiddish-speaking intellectual to advocate Yiddish in the city. His establishment of two Yiddish newspapers in Cracow, *Der reflektor* and, later, *Di post*, were responses to the linguistic assimilation in Cracow that had made the language question much less a burning issue than in other cities. Cracow's Jews read a Polish-language Jewish newspaper; Blekher provided them with another option. Blekher's newspapers, discussed further in the next chapter, stand as a reminder that Jewish intellectuals did not always so passively accept widespread polonization. Blekher's desperate tone in his newspapers attests to the polonization that had already occurred in Cracow but also provides an important example of a dissenting voice. Most representative of the polonization Blekher rejected was *Nowy Dziennik*, whose writers cared more about the content of Jewish nationalism than the form in which that nationalism was expressed.

THE DECISION TO PUBLISH IN POLISH

Nowy Dziennik quickly became the primary medium of Cracow's Jewish community. While *Nowy Dziennik* is evidence of the linguistic and cultural assimilation of Cracow's Jewry, its founders and editors did not live on the margins of the Jewish community. Indeed, the paper was one of the most important Jewish institutions in all of Poland. In acculturating, the Jews of Cracow were adapting to the political and cultural realities they found themselves in. But, as they themselves asserted, acculturation did not mean assimilation. Prompted by the anti-Jewish violence in Eastern Galicia after the First World War, Berkelhammer and other Jewish community leaders established *Nowy Dziennik* to support and defend the Jewish community.

The death of an Orthodox Jew at the hands of Piłsudski's Legionnaires led immediately to the founding of *Nowy Dziennik*. When the liberal Polish paper *Nowa Reforma* glossed over the cause of the Jew's death, claiming it was a heart attack, Jews demonstrated and demanded a daily Jewish newspaper in the Polish language.[34] Jewish newspapers in Polish had appeared before, most notably the weekly *Izraelita*, and, in Cracow, the short-lived *Dziennik Krakowski*, edited by Wilhelm Feldman from 1896 to 1897. *Nowy Dziennik* was the first of the three Polish-language Jewish dailies that came to be so influential in inter-war Poland. *Chwila* [*Moment*] appeared in Lwów in 1919 and, after ill-fated attempts to establish a Polish-language Jewish daily in Warsaw, *Nasz Przegląd* [*Our Review*] was finally successful in 1923. In founding *Nowy Dziennik*, Cracow's Zionist leaders asserted their Jewish identity, even as they moved Cracow Jewry closer to Polish culture.

The daily first appeared on 9 July 1918, when the primary concern of the editors, and no doubt readers as well, was the conclusion of four years of war. The Zionist leader Pinchas Goldwasser has been credited with the idea for a Polish-language Jewish daily as early as 1916. Other Zionist leaders argued that there was simply no demand for a Jewish daily newspaper in Polish and suggested a bi-weekly publication instead.[35] The men who founded the newspaper came from as far outside Cracow as Lwów and Drohobycz and from such closer locations as Wieliczka, Nowy Sącz and Tarnów.[36] Among the founders who insisted that the newspaper be a daily were Berkelhammer, Ozjasz Thon and the Jewish politician Michał Ringel. Because anti-Semitism led to difficulties in finding a publisher in Cracow, *Nowy Dziennik* was first published in the Czech town of Moravská Ostrava from July 1918 to January 1919. From February 1919 to February 1920, the newspaper was published in Cracow, and then from February 1920 on by *Nowy Dziennik*'s own press.[37] The paper appeared daily except on the Sabbath, though there were times in the paper's first years when it did not appear on Mondays. The number of pages in the initial issues varied, until it was finally decided that *Nowy Dziennik* should be a twelve-page newspaper.

The founders of *Nowy Dziennik* intended from the beginning to publish in Cracow. Publishing in Moravská Ostrava was problematic and only a temporary solution. The paper was printed at two in the morning and then sent to Cracow, where it arrived at six and then went on to Warsaw, Lublin and Lwów. In addition to distribution difficulties, publishing in Moravská Ostrava meant that the paper was subject to two different censors, one in Moravská Ostrava and one in Cracow. The difficulty was that if it was stated on the newspaper that it was printed in Cracow, officials in Cracow had the right of censorship. But, since it was published in Moravská Ostrava, the officials there also could legally act as censors. Reflecting on the establishment of the newspaper, Wilhelm Berkelhammer recalled that someone had the idea to take Cracow off the title page to avoid this problem. He compared the newspaper's homelessness to that of the Jewish nation more generally: 'Since no one anywhere wanted to host us, we had to build our own home. The small group concentrated around *Nowy Dziennik* knew this, and the entire Jewish nation must constantly repeat this to itself.'[38] Though the founders of *Nowy Dziennik* were comfortable enough in the majority culture to publish in Polish, they still recognized the need for a daily newspaper that was explicitly Jewish.[39]

The Polish-Jewish political leader Michał Ringel, as well as Berkelhammer and Thon, made the claim that *Nowy Dziennik* was the first Jewish daily in a non-Jewish language, explaining that other Jewish newspapers, such as German-Jewish newspapers, were either not dailies or were not general-interest newspapers such as *Nowy Dziennik*. Other Jewish newspapers in Europe were simply community organs or, according to Ringel, concealed their Jewishness. Ringel wrote of the founding of *Nowy Dziennik*:

> Today it appears to have been rather simple, a usual consequence of the existence of the Zionist organization, but at the time it was a brave and risky step: a crossing of the Rubicon that separated the Jewish world from non-Jewish society. At the same time, it was the building of a bridge over a gulf separating two worlds ... It was the first [newspaper] which began to speak not only to Zionists and non-Zionist Jews, but simply to Polish society and its spiritual elite, appealing to the badly informed to better inform themselves.[40]

Perhaps somewhat immodestly, Ringel described *Nowy Dziennik* as the second step, after the publication of Theodor Herzl's *Die Welt*. While *Die Welt* had taken the slur of *Judenblatt* and transformed it into an honourable title, that paper was only a weekly. *Nowy Dziennik* filled a real gap. Jews were often able to read only Polish-language papers that were anti-Semitic. *Nowy Dziennik* was, from the start, a national Jewish newspaper, and its founders were clear that it would appear in the language of Europe, not the language of the ghetto.

Far from isolating themselves in a cultural ghetto, Cracow's Jewish leaders reached out to the non-Jewish community by publishing in the majority language even as they created a new venue for Jewish politics, opinion and thought. Berkelhammer wrote on the fifth anniversary of the paper's founding, 'It fell to us to create a completely new type of political periodical, to create a synthesis between the sphere of Jewish concerns and the sphere of general issues, so that our daily would become in some degree a Jewish tribune, defending courageously and openly the Jewish national and Zionist stance.'[41]

Nowy Dziennik did not focus exclusively on Jewish issues or Jewish politics. Its commitment was to represent the Jewish community to Polish society and, in turn, further to acquaint the Jewish community with the majority culture. The goals of the founders indicate that they sincerely hoped their newspaper would find an audience among ethnic Poles, although they were not naive. They recognized their effort as the first of its kind and knew that attracting readers, whether Jewish or Polish, would not be an easy task. The founders of *Nowy Dziennik* wanted to build the Jewish nation *and* reach out to the Polish community. *Nowy Dziennik* was their attempt to meet both goals. The editors were more successful in 'building their own home' than in gaining the full acceptance of the majority community. *Nowy Dziennik* was most likely not well known among Poles, but as an initial effort to develop a Polish-language Jewish journalism, it stands as a remarkable achievement.

The editors of *Nowy Dziennik* declared that they could not understand how the Jewish community could live among Poles if they were not able to conduct their affairs in Polish. The decision to publish in Polish was intended to aid the Jewish community in improving its relations with the Poles. The decision was taken for specific reasons, namely, because publishing in Polish would be more likely to effect the programme the newspaper set for itself. This programme included 'a defence of the weak and the hurt, among these, the Jews; support for the moral and material good of broad layers of society; agreement between peoples; brotherhood among nations; the self-determination of nations; and a just and lasting peace'.[42]

Writing with cautious optimism on the fifth anniversary of

the paper's founding, Berkelhammer explained the decision to use a non-Jewish language for a Jewish newspaper:

> Feeling a threatening storm in the air as an inevitable side effect of the approaching political changes, and feeling that the wall between Jewish society and the Polish nation that was built as a result of years of misunderstanding and deliberate lies and slander must start to fall down, if not be removed immediately – we decided to begin publishing our newspaper in Polish.[43]

For the editors and writers of *Nowy Dziennik*, national identity could be built, developed and changed using the tools of another nation. Berkelhammer defended the newspaper against charges that it was simply an instrument of assimilation. He wrote:

> We deny most assuredly that a Jewish newspaper in the Polish language is an instrument of linguistic assimilation or that it contributes to the growth of assimilation. Even if this were so, a Jewish newspaper in Polish is so important and necessary that we would take the risk of a 'surplus' of assimilation and find some other way to treat or neutralize it. Three million Jews cannot live among a twenty million Polish majority and not be in constant and immediate contact with it.
>
> Moreover ... in light of our actual multilingual ability, it is clear that perhaps even a very significant number of Jews can read only or almost only a daily in the Polish language. Whoever thinks that *Nowy Dziennik* with its Polish language is not a very serious instrument in the fight against assimilation is simply mistaken. We would remind the linguistic fanatics among us of the national fight of the Irish, conducted in English ... A multilingual nation *must* have a multilingual press.[44]

Berkelhammer's insistence on the multilingual identity of the Jewish community was, for him, a frank assessment of Jewish language use in Poland. Further, the attempt to reach a Polish audience signalled a changing Jewish community that was aware of its political and social position in a changing Poland.

The need for a Polish-language voice of Polish Jewry was not limited to Cracow. Jewish editors such as Berkelhammer published in Polish because of a (perhaps mistaken) notion that the Jewish community read only Polish and because of a desire to build a bridge to Polish society.

The editorial staff of *Nowy Dziennik* remained fairly stable throughout the 20 years of its existence. Wilhelm Berkel-hammer was the founders' first choice as editor and, but for the years 1921–25, served in that post until his death in 1934.[45] As a student in Tarnów, Berkelhammer had contributed to Zionist publications and was an active journalist, publishing in such German- and Polish-language journals as *Welt* [*World*], *Moriah*, *Jüdische Rundschau* [*Jewish Review*], and *Wschód* [*East*].[46] He also personally supervised the editing of *Nowy Dziennik's* literary supplement, publishing Polish, Hebrew, Yiddish and foreign literature, in a reflection of his worldview that Jews belonged to all of humanity.[47] In addition to Berkelhammer, the original editorial staff included Zygmunt Ellenberg, Jakob Freund and Jechiel Halpern. The first theatre critic was Wilhelm Fallek, and the first music critic was Franciszka Sonnenscheinówna. (Mojżesz Kanfer succeeded Fallek as theatre critic and the lawyer Henryk Apte succeeded Sonnenscheinówna as music critic.) Henryk Leser served as sports editor for many years. Supplementary sections throughout the years featured articles on economics, literature, sports, home health, radio, film, chess, women's issues, children and youth. In 1921, the West Galician Zionist leader Ignacy [Yitzhok] Schwarzbart replaced Berkelhammer as editor, in which position he served until 1925.

In its first issue, the editors of *Nowy Dziennik* set forth the programme for which they were working and outlined the goals of the newspaper. *Nowy Dziennik* was to be the voice of the Jews in Polish society. The time had come when understanding between Poles and Jews was necessary.[48] Polish Jews were not under-age children, an editorial pointed out. They were capable of addressing the Polish community and expressing their own intentions and goals; the time had come to do so. Berkelhammer wrote explicitly that the goal of the paper was to serve as a watchdog for Polish Jewry and to serve faithfully the Polish Republic.[49] Whether or not it expressed the beliefs of the Jewish masses, *Nowy Dziennik* appointed itself a defender of the Jewish community and a conduit for the most general kind of nationalist ideas.

Its task was an important one, given the anti-Semitic climate of the years immediately following the First World War. After the pogroms of November 1918, a group of Cracow city council members demanded the suspension of the paper and railroad workers in Tarnów destroyed packages that held copies of *Nowy Dziennik*, allegedly in response to the paper's anti-Polish stance.[50] For a time, postal privileges were suspended and in place of *Nowy Dziennik*, a new paper, *Gazeta Żydowska*, appeared for a period of 15 days, after which *Nowy Dziennik* could again be circulated in Western Galicia. In spite of these early difficulties, the editors and writers of *Nowy Dziennik* persisted in their pioneering efforts.

The Polish-language publication efforts in Cracow, Warsaw and Lwów were new attempts to strengthen Jewish culture in the face of anti-Semitism and to reposition the Jewish community *vis-à-vis* the Polish state and nation. The linguistic assimilation these publications represent reflects the continuing process of adapting to the culture of the majority. As Herbert Gans has written of Jewish identity in the United States, 'new constructions of ethnicity are themselves potential evidence of continuing acculturation'.[51] The rhetoric of early editorials in each of the three major Polish-language Jewish dailies is strikingly similar, though the local situations were often very different. While *Nowy Dziennik* was born as a result of a specific anti-Semitic incident, *Chwila* was formed in response to the conflict between Poles and Ukrainians and the consequent violence against Jews in 1918–19.

In December of 1918 Zionist members of the Jewish National Council in Lwów formed a committee, including the political leaders Leon Reich and Michał Ringel, to discuss the preparation of a series of publications that would explain to the non-Jewish public the real reasons for the behaviour of the Jewish people. Recognizing that similar single-issue publications had appeared before, Gershon Zipper suggested the establishment of a daily newspaper that would highlight 'new problems and concerns in relation to Jews and non-Jews'. The paper appeared for the first time on 10 January 1919. The paper reflected the political programme of Reich, a delegate to the *Sejm*. As described in a fifteenth-anniversary issue, this programme included a struggle for 'the idea of harmony and Polish-Jewish coexistence, the educating of Jewish society in Poland in the love of the work of citizenship for the Polish state and the acquiring among Poles of a sympathy and understanding of the national tasks and ideals of Jews'.[52] Given the contemporary context, articles in *Chwila* understandably focused on the neutrality of the Jews in the conflict between Poles and Ukrainians, devoting much more attention to the ongoing violence after the First World War. The paper itself, though, was the Jewish community's attempt to do the same as *Nowy Dziennik*: educate its own people and non-Jewish society about their community's goals.

In contrast, *Nasz Przegląd* was born in a political context that had already become significantly more stable. Attempts to establish a Polish-language Jewish daily in Warsaw in 1918 and 1919 failed; only in 1923 with the appearance of *Nasz Przegląd* did the city's largest Jewish community achieve what the largest cities in Galicia had already established. *Nasz Przegląd* is notable for its size and influence within the Jewish community but, more importantly, it was an independent, non-partisan newspaper. Both *Chwila* and *Nowy Dziennik* were Zionist. Though they became, arguably, the most important voices of their communities, they were decidedly partisan. The editors of *Nasz Przegląd* strove to keep their newspaper open as a forum for all kinds of views, declaring that their only enemies were anti-Semites. The editor Jacob Appenszlak noted the newspaper's goals in its first issue:

> We want to strengthen national feeling and broaden the consciousness of our creative will and Jewish spiritual welfare. We long to make accessible to Polish society an understanding of our national self, rights, and ideals. As citizens of the Republic, we want a strong, lasting and free Poland, one where freedom thrives and its might and well-being derives from the harmonious co-operation of all of its citizens, without regard to confession, nationality or views.[53]

NATIONAL IDENTIFICATION IN *NOWY DZIENNIK*

The prominent Zionist leader Ozjasz Thon clarified the reasons for the decision to found a newspaper like *Nowy Dziennik* in an article published for the newspaper's ten-year anniversary. Thon wrote that the first and foremost reason was the desire for a 'conversation, from nation to nation'.[54] This wish to undertake an ongoing dialogue with the Polish nation necessitated the use of Polish, however much one might wish the majority to learn minority languages. The first step in reaching out to Poles would be to speak their language and to educate them about Jewish issues. Second in Thon's list of priorities was the Zionism of the paper's founders and their recognition of the need for an independent newspaper. This allowed for the formation of principles of citizenship and nationality for Polish Jews. This was a change from the political positions of Cracow's pre-war Jewish assimilationist leaders who, according to Thon, introduced Jews to the political marketplace as though they were goods to be traded. Thon wrote, 'Patriotism was not for us a product for which one longs to get the highest price, as it was treated by our assimilationist predecessors; rather, it is a simple, ethical obligation, one which we fulfil sincerely.'[55] Thon objected to the pre-war assimilationists who, in his view, did not recognize that other Jewish groups expressed loyalty to the Polish state, but were also working to develop political and cultural institutions that would represent the Jewish nation. The Zionist leaders of inter-war Cracow gradually asserted their influence over the pre-war assimilationists, arguing that they could represent the Jewish nation and be patriotic to the Polish nation at the same time. While they wrote in Polish, they acted as Jews and wished to engage Poles on equal terms.

From the very beginning, *Nowy Dziennik* reflected the desire to effect a rapprochement with Polish society and the need to develop principles of nationality for the Polish Jewish community. While on the surface the founding of a Polish-language Jewish newspaper seems like a normal phenomenon, *Nowy Dziennik*'s desire to engage the Polish nation and develop the Jewish nation at the same time was quite radical. Thon and the other Zionists of *Nowy Dziennik* placed their Jewish nation on the same level as the newly established independent Poland. Thon's

call to develop principles of citizenship and nationality among
the Jews was a call for civic equality, just as the very founding of
Nowy Dziennik was an explicitly national act by a national
minority without political sovereignty. Refusing to reject their
obligations as either Jews or Poles, Thon and the writers of *Nowy
Dziennik* reached out to the Polish community as part of their
efforts to live as a national minority within the nationalizing
state of Poland.

Nationalism for the editors of *Nowy Dziennik* arose from the
desperate conditions the people found themselves in because of
war and economic discrimination. Economic conditions made
coherent nationalist goals necessary and vital. These goals
included calls for some form of national autonomy, which
themselves were a response to Polish pressure to assimilate and
a refusal to be appeased by the less than perfect application of
constitutional guarantees for free religious and cultural
expression.[56] National autonomy within a Polish state was not,
however, an idea extensively detailed in the pages of *Nowy
Dziennik*. Instead, their goal was primarily to improve the moral
and material well-being of the Jewish masses. Cracow's Zionists
committed themselves to the ideal of the creation of a homeland
for the Jews in Palestine, but, in the Zionist tradition of
Gegenwartsarbeit (or work for Jews in the Diaspora), they also
committed themselves to work at home.[57] They did not, indeed
could not, choose Palestine over Poland. For the Jewish
intellectuals writing for *Nowy Dziennik*, nationality was not
connected to political rule or political borders between different
countries. Nationality was not even necessarily based on
language. They assumed the existence of a Jewish nation based
on the shared social, religious and political heritage of the Jewish
people, no part of which was ever specifically rejected by
Cracow's Jewish nationalist leaders.

The Jewish nationalism of the writers of *Nowy Dziennik*
echoed, to some extent, Polish nationalism. An article in *Nowy
Dziennik* delineated two different types of Polish nationalism, one
exemplified by the rightist National Democratic leader Roman
Dmowski (1864–1939) and the other by the romantic nationalism
of Poland's nineteenth-century poet from Lithuania, Adam
Mickiewicz (1797–1855).[58] Dmowski's form of nationalism
expressed that Polish nationalist's love for his own nation but

only hatred for other nations. The nationalism Dmowski espoused was 'egoistic, brutal and zoological'. But nationalism was not always negative, according to the writer – it could be more like the nationalism of Mickiewicz, which expressed a love for other nations and a desire not to hurt other nations. The nationalism of Mickiewicz did not know hatred. The anonymous author wrote, 'Nationalism, which is not national chauvinism, does not know slogans of hate.' Indeed, nationalists should work in co-operation with other nations and respect the other nations' equal rights. The nationalism of *Nowy Dziennik*, according to this author, was like that of Mickiewicz. Its goal was to improve the conditions of the members of the nation, but not at the expense of members of different ethnic or national groups. The comparison to Polish nationalism recognized that not all Polish nationalist sentiment was identical. In appealing to the more positive (and at least somewhat idealized) form of Polish nationalism, the writer allowed for a conception of Jewish nationalism that permitted an identification with Polish culture.

The existence of a noble strain of Polish nationalism helped to justify the decision to publish in Polish. Bridging the gap between the two different worlds, *Nowy Dziennik* illustrated how the two different nations were not so far apart in their conceptions of nationalism. The generally expressed nationalist goals assured the Jewish 'masses' of the nationalists' concern, while the comparison to Polish nationalism may have been intended at least partly for the non-Jewish audience the editors hoped to attract. Further, by limiting Jewish nationalist goals within Poland to the improvement of Jews' material and moral well-being, the writers of *Nowy Dziennik* allowed for a Jewish nationalism that could exist alongside Polish nationalist thought.

In publishing the writing of some of Polish Jewry's most successful political leaders and journalistic talents, including Berkelhammer, Thon and the Zionist leader Apolinary Hartglas, *Nowy Dziennik* presented a Jewish national identity combined with a fervent Polish patriotism. Describing in 1924 what patriotism meant to the Jewish intellectuals of *Nowy Dziennik*, Berkelhammer quoted the Belzer Rebbe, who said that the Orthodox 'serve Poland, just as we served Austria'.[59] Like Thon objecting to the trading of patriotism as a political good, Berkelhammer asked whether patriotism that was so easily transferred could really be patriotic. Significantly, Berkelhammer disparaged the Rebbe for speaking in a 'very heavy indistinct jargon' (Yiddish), claiming that if the Orthodox do not speak the majority language they cannot be truly patriotic. The patriotism of the Orthodox, in Berkelhammer's description, was passive, emerging from a social and spiritual ghetto. In contrast, the patriotism of *Nowy Dziennik* was presumably more active and positive and, at least, expressed in the Polish language. Berkelhammer shows here that *Nowy Dziennik*'s support of other Jewish cultures had its limits. His disparaging comments regarding Yiddish speakers indicate that he privileged Jews who spoke Polish. His advocacy of Polish, however, does suggest his strong connection to Polish culture, just as Thon's insistence that patriotism cannot be traded indicates his attachment to Poland, the country in whose parliament he served many years as an elected representative of the Jewish community.

Nowy Dziennik would become increasingly, more explicitly, Zionist in its later issues, but it also gave its support to the Polish state and encouraged the expression of Jewish culture in Polish. Indicating that the distinction between nationalism and patriotism was more than simply semantic, *Nowy Dziennik* often included coverage of Polish cultural events, Polish literature and Polish theatre. For the group of Jewish intellectuals associated with *Nowy Dziennik*, different nations could coexist in the same state; the nations did not necessarily have to interfere with each other's development. The writers of *Nowy Dziennik* saw themselves as citizens of Poland and members of the Jewish nation and were unwilling to compromise either of these identities.[60]

This insistence on a Jewish national identity as well as a patriotic affiliation with the Polish state and culture challenged both Jews and Poles. In short, Poles and Jews differed over how they wished to define the Jewish community within the Polish state. Using the Latin terms, the Poles wanted the Jews to be *Gente Judaei, natione Poloni* (Jews by birth, Poles by nationality), while the Jews desired to be *Cives Poloni, natione Judaei* (Poles by citizenship, Jews by nationality).[61] This idea of a civic, or administrative, identity, expressed in the Polish term *państwowy*, is especially important for the Jews associated with *Nowy Dziennik*. This conception of an identity that could be separated from an ethnic or national identity allowed the writers of *Nowy Dziennik* to assert their own Jewish nationalism without sacrificing their commitment to Polish patriotism, Polish culture and Polish identity. The Jews were undergoing what Milton Gordon would describe as civic assimilation. The Jews did not need to become citizens, since they had already attained that status, however compromised their rights as individuals and as a group. The Zionist leaders of *Nowy Dziennik* fought to develop, enact and preserve their rights as Polish citizens just as they fought to develop, enact and preserve their national identity as Jews.

While *narodowość* (nationalism), for the writers of *Nowy Dziennik*, was organic, *państwowość* (implying citizenship in a political state) was practical.[62] One was a part of a nation just as one was a member of an extended family; this was a relationship that could not be altered. Loyalty to the state in which one lived was not only possible – it was an ethical obligation. Given this reasoning, Jewish nationalists were able to think of themselves as having an organic national Jewish identity as well as a civic Polish identity. Poland could be a place of faithful citizens of Jewish nationality. Expressing the perpetual conflict of dual loyalty, one author assured the Poles that Jews would always stand beside them, while assuring Jews that the Jewish leaders would not betray them.[63]

The distinction between the Orthodox definition of patriotism as a feeling that can be transferred from one government to another and the characterization in *Nowy Dziennik* of *państwowość* as practical is a fine one. Nevertheless, it was a distinction that was important to make. It allowed the Zionists of *Nowy Dziennik* to define themselves on their own terms. Just as Jews in the United States in the early twentieth century were learning to be Jewish within a specific cultural context, so Jews in Poland were confronting issues peculiar to their own history. The attachment to Poland expressed in the pages of *Nowy Dziennik* may have been all the stronger because of Jews' awareness of Poland's partitioned past. The writers of *Nowy Dziennik* may have thought that loyalty to a state with such fragile boundaries might be particularly appreciated by an often hostile Polish government. Poland was a multi-ethnic society, but it was not a nation of immigrants. Jews in Poland, however much they acculturated and assimilated linguistically, would always remain not just ethnically distinct from the majority population but nationally distinct as well. Their religious, linguistic, cultural and, indeed, national distinctiveness assured that they could not 'melt' into society or mix easily with Poland's other ethnic and national minorities. The insistence on both Jewish nationality and Polish patriotism was an attempt to finesse their difference, to be a part of one nation even as they developed another.

But does this distinction between a national identity and a civic identity apply to the Jewish masses? As one anonymous author in *Nowy Dziennik* suggested, the Jewish religion was 'the alpha and the omega' of the Jewish masses.[64] There were certainly no doubts as to the Jewish identity of the majority of the Jewish population, but in what way were the masses Polish? Jews accepted a form of Polish identity as citizens of the Polish state and began the process of linguistic assimilation, but that does not mean that they had to 'denationalize' (*wynarodowić się*). As this author explained, 'If we state that the Jewish people in Poland are Polish in the sense of belonging to the state, and Jewish nationals at the same time, we are only demanding recognition of and respect for something that only greedy, chauvinistic imperialism dares to uproot in human history.' Thus the author implies that anyone denying the Jews their own national identity as well as a Polish civic identity is a greedy and chauvinistic imperialist. The admission of a governmental or civic identity as Poles could not truly jeopardize Jewish national identity. For this writer, learning Polish did not necessarily mean any compromise of Jewish identity. The difficulty for Jewish nationalist leaders was defending this notion to both Jewish and Polish audiences. Jews have long struggled with how to proclaim allegiance to their own people and to the non-Jewish state in which they live. The editors of *Nowy Dziennik* offered an explanation of Jewish national identity that, for them, solved this problem. They clearly showed they thought of themselves as members of the Polish state as well as the Jewish nation, a national community separate from Poles.[65]

Divisions within the community were part of the reason this conception of Jewish national identity was, and still is, difficult for many to accept. The nationalists of *Nowy Dziennik* had to explain to the larger Jewish community and to Jews who had already assimilated and rejected their Jewish background why they persisted in promoting ideas of Jewish nationalism. According to the editors of *Nowy Dziennik*, it was a mistake to divide Jews into two different groups, assimilationists and nationalists. Jews who had converted or who considered themselves as Poles of the Mosaic faith were in no way numerous among the Jewish community or, indeed, a part of the Jewish community at all, having already rejected it in favour of Polish culture. Indeed, the editors repeatedly stressed this rejection of assimilationists in later issues.

Jewish nationalists were not active enemies of Poles. The explicit division into two groups, assimilationists and nationalists, denied the fact that the Jewish masses were really *Jewish*. The writers of *Nowy Dziennik* realized that the Jewish masses did not possess European enlightenment; their Jewish roots were very deep and one could not expect them to be assimilated even within the next ten years. The poverty of war, however, increased the pace of nationalism and broadened the horizons of the masses.

Each day, the masses were less withdrawn, less isolated, asserted one author. Nationalism sought simply to improve the quality of life of the Jewish masses. It did not demand equal rights or some form of national autonomy for cultural minorities. Rather, the call was simply to lead the Jews into the next decades with an increased identification with Jewish national goals as well as a greater level of participation in Polish society.

In accounting for their Jewish nationalism, the writers of *Nowy Dziennik* compared themselves to Polish nationalists. Proclaiming that the organizational life of the Jewish community was so intense and active due to the devastation of the war, one author asserted that in spirit the new Jewish nationalists (the writers and, presumably, some of the readers of *Nowy Dziennik*) were actually more like the Poles working towards Polish independence and statehood than the Poles of the Mosaic faith. In placing themselves as Jewish nationalists on the same level as Polish nationalists, the writer subtly made their case for the existence of a separate national community and civic equality.

With a conception of Jewish national identity that allowed for a genuine identification with Poland, Cracow's Jewish nationalists could enthusiastically support the Polish state alongside their promotion of Hebrew, Yiddish and general Jewish culture. To celebrate twenty years of Polish independence, *Nowy Dziennik* ran an article by the Zionist politician Apolinary Hartglas, who praised the extraordinary growth of the Polish state, as well as the Polish victory over the Bolsheviks.[66] In an answer to why Jewish political leaders were willing to participate in Polish politics after the establishment of the state, he responded it was because of the obligation implied by Polish citizenship and a general solidarity with Polish national ideals. Hartglas wrote, 'Jews see in the liberation of Poland an act of historical justice, such as they expect for themselves.' Further, 'We have done everything as befits any good citizen, and we have done more than other citizens, because no other's citizenship is questioned as much daily as is ours.' Jews rejoiced, 'not only as citizens, but also as nationalist Jews … because our joy with all of Poland flows from the same source as the belief in the liberation of our own nation, from a deep conviction that justice and freedom must finally triumph!' Statements such as these by Hartglas simply reflect the real dilemma of Diaspora politicians who were forced to figure out how to live as citizens of one nation-state while proclaiming loyalty to Zionist ideals.

It is tempting to dismiss this enthusiasm for the Polish state as mere kowtowing to Polish government officials, but such declarations were not mandatory. Rather, these comments reflect a general appreciation of the fact that the Jews' fate in Poland relied to a significant extent on good relations with the Polish state. Not surprisingly, a 1921 editorial marking the anniversary of the Polish constitution of 3 May 1791, praised that document as the 'best moment of the Polish spirit'.[67] The constitution adopted in 1921 was not quite as good as that of 1791, primarily because those who championed it were 'not only able to love their own nation, but also to hate other nationalities'.[68] Cognizant of their enemies within Polish society, Polish Jewish leaders appealed to what they defined as the positive, tolerant aspects of Polish nationalism while spreading Jewish nationalism to the larger community. Furthermore, for Hartglas, the re-establishment of a Polish national state was a harbinger of the likely re-establishment of a Jewish national state, because, for him, Jewish claims to statehood had the same basis as Polish claims.

Even when the situation of the Jews in Poland worsened significantly in the late 1930s, *Nowy Dziennik* still argued that everyone, regardless of nationality, should defend the Polish nation. At a time when pogroms against the Jewish population were making the front pages, and when economic anti-Semitism on the part of the Polish government became more evident, Jewish allegiance to the Polish state stands out as singularly idealistic, if not foolhardy. One Cracow Jewish leader wrote,

But we dare to doubt that insulting the blue and white flag and rejecting Jewish youth in the idea of national defence [referring to the Polish nation] is in line with the programme of General Rydz-Śmigły which he so beautifully expressed in the pithy slogan: To lift Poland higher ... However, in spite of all the bitterness we feel in light of certain offensive and unjust acts, we respond to the appeal, and we offer our sacrifice for the goal of the defense of the state. For we consider that the slogan of the defence of the state before dangers that threaten it should unite all its citizens. Nobody can escape from this obligation.[69]

In committing themselves to serve the Polish state rather than the Polish nation, Cracow's Jewish leaders were upholding ideals of Polish nationalism that they felt should apply to the Jewish national community as well.

The tragedy here is that Polish nationalism of the 1930s differed markedly from the romantic nationalism of the nineteenth century. Brian Porter's work has demonstrated how some Polish nationalists turned towards the right and allowed for the hatred of other communities well before the inter-war period.[70] While Piłsudski's *Sanacja* regime kept the extreme nationalists out of power, it could not stop the spread of the nationalist movements that attracted the youth and students often responsible for the beatings of Jews on university campuses and anti-Jewish violence in city streets. The Polish-Jewish literary critic Henryk Vogler later described his experience of such violence, having been caught up in a group of Jewish students being chased by a crowd. Vogler explains the effect of that event on his own identity: 'In that moment I became a Jew.'[71] The comments of Hartglas were made in a political environment that tolerated and supported proposals for anti-Jewish legislation and challenges to Jewish citizenship in the Polish state. Moreover, Jewish politicians and writers were not unaware of the fate of the Jews in Nazi Germany. Many German Jews crossed the border into Poland, fleeing the Nazi regime. Polish Jewish leaders knew that constitutional republics could turn into dictatorial regimes quite easily; Piłsudski's 1926 coup itself had shown how rapidly the political situation could change.

'WITH THE NATION – OR AGAINST IT!'

In comparing their cause to Polish nationalism, Jewish leaders hoped to make their own goals more understandable and more acceptable to both the Polish and Jewish public. Commitment to the Polish state was simply a condition of existence as a national minority in a multi-ethnic Polish state and so was expressed in the hopeful early years of 1918 as well as in the difficult years of the late 1930s. This commitment was a reflection of a real conviction in the potential of nationalism – whether Jewish or Polish – to deliver a people from exile and not without serious implications for the development of the Jewish community in Poland. The sincerity of the Zionists' commitment to Poland and Polish causes was part of Jewish nationalist idealism. From the very start, hopes for an independent Polish state influenced the Cracow Zionists' decision to publish a Jewish newspaper in Polish. The Polish national resuscitation of 1918 provided a model for the Jewish people who similarly had been deprived of a state for an even longer period of time. Given local historical circumstances, the Polish national 'rebirth' meant more for the Jewish community of Cracow than of Lwów, where Jews knew to walk the careful line of neutrality between Poles and Ukrainians during the immediate post-war period. In Cracow, the influence of the Polish community can be seen in public and private education and in the control exercised over Jewish organizations, as described in following chapters. Living among the Polish majority conditioned the Jewish nationalism developed in inter-war Poland, as evidenced by the formation in *Nowy Dziennik* of a Jewish nationalism that allowed for the expression of a Polish civic identity. At the same time, living among Poles did not prevent the development of a Jewish nationalist identity that meant to nurture, protect and defend the Jewish people. The Zionism of *Nowy Dziennik* hoped both to improve material conditions for the Jews in Poland and to prepare its community for emigration to Palestine. They committed both to the state in which they lived and the Zionist dream of a homeland.

The insistence on an identity as both Jews and Poles required a new relationship with Poles, one that recognized both Jewish similarities to Poles and fundamental differences. That Jews defined themselves against other nations is not surprising. Poles, and so many others, did the same in their own national development. Important for the discussion here is the effort made by Cracow's Jewish nationalists to affirm both a Jewish and a Polish identity, however differently they may have defined each. The articles in *Nowy Dziennik* regarding assimilation often argued that the Zionists were developing a real relationship with the Poles, something never attempted by the pre-1918 assimilationist leaders.[72] In short, the Jews of Cracow were trying to have it both ways, to enter the majority culture without giving up their own.[73]

This refusal on the part of Jewish nationalist leaders in Cracow to relinquish one national identity even as they adapted to life in the new state of another nation challenged both the minority and majority cultures. It is this challenge that makes *Nowy Dziennik* so significant. In refusing to give up either their separate identity as Jews or the Polish language, literature and culture to which they lay claim, the Jewish intellectuals around *Nowy Dziennik* posited a Jewish identity that not all Jews, and certainly not all Poles, were likely to accept. Yet in publishing in Polish, Berkelhammer and the others gambled successfully. Recognizing that Polish political rule would not always benefit the Jewish community, they hoped to stem assimilation by insuring that Polish-speaking Jews would be able to express a Jewish national identity in Polish. They were able to accept the breakdown of the language boundary between Jews and Poles because in doing so they created another one. The assertion of the nationhood of the Jews, they hoped, would prove to be another boundary between the two communities – but one that would not prohibit communication with the majority population.

Writing in Polish, the writers of *Nowy Dziennik* were vulnerable to charges that the newspaper was simply an instrument of assimilation. In response, they recognized their position as Jews in Poland as unique, as differing from that of the relatively more assimilated Jews in Western Europe as well as from Poles and other non-Jews in Poland. They acknowledged that Polish Jewry could not remain the same economically and culturally in the face of the political, economic and social changes that followed the First World War, but they did not compromise their ethnic and national identity. They set themselves firmly against organizations like the Association of Poles of the Mosaic Faith, assimilationist leaders within the community who worked against any form of national autonomy and viewed Jews only as a religious group, not as a nation.[74] That the writers of *Nowy Dziennik* should be so concerned with defining themselves against assimilationists makes sense. This was necessary if their efforts to act as the unquestioned voice of Cracow Jewry were to be successful. Before 1918, assimilationist leaders in Cracow had attained positions on the Cracow city council and represented the Jewish community to the Polish public. If the Zionists were to replace them as the leaders of the Jewish community, they would first need to distinguish themselves from the community's acknowledged leaders.

The pre-war assimilationist leaders had presented themselves as the only intermediaries between Jews and Poles. According to the editors and writers of *Nowy Dziennik*, the assimilationists had not been successful because they did not respect the commitment of the Jewish masses to a separate Jewish identity. The Jewish nationalists of *Nowy Dziennik* considered assimilation a fiction. The fact that the Jewish 'masses' led a separate life, that they felt Jewish and thought Jewish, according to one writer in *Nowy Dziennik*, indicated that they were not Polish culturally or nationally and that the Jewish nationalists of *Nowy Dziennik* were the most appropriate group to appeal to the Jewish masses.[75] Educated in both Polish and Jewish cultures, they were able to reach out to the Jewish masses in ways that the assimilationist leaders did not.

The writers of *Nowy Dziennik* exploited the categories of 'nationalist' and 'assimilationist' in their effort to define themselves against the older, entrenched leadership of the

Cracow Jewish community. One writer charged a group of 'indifferent' Jews in Cracow with having assimilated 'cosmetically'. These Jews played with identity just as some played with make-up. This group would neither confirm nor deny a Jewish identity; similarly, they would not accept any kind of Polish identity. In humanitarian, philanthropic, professional and social institutions, the indifferent Jews would claim to be better Jews than the best Zionists. But when asked about belonging to the Jewish nation, they would remain silent.[76] Neither did they offer a response when they were asked if they belonged to the Polish nation. The anonymous author urged these Jews, 'Take off your mask! For Palestine or against it! With the nation – or against it! Clearly, openly, with a manly confession of faith. On this or on that side of the great effort of the history of our nation! One should have the courage of strong political belief.'[77]

Unfortunately, this 'party of the indifferent' was particularly strong in our beloved Cracow, the author continued. The appeal to the Jewish community here is to identify themselves as Jews; the target audience for this article is precisely those Jews who, the article asserted, were 'indifferent'. A significant part of the Jewish population, in between those completely assimilated to Polish identity and the Zionists of *Nowy Dziennik*, did not respond to Jewish nationalist appeals. The writers of *Nowy Dziennik* tried to speak for all of the groups within the Jewish community, but they continually railed against those they termed politically 'indifferent' and the more assimilated (or less nationalist) they were so decidedly against. Indifference, according to this author, was even worse than real assimilation, which was at least a clear enemy against which one could fight. The widespread phenomenon of indifference was naturally threatening to the Zionists. Zionism was a political expression of commitment to the Jewish people; indifference threatened the political success of the Jewish community. Jews in Poland struggled for their very existence; this was 'no time or place for a womanly, cowardly, sentimental neutrality in light of the most essential problems of Jewish life. With a thousand voices we call: Everybody to the front!'

A lack of politicization leading to indifference could not solve the problems of the Jewish community as the Zionists perceived

them. The Zionists saw themselves in a fight for the support of
the Jewish 'masses' and the assimilated and 'indifferent'
intellectual leaders only hindered Zionist success. The gendered
language throughout this article suggests that the author
equated a strong Jewish nation with common notions of
masculinity. The author insulted the indifferent enemy as
'womanly' and literally called Jews to battle. Articles such as this
one in *Nowy Dziennik* were tools in the Zionist battle for political
dominance in Cracow and throughout Poland, part of how the
Zionists hoped to gain support for their cause. It is questionable,
however, whether such rhetoric brought them closer to their
goal. They themselves were presenting a form of nationalism
that combined an affiliation to the Polish state, an idea that
challenged those Zionists and other Jews who did not have such
a connection to Poland or who found themselves frequently
reminded of Polish anti-Semitism. They declared themselves for
Palestine, not against Poland.

This position is somewhat qualified by the memoirs on *Nowy
Dziennik* written by David Lazer, the paper's editor in the late
1930s. Calling his newspaper 'an Israeli daily in the Polish
language', Lazer noted that *Nowy Dziennik* employed no fewer
than seven regular correspondents in Palestine.[78] Lazer writes
that, as the situation for Jews in Poland worsened during the late
1930s, the staff of *Nowy Dziennik* would have gone to Palestine
but for the need to serve the Jews in Poland they would have left
behind.

Still, the attachment to Poland was a strong one, as strong as
the attachment many German Jews felt for Germany. Ezra
Mendelsohn has described Jewish politics in the early twentieth-
century history of the United States as integrationist, in
opposition to the Jewish nationalist politics of East Central
Europe.[79] Unlike Jewish political leaders in the United States
such as Cyrus Adler, Jacob Schiff and Louis Marshall, Thon and
the Zionists of Cracow viewed the Jews first and foremost as a
nation. But like Adler, Schiff and Marshall, Thon wanted to
integrate. Indeed, there is evidence that he even felt that
integration had already taken place or at least had already
begun. In 1936, *Nasza Opinja* [*Our Opinion*], a weekly Polish-
language Jewish newspaper covering Jewish affairs throughout
Poland, published a special issue devoted to Cracow. The cover

story predictably featured the writings of Ozjasz Thon. Chosen to represent the famous rabbi's work was a speech Thon gave at a memorial service for Władysław Steinhaus, a young Jewish soldier who fought with Piłsudski's legions during the First World War in spite of a doctor's permission exempting him from any obligation to serve militarily. Steinhaus subsequently died a hero's death and was buried in Cracow's Jewish cemetery. In his speech Thon recalled the words Steinhaus is said to have spoken to his father when he was near death: 'I am happy to die as a Pole and as a Jew.' Thon's speech honouring a man who gave his life for the freedom of his 'native country' made clear Thon's respect for those who died for the ideal of a free and just Poland.

Jewish leaders such as Thon and the editors of *Nowy Dziennik* found a way to assert their national difference in Poland without yielding their rights or obligations as Polish citizens. In inter-war Poland, the Jews as a nation had to learn to survive in a multinational community. That survival was precarious in difficult economic times. They adopted Polish language and literature and created their own version of a Polish civic identity. By making these concessions to the reality of their lives in Poland, they hoped to maintain their uniqueness as a separate national group. Though vehemently opposed to assimilation, they did not reject acculturation; they looked for ways to integrate their national, linguistic, religious and cultural identities without doing violence to any of these important aspects of their lives.

Nowy Dziennik's plea to the indifferent Jews of Cracow may very well have resonated with some in the community. The call for a more active Jewish nationalism in the city was certainly part of how Cracow's Jews motivated their community to adapt to the changing circumstances of inter-war Poland. So, too, was an attack on the traditional heders (*kheyder*, singular, the Jewish schools of Eastern Europe), long a target of reform within the Jewish community. Jewish schools had to get 'out of the darkness' and end their 'withdrawal' from society. Those who might defend the heder were 'medieval'. Jewish education in Poland, according to the editors of *Nowy Dziennik*, was due for a radical transformation. Any modernization of Jewish schools entailed a co-operation with Polish authorities that would, necessarily, qualify Jewish control of private Jewish schools.

More importantly, Jewish education was needed for the making
of citizens, Polish citizens. Improvements in Jewish education
were vital for the success of the newspaper's 'programme,' the
defence of the weak and injured and the improvement of the
material conditions of Polish Jewry: 'As nationalist Jews, as
Polish citizens, as people of progress and culture, we aim for the
development of Jewish schools, without which the making of
Jews into citizens will never take place!'[80] In their refusal to
assimilate according to the Western model and in their
realization that change was necessary in order to educate Jews in
proper Polish citizenship, the writers of *Nowy Dziennik* were
transforming Jewish national identity in Poland. The conception
of a civic identity, tied to the newly established, independent
Polish government, allowed for the expression of a Jewish
nationalism that could work towards the betterment of the
political, social and economic conditions of the Jews in Poland as
well as in Palestine. Civic assimilation could forestall structural
assimilation. It allowed the Jews to be both Poles and Jews. The
efforts of Cracow's Jewish leaders demonstrate that they were
working to become a part of the Polish political state without
sacrificing their desire to be a part of the Jewish nation.

ATTACKS ON CIVIL SOCIETY

In May 1923, right-wing Polish terrorists bombed the offices of
Nowy Dziennik. The bombing was just one of a series of
bombings that occurred in Cracow that spring and part of a
wave of attacks on the offices of private Jewish institutions
throughout Poland. The first bombing targeted a local Jewish
activist in the city of Sosnowiec; a second bombing, the Jewish
political leader Leon Weinzieher from Będzin. The Sosnowiec
offices of the Jewish sports organization Makkabi were next.

Three bombings in Cracow followed these events.[81] The first
site hit in Cracow was the home of Dr Władysław Natanson,
rector of Jagiellonian University and an opponent of the *numerus
clausus*. The bomb damaged the door and steps to his personal
residence, but Natanson was most certainly not the original
target of the attack. The anti-Semitic group Rozwój [Develop-
ment] had warned in the anti-Semitic Cracow newspaper *Głos*

Narodu [*Voice of the Nation*] that there would be some kind of attack if the visiting Yiddish theatre troupe, Vilner Trupe, performed as scheduled in the city's Bagatela theatre. When the performance was cancelled specifically because of fears arising from this threat of violence and the thought of a bomb going off in a crowded theatre, Natanson's house, very near the theatre, became an alternate target. An attack on a Jewish workers' group with an office in Cracow's Hotel Keller followed. A bomb placed on the floor above the offices of the Association of Jewish Trade Unions damaged doors, furniture and window panels, and created a hole in the floor. As no reason to target the hotel owner or other occupants of the hotel was ever put forward, it was clear the trade unions' association was the target.

Nowy Dziennik was the third bombing in the city in a little less than two months. Because the paper did not appear the day after the bombing, it is necessary to piece together the actual events from later reports in *Nowy Dziennik* and from other newspapers.[82] On 16 May 1923, a bomb exploded in the offices of *Nowy Dziennik* at Orzeszkowa 7 at nine in the evening. The third floor suffered the greatest damage. The ceiling had fallen in, so that the sky could be seen from the interior of the building. A door had been blown out and two walls on the second floor had been destroyed. No one was killed but the explosion occurred only ten minutes after an editorial meeting had taken place. The police had been on duty for ten days guarding the offices of *Nowy Dziennik* and the socialist newspaper *Naprzód*, but though the policeman had seen two men near the building, they could not say for certain that these men had planted the bomb. Fortunately, the printing press on the ground floor was not damaged.

Most distressing to the Jewish community after these events was the response of the police, who were hesitant to question and arrest the members of the Endecja who were most likely responsible for the crimes. After the initial arrest of the Endek youth leaders the police suspected of involvement, five hundred people gathered in front of the main building of Jagiellonian University and shouted 'Down with the Jews' in response. Editors at the city's newspapers received letters as well, threatening retaliation if they printed anything against the perpetrators of the bombing.[83] The Jewish press, political leaders such as Ozjasz Thon, and the Polish Socialist Party all chided the police for searching for the perpetrators in other Polish cities and not in Cracow and for considering seriously that the perpetrator of the bombings in Cracow could have been Jewish. At a meeting of the *Sejm*, Thon pointed out that, after all, Cracow was a small city, not Paris or London. Surely, he claimed, the police should not be experiencing such great difficulty in finding those responsible. Thon was openly shouted at in response, but he also drew laughter – when he pointed out that it was possible that the falling doors of *Nowy Dziennik* could have hit a passing Endek.[84]

Nowy Dziennik recognized the threat of such terror to the foundations of the Polish state. The bombings occurred in an already charged atmosphere, less than six months after the December 1922 assassination of President Gabriel Narutowicz. Right-wing political groups attacked Narutowicz for having won his position with the support of Jewish votes from Yitzhok Gruenbaum's National Minorities Bloc. As one writer asked, 'Where are we living? In what kind of times? In what kind of relationships?'[85] Such attacks would inevitably lead to the ruin of ethics and the foundation of the state, 'of which we are citizens', the author stressed.[86] Writing from Lwów in *Chwila*, Henryk Hescheles, the editor of that paper, lamented Cracow's transformation from a city of royal gardens and the most beautiful cultural traditions into a city in the middle of a battle.[87] *Nowy Dziennik* was not the only Jewish organization targeted, but the newspaper was under attack as a specifically Jewish institution playing a visible role in improving Jewish life. Victims of the bombings included groups and institutions from various areas of Jewish life, whether sports clubs, the press or workers' groups. *Nowy Dziennik* was not necessarily targeted because of its status as the city's only daily newspaper or because it was seen as representative of a majority Jewish viewpoint. It was simply included in right-wing attacks on Jewish society.

At the heart of the conflict, according to the Jewish press, was a battle for the home in which both Poles and Jews lived. The Endecja, according to the Jewish press, simply did not recognize that violence on the streets precluded any feeling of safety, among both Jews and Poles:

> During the bombings in Cracow, the Endek press behaved like the resident of a home who refuses to help his

neighbour during a fire, because the fire did not start in his apartment, but in his neighbour's. The Endeks do not see that this is one home. The Endeks always segregate Polish and Jewish and, in their incomprehensible blindness, forget that each home standing in the lands of Poland – is Polish, that every part of the home is Polish, though in it may live Jews, Ukrainians, or others.[88]

Almost exactly a year later, in the spring of 1924, Polish authorities finally charged a right-wing lawyer with the Cracow bombings.[89] The lawyer, known as Abłamowicz, was known for his involvement with right-wing groups that supported Eligiusz Niewiadomski, the assassin of President Narutowicz.

The attacks in Cracow were not the last of 1923. Incidents in Warsaw, including one at the university, kept the issue of violence against Jews alive in the Jewish and Polish press throughout the year. The events were seemingly unrelated, but because both individual Jewish activists and groups and sympathetic non-Jews were attacked, they were linked to the earlier incidents in Cracow. One clear similarity among the events was the hesitancy of Polish police officials to question or arrest Endek students. In Warsaw, the police justified this hesitancy because of the Endek demonstration that was the reaction to the questioning and arrest of Endek students in Cracow. The police also received threats, warning them not to investigate the incidents seriously. Such attacks occurred throughout the inter-war period in other contexts; *Nowy Dziennik* was not the only Polish-language Jewish newspaper in inter-war Poland to be the target of a bombing. The offices of *Chwila* were attacked in June 1929, in the riots that occurred after the alleged disruption of a Corpus Christi procession by Jewish students in Lwów. This attack on *Chwila* was even more devastating than the one on *Nowy Dziennik*. Like the attack on *Nowy Dziennik*, it occurred as part of a series of events. These incidents of violence, directed at the newly visible institutions of Jewish civil society, naturally call into question the process of integration that those behind *Chwila* and *Nowy Dziennik* supported. Violence against Jews provided a compelling reason for the development and maintenance of a separate Jewish civil society even as emerging Jewish leaders spoke eloquently of the need to participate in the larger society.

Given the lack of other Jewish political alternatives in Cracow, the influence of *Nowy Dziennik* among the city's Jewish elite is difficult to overestimate. Its influence on the Jewish 'masses' the writers of *Nowy Dziennik* hoped to win to their cause is much more problematic to determine. No other group in Cracow had a comparable daily newspaper to rival the Zionists. *Nowy Dziennik* was the leading voice of the Cracow Jewish community. This is precisely why the efforts of its editors and writers to bring about a conception of Jewish national identity that included elements of Polish culture are so significant. The Zionists of *Nowy Dziennik* represent the acculturation of the Jewish community in Cracow, an acculturation qualified by the development of an active Jewish national (not simply ethnic) identity. Those writers gathered around *Nowy Dziennik* wanted to belong to both the Jewish and Polish nations, to be both Jews and Poles.

Because of the Zionist longing for Palestine, the attachment of the Jews of Cracow to a Polish civic identity is indeed difficult to understand. This attachment, however, is but one aspect of *Gegenwartsarbeit*, or Zionist work to improve the conditions of local Jews. The Jews of the Diaspora were not to be sacrificed for Zionist goals; the Zionists of Cracow focused their efforts just as much on improving conditions for Jews in Poland as on the establishment of a Jewish home or state in Palestine. The key to understanding how Zionism can be compatible with a loyalty to Poland, a desire for a Polish civic identity, and even a willingness to defend the Polish state lies in an acceptance of the Jews' status as citizens of Poland – with both the opportunities and disabilities that implies – and in an understanding of their assertion of a separate national identity in a multinational state. Jews were not as alienated from Poland and Polish culture as our understanding of the subsequent, and horrific, events of the wartime years might lead us to assume. It did not take long for Jews to grow disillusioned with the Polish political system in the 1920s, but co-operation with the majority government and participation in the majority society was still necessary, a fact acknowledged in the pages of *Nowy Dziennik*. From the beginning to the end of the inter-war period, *Nowy Dziennik* reflected a desire to develop Jewish national life and to participate in the building of the Polish state.

Others in the Jewish community, however, did not always support the ideas expressed in *Nowy Dziennik*. While those writing and reading *Nowy Dziennik* were an influential segment of the Jewish community, they were outnumbered by the Jewish 'masses'. The group of writers and intellectuals gathered around *Nowy Dziennik* did not represent the Jewish community in all its social and economic diversity. While the founders of *Nowy Dziennik* responded to the phenomenon of assimilation by asserting their nationalist ideas yet remaining loyal to the Polish state, other groups in Cracow responded in different ways, affirming other boundaries between Jews and Poles, both linguistic and religious. These voices were in Yiddish and they reveal the continuing importance of religious tradition within the Jewish community and the emergence of a Yiddish cultural politics in polonized Cracow.

NOTES

1. Chone Shmeruk, 'Hebrew-Yiddish-Polish: A Trilingual Jewish Culture', in *The Jews of Poland Between the Two World Wars*, ed. Yisrael Gutman et al. (Hanover, NH: University of New England Press, 1989), 308–9. In a general article on the Polish-Jewish daily press, Michael Steinlauf has raised significant questions of linguistic assimilation. Steinlauf asserts that linguistic assimilation had advanced considerably during the twenty years of the Second Republic, a conclusion my study of the press in Crakow confirms. Michael Steinlauf, 'The Polish-Jewish Daily Press', *Polin*, 2 (1987): 219–45. Also see Marian Fuks, *Prasa żydowska w Warszawie, 1823–1939* (Warsaw: Państwowe Wydawńictwo Naulowe, 1979) and 'Prasa żydowska w Polsce wydawana w języku polskim – jej rola i znaczenie w kształtowaniu stosunków polsko-żydowskich (do 1939 r.)', *Biuletyn Żydowskiego Instytutu Historycznego*, 3–4 (July–December 1985): 135–42.
2. Piech, *W cieniu kościołów i synagog*, 17. Also see *Skorowidz miejscowości Rzeczypospolitej Polskiej opracowany na podstawie wyników pierwszego powszechnego spisu ludności z dn. 30 września 1921 r. i innych źródeł urzędowych*, t. 12, *Województwo Krakowskie i Śląsk Cieszyński* (Warsaw, 1925), 17.
3. *Ogólne wyniki spisu ludności, domów, budynków, mieszkań i zwierząt domowych w Krakowie z 30 września 1921 r.* (Cracow: Biuro Statystyczne Miasta Krakowa, 1924), 112.
4. *Drugi powszechny spis ludności z dn. 9 XII 1931 r. Miasto Kraków, Statystyka Polski*, Seria C, zeszyt 64, tab. 10–11 (Warsaw, 1937).
5. Jacob Lestchinsky, 'Di shprakhn bay yidn in umophengikn poyln: an analiz loyt der folkstseylung fun 1931', *YIVO bleter*, XXII, no. 2 (November–December 1943), 157.

6. Steinlauf, 'The Polish-Jewish Daily Press', 234. As Steinlauf writes, 'That is, for the sake of Jewish national interests, the Polish-Jewish press opposed documentation of the fact that many of its own readers existed!'
7. 'Nokh der folks-tseylung in kroke', *Dos yidishe vort*, 11 December 1931, 4.
8. 'Język ojczysty', *Nowy Dziennik*, 29 November 1931, 10.
9. Lestchinsky, 'Di shtotishe bafelkerung in poyln 1921–1931', *YIVO bleter*, XX, 1 (September–October 1942): 1–29; 'Di shtotishe bafelkerung in poyln 1921–1931', *YIVO bleter*, XXI, 2 (March–April 1943): 20–47.
10. Rafael F. Scharf, *Poland, What Have I to Do with Thee* ... , 4.
11. See Lestchinsky, 'Di shprakhn bay yidn in umophengikn Poyln', *YIVO bleter*, XXII, 1943, 147–62 and Steinlauf, 'The Polish-Jewish Daily Press', n. 3, 235–6 and n. 24, 239.
12. Alfred Döblin, *Journey to Poland* (New York: Paragon House Publishers, 1991), 157.
13. Ibid., 104–5.
14. Holger Nath, 'Yiddish as the Emerging National Language of East European Jewry', *Sociolinguistica*, 6 (1992): 58.
15. Czesław Brzoza, 'Jewish Periodicals in Cracow (1918–1939)', *Bibliographies of Polish Judaica International Symposium Cracow 5th–7th July 1988 (Proceedings)* (Cracow: Research Center of Jewish History and Culture in Poland, 1993), 55–111. This bibliography of the Jewish press of inter-war Cracow is based on extensive research in city and state archives. Brzoza lists the dates of publication, noting any interruptions, as well as the likely circulation based on police registers and any supplements that the newspapers might have published. This collection of bibliographies also includes the helpful bibliography compiled by Ewa Bąkowska, 'Polish Language Jewish Press in the Holdings of the Jagiellonian Library', 111-83. See also Brzoza's 'The Jewish Press in Kraków (1918–1939)', *Polin*, 7 (1992): 133–46 and his *Polityczna prasa krakowska* (Cracow: Uniwersytet Jagielloński, 1990). Brzoza utilized the bibliographical work of Paul Glickson and Yechiel Szeintuch. See Glickson, *Preliminary Inventory of the Jewish Daily and Periodical Press Published in the Polish Language 1823–1982* (Jerusalem: Magnes Press, 1983) and Szeintuch, *Preliminary Inventory of Yiddish Dailies and Periodicals Published in Poland Between the Two World Wars* (Jerusalem: Hebrew University of Jerusalem, 1986).
16. Brzoza, *Polityczna prasa krakowska*, 169. One of the Polish titles read most widely by Jews was the popular *Ilustrowany Kuryer Codzienny [Illustrated Daily Courier]*.
17. For example, Brzoza cites a circulation of 1,000-2,000 copies for *Rękodzieło i Przemysł* from 1923–1936, but only 500–700 for *Dos yidishe vort* and 1,000 for *Di post*.
18. In later years, these sections often increased in the number of pages.
19. Shmuel Werses explains the difficulties the Hebrew press faced in inter-war Poland in his article, 'The Hebrew Press and Its Readership in Interwar Poland', in *The Jews of Interwar Poland Between the Two World Wars*, ed. Yisrael Gutman et al. (Hanover, NH: University of New England Press), 312–33. Foremost among these reasons are financial strains, a limited readership and competition from both the Yiddish and Polish press.
20. See Gershom Bader, 'Der "Hamagid" hot genumen dershaynen in Kroke', *Mayne zikhroynes*, 394–400 and David Lazer, 'Hamitzpah', in *Di yidishe prese vos iz geven*, ed. David Flinker et al. (Tel Aviv: Velt farband fun di yidishe zhurnalistn, 1975), 297–301.
21. See Samuel J. Imber, *Asy czystej rasy* (Cracow: Bibljoteka S. J. Imbera, 1934).
22. Löw adopted the name Leon Przemski in post-war Poland.
23. Khaim Lev (Chaim Löw), 'Nakhman Mifelew – Der mentsh', *Di Post*, 17 September 1937, 4.
24. The circulation numbers are taken from police registers from 1918 to 1939, which

might explain the huge variation, assuming the lower numbers for the newspaper's early years. In 'The Jewish Press in Kraków', Brzoza explains that *Nowy Dziennik* 'achieved the peak of its potential in 1929, when its circulation reached 11,000–18,000'. Brzoza, 'The Jewish Press in Kraków', 146. To compare, the most popular non-Jewish Polish-language daily, *Ilustrowany Kuryer Codzienny*, had a nationwide readership of 229,619 in 1931. Brzoza, *Polityczna prasa krakowska*, 131.

25. According to an article from 1930 regarding a conflict between Thon and the Hasidim of Crakow published in *Dos yidishe vort*. 'Di "bebe" bokhurim (beltsbobov) organizirn demonstratsies gegn dep. dr. Thon', *Dos yidishe vort*, 28 November 1930, 3.
26. David Lazer, 'Nowy Dziennik', *Di yidishe prese vos iz geven*, 311.
27. Mojżesz Kanfer, the theatre critic for *Nowy Dziennik*, also founded the Cracow Yiddish Theatre Society. His work is discussed extensively below in Chapter 7.
28. Wilhelm Berkelhammer, 'Nasz problem językowy', *Nowy Dziennik*, 28 January 1925, 5.
29. Quoted in Michael Steinlauf, 'The Polish-Jewish Daily Press', n. 20, 238; taken from David Lazer, 'Nowy Dziennik, 1918–1939', *Di yidishe prese vos iz geven*, 311.
30. 'Na powitanie Dnia hebraistów w Krakowie', *Nowy Dziennik*, 26 June 1927, 5–6.
31. Benzion Katz, 'My, a nasza literatura', *Nowy Dziennik*, 26 June 1927, 5.
32. 'Der budzhet-debate in kahal rat', *Dos yidishe vort*, 17 December 1926, 1.
33. 'Unzer nayer shprakhen-kamf', *Dos Yidishe Vort*, 1 March 1929, 2.
34. Steinlauf, 'The Polish-Jewish Daily Press', n. 28, 301–2.
35. Pinchas Goldwasser, 'Przyczynek do historji Jubilata', *Nowy Dziennik*, 16 July 1928, 22.
36. Czesław Brzoza, *Polityczna prasa krakowska*, 159.
37. Zygfryd Moses, 'Nowy Dziennik – nieco historji i statystyki', *Nowy Dziennik*, 16 July 1928, 21.
38. Berkelhammer, 'Narodziny Nowego Dziennika (Wspomnienie)', *Nowy Dziennik*, 11 July 1923, 6–8.
39. Steinlauf addressed the reasons why Polish Jews felt they needed a daily newspaper in 'The Polish-Jewish Daily Press', 222–3. Steinlauf concludes that the daily newspaper was 'a commonplace of everyday life', and he quotes the Yiddish journalist Sh. V. Stupnitski, who called the establishment of a Jewish press in Polish 'an act of national self-defence'. The Stupnitski quote is taken from that writer's article in *Nasz Przegląd*, 'W młynie opinji. Czy potrzebne jest pismo polsko-żydowskie?', 14 June 1928.
40. M. Ringel, 'Pierwszy dziennik', *Nowy Dziennik*, 16 July 1928, 2.
41. Wilhelm Berkelhammer, 'Narodziny Nowego Dziennika (Wspomnienia)', 11 July 1923, 7.
42. 'Nowy Dziennik', *Nowy Dziennik*, 9 July 1918, 1.
43. Wilhelm Berkelhammer, 'Narodziny Nowego Dziennika (Wspomnienie)', 11 July 1923, 6–8.
44. Wilhelm Berkelhammer, 'Nasz posterunek, Z okazji jubileuszu', *Nowy Dziennik*, 15 July 1928, 9.
45. 'Wilhelm Berkelhammer', *Nowy Dziennik*, 29 August 1934, 2.
46. Ibid.; Wilhelm Fallek, 'Berkelhammer – Drogowskaz dla obecnych i następnych pokoleń', *Nowy Dziennik*, 3 September 1934, 3.
47. Fallek, 'Berkelhammer – Drogowskaz dla obecnych i następnych pokoleń', 3 September 1934, 3.
48. 'Nowy Dziennik', *Nowy Dziennik*, 9 July 1918, 1.
49. Wilhelm Berkelhammer, 'Nasz posterunek, Z okazji jubileuszu Nowego Dziennika', *Nowy Dziennik*, 9.
50. Brzoza, *Polityczna prasa krakowska*, 160.
51. Herbert Gans, 'Symbolic Ethnicity and Symbolic Religiosity: Towards a Comparison

of Ethnic and Religious Acculturation', *Ethnic and Racial Studies*, 17, no. 4 (October 1994): 580.

52. Henryk Hescheles, 'W piętnastolecie pracy', *Chwila*, 15 January 1934, 2.
53. Jacob Appenszlak, 'Na posterunku ... ', *Nasz Przegląd*, 25 March 1923, 2.
54. Ozjasz Thon, 'Po latach dziesięciu', *Nowy Dziennik*, 16 July 1928, 1. Thon's phrase was '*rozmowa „ od narodu do narodu".*'
55. Ibid.
56. 'Cives Poloni, natione Judaei, Obywatele polscy, narodowości żydowskiej', *Nowy Dziennik*, 22 September 1918, 3.
57. As Ezra Mendelsohn explains, 'The dual commitment to classic Zionist aims (for example, aliyah and the revival of Hebrew) and to the local political struggle for Jewish civil and national rights in Poland (implying a commitment to the struggle for Polish democracy) was a serious source of tension within East European Zionism.' Ezra Mendelsohn, *On Modern Jewish Politics*, 57.
58. 'Nacyonalizm i nacyonalizm', *Nowy Dziennik*, 16 September 1919, 1.
59. Wilhelm Berkelhammer, 'Ortodoksya a patryotyzm', *Nowy Dziennik*, 1 September 1924, 1. On Jewish loyalty to Habsburg Austria, see Rozenblit, *Reconstructing National Identity*.
60. 'Przynależność państwowa a narodowa', *Nowy Dziennik*, 6 September 1919, 1.
61. 'Cives Poloni, natione Judaei, Obywatele polscy, narodowości żydowskiej', *Nowy Dziennik*, 22 September 1918, 3.
62. 'Państwowość a narodowowość', *Nowy Dziennik*, 18 August 1918, 1.
63. 'Cives Poloni, natione Judaei', *Nowy Dziennik*, 22 September 1918, 3.
64. 'Przynależność państwowa a narodowa', *Nowy Dziennik*, 6 September 1919, 1.
65. 'Parę słów wyjaśnienia', *Nowy Dziennik*, 15 July 1918, 1.
66. Apolinary Hartglas, 'Z jednego źródła', *Nowy Dziennik*, 11 November 1938, 5. For more on Hartglas, see his memoir *Na pograniczu dwóch światów* (Warsaw: Oficyna Wydawnicza Rytm, 1996).
67. This, in spite of the fact that the 1791 constitution did not emancipate the Jews.
68. '1791–1921', *Nowy Dziennik*, 4 May 1921, 1.
69. 'Pod znakiem obrony narodowej', *Nowy Dziennik*, 14 June 1936, 2–3. Rydz-Śmigły was one of the main political leaders of Poland in the late 1930s after the death of Marshal Józef Piłsudski in 1935.
70. Brian Porter, *When Nationalism Began to Hate*.
71. Henryk Vogler, *Wyznanie mojżeszowe* (Warsaw: Państwowy Instytut Wydawniczy, 1994), 97–8. Vogler also writes how, at the end of his life, he views his identity differently, not simply as either Pole or Jew, but as both, writing, 'I am a Pole as well as a Jew.'
72. Ludwik Oberlaender, 'Asymilacja', *Nowy Dziennik*, 22 January 1928, 1.
73. For a discussion of the difficulties associated with this task, see Zygmunt Bauman, 'Exit Visas and Entry Tickets: Paradoxes of Jewish Assimilation', *Telos*, 77 (Fall 1988): 45–77.
74. For more on the Association of Poles of the Mosaic Faith, see Celia Heller, *On the Edge of Destruction: Jews of Poland Between the Two World Wars*, 185–6.
75. 'Legenda asymilacyi', *Nowy Dziennik*, 1 September 1919, 1.
76. Unfortunately, the author does not identify precisely who was included in this group. The author distinguished between those Jews who accepted assimilation as a desired political alternative, the group of the 'indifferent' and the Zionists.
77. 'Szminkowana asymilacya', *Nowy Dziennik*, 18 January 1925, 1.
78. David Lazer, 'Nowy Dziennik', *Di yidishe prese vos iz geven*, 315.
79. Ezra Mendelsohn, *On Modern Jewish Politics*, 16–17.
80. 'O szkołę żydowską', *Nowy Dziennik*, 24 July 1919, 1.

81. The relevant articles in *Nowy Dziennik* concerning these events: 'Szczegóły tajemniczego wybuchu przy ul. Studenckiej', 23 April 1923, 5; 'W sprawie zamachu na dom rektora dra Wł. Natansona', 27 April 1923, 4; 'Drugi wybuch bomby w Krakowie, Eksplozya w hotelu Kellera – Ci sami sprawcy, co przy ul. Studenckiej', 8 May 1923, 4.

82. See 'Szukamy sumienia … ', *Nowy Dziennik*, 19 May 1923; 'Bomba w redakcyi Nowego Dziennika', *Chwila*, 17 May 1923, 1; 'Terror w Krakowie', *Chwila*, 18 May 1923, 1; 'Krokever yidn lebn in shrek', *Togblat* (Lwów), 19 May 1923, 5; 'Dokoła zamachu dynamitowego na Dziennik Nowy', *Nasz Przegląd*, 17 May 1923, 1; 'Bomba krakowska', *Nasz Przegląd*, 17 May 1923, 2; 'Wybuch trzeciej bomby w Krakowie', *Ilustrowany Kurier Codzienny*, 18 May 1923, 1; 'Śledztwo w sprawie wybuchu bomby w redakcji Nowego Dziennika', *Ilustrowany Kuryer Codzienny*, 18 May 1923, 5.

83. 'Terror w Krakowie', *Chwila*, 18 May 1923, 1.

84. 'Prawo bomb', Przemówienie posła Thona na posiedzeniu sejmowem w dn. 23 b. m. *Nasz Przegląd*, 25 May 1923, 2.

85. 'Szukamy sumienia … ', *Nowy Dziennik*, 19 May 1923, 2.

86. Ibid.

87. H.H., 'Hańba,' *Chwila*, 19 May 1923, 1.

88. 'Wobec zamachów warszawskich', *Nowy Dziennik*, 27 May 1923.

89. 'Sprawa Abłamowicza', *Naprzód*, 12 April 1924, 1.

3

The Yiddishist Reaction to Assimilation:
Religious and Cultural Responses

Do you not know that your grandparents blessed their dearest and most beloved children and grandchildren before the Kol Nidre of Yom Kippur only in Yiddish?!
Letter to the editor of *Di post*, signed 'A Polish Jew',
17 September 1937, 7

Like *Nowy Dziennik*, the Yiddish newspapers in Cracow were founded with individual missions, as responses to what their publishers saw as the tragic circumstances, indeed as the crisis, of modern Polish Jewry. The most important Yiddish periodicals reflected a concern with the self-definition of the Jewish community, the editors declaring these publications advocates for one or another kind of specific Jewish communal identity. For *Dos yidishe vort* [*The Jewish Word*] and *Di yidishe shtime* [*The Jewish Voice*], the concern was to guard Jewish tradition at a time of immense change. For *Der reflector* [*The Reflector*, or *Mirror*] and *Di post* [*The Post*], the issue was the development of a modern Yiddish culture in a city the Jewish population of which was becoming increasingly polonized, at least in terms of language.[1] The emphasis on guarding the traditions of the community, whether religious or linguistic, is not surprising given the real changes Polish and Jewish society experienced after the First World War. While Polish-language Jewish writers advocated Jewish participation in the Polish state, Yiddish-language Jewish writers were likely to care more about traditional Jewish religious Orthodoxy or the Yiddish theatre. *Di yidishe shtime* appealed to those Jews who strongly identified with Jewish religious tradition and *Der reflektor* and *Di post* served as the standard bearers of Yiddish secular culture in Cracow. *Dos yidishe vort* combined religious Judaism with secular Zionism.

The Yiddish press allows us a glimpse into a cultural community that was divided in its approach to language, religion and cultural tradition.

Each of the Yiddish newspapers made claims to being the 'only' Yiddish newspaper or the 'first' Yiddish newspaper to be published in the city of Cracow or region of Western Galicia in twenty years. This was perhaps so because each Yiddish title differed markedly from the others. Still, the strength of the denials indicates that it was also because of the editors' ideological need to be the first to address the important issues of Jewish life. In fact, the Yiddish word had not been silent in Cracow in the previous two decades, despite the claims of Moyshe Blekher when he first published *Der reflektor* in 1935.[2] Samuel Probst's *Dos yidishe vort* had been in publication since 1925. While Blekher's cultural concerns were very far removed from Probst's more pedestrian interests in Jews' religious faith and economic survival, *Dos yidishe vort* was a successful, regularly published newspaper, the most important Yiddish title in Cracow in the 1920s. It may be possible that it was beyond Blekher's purview as a Yiddish-speaking intellectual, but it is rather unlikely. That Blekher did not recognize *Dos yidishe vort* as a competitor, let alone a worthy one, illustrates his disdain for other Yiddish cultural efforts, a central theme in both *Der reflektor* and its successor, *Di post*. Blekher's dismissal of the Orthodox Yiddish press also reflects the distance between traditionally religious Yiddish speakers and Yiddish-speaking Jewish intellectuals.

The Yiddish-speaking community encompassed more than those Jews who were traditionally religious and those oriented towards high Yiddish culture. Zionist groups in Cracow also published in Yiddish. The most notable of these efforts was *Arbayter vort* [*Workers' Word*], published from 1921 to 1922.[3] *Arbayter vort*, the newspaper of the Independent Social Democratic Workers' Party Poale Zion in Poland, appeared weekly for nearly a year. Strikingly, the paper was not simply a political tool. Its editor, Naftali Birnhack, developed a newspaper that served Zionist ideals, informed readers of important local issues, and educated its readers about Yiddish culture, including the emerging Yiddish theatre scene. *Arbayter vort* is an important indicator of the socialist Zionist presence in

Cracow. Unlike other Zionist publications in Yiddish, such as *Der Ruf* [*The Call*] and *Di naye tsayt* [*The New Times, Arbayter vort* was not simply a Yiddish mouthpiece for the writers of *Nowy Dziennik*. It was a genuine effort to be a strong, local newspaper with a specific political viewpoint. Like *Nowy Dziennik, Der Ruf* and *Di naye tsayt* were efforts to reach out to a large part of the community that may not have defined themselves as either exclusively religious or exclusively secular. *Der Ruf*, published briefly in 1934, was focused squarely on Zionism and Palestine. *Di naye tsayt*, which appeared briefly in 1928, reads like a Yiddish version of *Nowy Dziennik* and includes articles by some of the same writers. The articles in *Di naye tsayt* focused on the conflict between the Zionists and Agudes yisroel (the modern political party of the Orthodox) and praised Ozjasz Thon, one of the most important contributors to *Nowy Dziennik*. Yiddish readers, however, do not appear to have been much interested in *Di naye tsayt*. It ceased publication after only a short time.

While none of the other Yiddish titles was as successful as *Nowy Dziennik*, some managed to stay in publication for one or more years, in the case of *Di yidishe shtime, Dos likht* [*The Light*] and *Di post*, or for several years, in the case of *Dos yidishe vort*. Judging from length of publication and circulation, the most important Yiddish newspapers, then, were either expressions of a traditional religious identity forced to confront modernity or a Yiddish cultural politics that sought to create a high Yiddish culture. While polonized intellectuals founded *Nowy Dziennik* to express their desire to integrate with Poles yet remain apart as well, others reasserted their connection to the Jewish religion or the Yiddish language. *Dos yidishe vort* was the only Yiddish newspaper that published regularly in Cracow in the late 1920s and early 1930s. The other significant Yiddish title of the inter-war period, *Di post*, appeared only from 1937 to 1939, but, as mentioned, it was different in orientation from *Dos yidishe vort*. Examining the various Yiddish titles of the Jewish press reveals how groups within the Jewish population other than the Zionists expressed an affiliation with the Jewish community. This study of the press shows the wide variety of Jewish subcultures within the Yiddish-speaking community and within Cracow.

THE PERSISTENCE OF RELIGIOUS TRADITION

Dos yidishe vort served as the city's primary Yiddish voice until the publication in the 1930s of *Dos likht, Der reflektor* and *Di post*. Czesław Brzoza has noted that, as listed in government registers, *Dos yidishe vort* appeared until 1939, but only issues until 1935 are extant; thus, it is difficult to determine the regularity with which the newspaper appeared from 1935 to 1939.[4] According to police registers, its circulation was significantly lower than that of *Nowy Dziennik*, 500 to 700 copies as opposed to several thousand.[5] Thus, *Nowy Dziennik* was the leading newspaper among Jewish readers and one cannot reasonably make any direct comparisons between *Nowy Dziennik* and other Jewish newspapers in terms of influence. Still, *Dos yidishe vort* endured for many years and, in spite of its low circulation, was Cracow's longest-lasting Yiddish newspaper. It is a significant indicator of the presence of a more religious, traditional Jewry in Cracow.

Though it could not compete in circulation with *Nowy Dziennik, Dos yidishe vort* found its place in the city's Jewish press as a local newspaper. In political orientation, *Dos yidishe vort* was the newspaper of the religious Zionists, or Mizrakhi. In general, though, it was much more insular than *Nowy Dziennik*, echoing the concerns of the Cracow community by focusing on Jewish issues of local importance (such as complaints from members of the community about the desecration of the Sabbath) more often than on issues of international significance. Samuel Probst, the editor of *Dos yidishe vort*, was more likely to sponsor a survey asking readers to identify the five most popular Jewish figures in Cracow than to ponder the intricacies of international Zionist politics or the meaning of Yiddish poetry. In addition, Probst reported regular meetings of the *kehillah* in great detail. The section of news briefs did much more than announce times and places of current lectures, theatre performances, or films. Short notices described the activities of different Jewish organizations and reported, sometimes amusingly, sometimes angrily, on ongoing projects of the Jewish community, whether the building of the Jewish hospital or conflicts over the appointment of rabbis in nearby towns.

Samuel Probst first published *Dos yidishe vort* in 1925, well after the end of the First World War. Unlike *Nowy Dziennik*, it was not founded as an immediate response to the war and the subsequent peace, but rather as an answer to a perceived, and real, need of the Jewish community in Cracow and Western Galicia for a Yiddish newspaper. Probst founded *Dos yidishe vort*, the only Yiddish weekly in Western Galicia, 'to guard Jewish tradition and the interests of Jewish merchants and craftsmen'.[6]

According to Probst, the Jews experienced a period of demoralization during and after the war and were just beginning once again to address the needs of their community. Previously, due to the conditions of war as well as the ongoing modernization of the Jewish community, the synagogues were empty, the heders, the traditional Jewish schools, had been closed, and children were being raised almost as *goyim* (non-Jews), according to the paper.

At the last moment (apparently some time before the first issue of the paper in March 1925), however, Jews began to return to the Jewish community, a movement of which *Dos yidishe vort* saw itself as a part. Probst wrote in his first editorial:

> It seems that today we have a full-blown repentance movement. The Jewish people have returned at the last moment to the old *yidishkayt*, finding it as the past generation tended it for us. The movement is not limited only to the Orthodox Jews or the older generation. No, it encompasses all groups, young and old, folk and intelligentsia, East and West, all feeling that they are too isolated, distanced from the source, from the ... way of earlier generations. They have attracted everyone's attention with their cries to halt this distancing from our fathers, in order not to reach the extreme point from which there is no way back.[7]

Probst does not explicitly define *who* is taking the leading role in this repentance movement, but the implication is that a new generation of Jewish leaders emerged in post-war Poland that rejuvenated the Jewish community. His editorial optimistically pointed out that, six years after the war, the synagogues were no longer empty, more and more students began studying in yeshivas, and students of all kinds, young and old, could learn Hebrew in different courses offered in all the larger cities. At the same time, it is likely that Probst overestimated the different groups he identified. Just as *Nowy Dziennik* claimed to speak for all Jews, so Probst assumed an emerging united front of the Jewish community. Probst's actions as a publisher are very clearly a private effort to address what he sees as a problem within his own community. His newspaper exemplifies the private initiative upon which Jews could act in inter-war Poland.

The politics expressed in *Dos yidishe vort* may account for its relative success. While running a newspaper of and for the Orthodox community, Probst was a Zionist, and his views indicate a sympathy with secular Jewish political movements. Probst often supported the work of Jewish organizations that were more secular and Zionist in nature than his own newspaper, such as the Hebrew gymnasium, a privately sponsored bilingual (Polish-Hebrew) school in Cracow. *Dos yidishe vort* was fairly conservative in its orientation, expressing traditional goals that had little to do with political concerns or the ongoing struggle between Zionism and Bundism. Probst did not associate the paper with Yiddishist ideology, such as the championing of Yiddish as *the* national language of the Jews or an advocacy of the working class. His efforts to straddle the border between Orthodoxy and Zionism, the challenge of the Mizrakhi party, probably struck a popular chord within a still traditional community undergoing rapid change. The content of the paper demonstrates that the editors were more concerned with questions of maintaining Jewish tradition in Cracow than with politics.

Evidence of this traditionalist position can be found throughout the paper. For example, Probst published an open letter in Hebrew regarding the Talmud Torah in Cracow, the religious school sponsored by the official Jewish community. In an editorial on the Talmud Torah school, Probst argued that the old traditions were vital for modern Jewish life and, therefore, the Talmud Torah should receive more support. At the same time, however, he recognized the importance of the *landes-shprakhe* (the language of the land, or Polish) and encouraged Jewish children to learn Polish in order to be able to function within the larger community.[8] Probst's willingness to admit that Jewish children needed to learn Polish was an important concession to the new political realities of inter-war Poland. Probst did not imagine that learning Polish precluded some form of Jewish identity. Many in Cracow's Jewish community had assimilated linguistically in the late nineteenth century; Probst was not, and did not want to be, a part of this group. He simply wanted to strengthen and maintain Jewish identity. Use of a non-Jewish language would not keep him from his goal.

As part of that goal, Probst continually advocated private Jewish education, expressing a fear of sending Jewish children to public schools and openly supporting the Zionist Hebrew gymnasium.[9] A Yiddish newspaper supporting a Hebrew gymnasium would have been unlikely in the context of the Jewish history of Warsaw or Łódź, where the language battle was much more fierce. Probst's support of the Hebrew gymnasium was an expression of the Mizrakhi position between the anti-Zionist Orthodox and anti-Orthodox Zionists. Part of the Yiddish-speaking community in Cracow (in fact, the only *active* Yiddish-speaking part of the community, at least until the late 1930s) not only supported the Hebrew gymnasium but also paid it the compliment of criticism.

In an effort to encourage improvement so that the school would better meet the needs of the Jewish community, Probst, in line with the religious orientation of *Dos yidishe vort*, accused the school of not being traditional enough.[10] He wrote that the Hebrew gymnasium 'took the Torah out of the phrase "People of the Torah"'.[11] He repeatedly complained about the high tuition fees and the complicated system of identification cards that singled out students who were not able to pay on time.[12] Fearing that the gymnasium would simply be a school where, for the price of fifty zlotys, a Jewish child could pass the *matura* (the entrance exam necessary for university study) without learning Hebrew, Probst challenged the school to live up to its ideals of helping Jewish children.[13] He argued sarcastically that the gymnasium should not act simply as a guesthouse for its students.[14] Private Jewish education was available only to those who could afford it; most Jewish children attended the public schools. Probst's argument highlights the class distinctions within the Jewish community and the editor's concern with developing Jewish institutions capable of instilling strong Jewish religious values. Probst wanted to ensure that all Jewish children, not just the children of wealthier Jews, would have the opportunity to become educated Jews.

Probst recognized the dilemma that faced Jewish educators. Now that Jewish society had greater and greater contact with the rest of European civilization, Jewish educators had to rethink how to raise the children, of both rich and poor, as Jews. Probst complained about the lack of Jewish tradition in the Hebrew gymnasium, without condemning the gymnasium's work. Probst upheld Jewish tradition without dividing the Jewish community even further.[15] If Probst was concerned about poor Jewish children not being able to receive a Jewish education in the Hebrew gymnasium, he none the less recognized that the youth attending the gymnasium would probably be future leaders of the Jewish community. In short, the editor of *Dos yidishe vort* legitimately cared more about the general welfare of the community than about any specific political or cultural debate. Like Wilhelm Berkelhammer of *Nowy Dziennik*, Probst placed more emphasis on attaining real progress for the Jewish community than on ideology.

Probst was not alone in his journalistic efforts to reach the area's more traditional religious Jewry. From 1927 to 1928, Benjamin Geizhals edited *Di yidishe shtime* and in 1931, Wolf Leib Urbach published *Dos likht*.[16] Both titles were clearly of a more religious nature than *Dos yidishe vort*. The strength of both newspapers was their strong support of traditional religious Jewry in Cracow and Western Galicia, unqualified by any concession to the increasing influence of the city's Zionists, as exemplified in the success of *Nowy Dziennik* and the Hebrew gymnasium and, to some extent, even by *Dos yidishe vort*.

While its contents reveal the international connections of the Jewish community, *Di yidishe shtime* was basically a local paper. The main concern of its editor was the elections to the *kehillah* in Cracow and the need for more representatives of religious Jews on the *kehillah* council. While the progressive Jews controlled the community during the inter-war period, they were constantly subject to the increased Zionist activity in the city and to the impatience of the Orthodox to have their own interests represented. That interest is made clear in the many articles *Di yidishe shtime* addressed to the community of religious Jews, calling them to unite against the acculturated Jewish leaders of the community and against the vocal Jewish nationalists.[17] The term 'religious Jews' comes from the Jewish community itself;

this was how the writers of *Di yidishe shtime* described themselves in opposition to the other Jewish groups in the city. This should not be taken to mean that the 'progressives' or 'Zionists' were not religiously Jewish in any way, simply that these groups had distinguished themselves from their co-religionists, whether by their acceptance of more liberal religious traditions, their participation in Polish society, or their views towards Jewish nationalism. It is likely that the progressive leaders of the *kehillah*, university graduates and professionals, had distinguished themselves from the readers of the Orthodox Yiddish newspapers by income level as well.

The defensive posture displayed in *Di yidishe shtime* is strong evidence of the process of secularization that was changing the very nature of Jewish life in Cracow and of the acculturation of Cracow's Jews to Polish culture. The content of *Di yidishe shtime* was primarily concerned with the internal divisions of the Jewish community and the maintenance of Jewish religious values, but Polish society was not infrequently a topic. Writing on the tenth anniversary of Polish independence, a journalist spoke of a sympathy for Poles, 'as Jews and fellow citizens'. Nevertheless, the journalist regretfully concluded that 'while it was unpleasant to talk about injustices at such a celebratory time, we are not equal in all respects, though for a moment, as citizens, we feel closer to each other'.[18] A Jewish identity as Polish citizens was real, however compromised by the disabilities placed on Jewish citizens by the Polish government. In *Di yidishe shtime*, Geizhals called for Poles to rectify the difficult conditions under which Jews lived, just as he called upon Jews to observe the traditions of their faith.

Cracow Jews themselves recognized the need to defend traditional religious values, as is evident in the complaints *Di yidishe shtime* made against those Jews they observed violating the Sabbath. Readers reported to the newspaper when they observed a Jewish store near Kazimierz open on the Sabbath. One reader expressed concern after observing the school board of the Hebrew gymnasium working on the Sabbath just as they did throughout the week.[19] Whatever the truth of these claims, such violations were taken seriously by the readers and editors of Cracow's Orthodox Yiddish newspapers. The papers themselves were weapons in the fight against such violations.

They brought the infractions to light and called the larger Jewish community to account for such behaviour.

Like *Di yidishe shtime*, *Dos likht*, published for the first and last time in 1931, was clearly of a more religious character than *Dos yidishe vort*. Like Agudes yisroel, *Dos likht* represents the entrance of traditional Jewry into a modern society that relied increasingly on an active press and political participation to attain its goals. Recognizing the success of secular Jewish political movements, traditional Orthodox Jews responded by establishing a newspaper and entering the dialogue about Jewish identity that had arisen as a result of tremendous change from within the Jewish community and from without. That Orthodox Jews made up the majority of the Jewish population in Poland is not in dispute. Nevertheless, they were unable to affect the larger Jewish community to the same extent as the Zionists in Cracow, Warsaw, London or Berlin.

More than Probst, Wolf Leib Urbach, the editor of *Dos likht*, emphasized his desire for his paper to become the voice of the Orthodox Jews in Western Galicia. Deploring the fact that other minority Jewish groups that did not represent the majority of Polish Jewry published their own newspapers, the editors in the first issue pronounced their goal 'to defend Jewish honour'. Sounding similar to Probst in *Dos yidishe vort*, an editor (presumably Urbach) wrote, 'Jewish holy places have been desecrated, violations of the Sabbath are spreading like an epidemic and threaten to infest the heart of Jewish Cracow – Kazimierz – and there is no Jewish newspaper to awaken us ... '[20] In publishing *Dos likht*, Urbach recognized the need of the Galician Orthodox to participate in a rapidly changing, modern society. The publication of the paper, like the election campaigning of Agudes yisroel, was a recognition that Jewish identity could no longer rely solely on the synagogue and *heder* for the transmission of Jewish culture. Like the editors of *Nowy Dziennik* and *Dos yidishe vort*, Urbach saw himself as a leader in a fight to define the Jewish community, to make the Jewish community what he felt it should be and not what it was becoming. The fight was a fight for Jewish honour, defined by each representative of the Jewish community in different ways, whether in terms of the general Zionism of *Nowy Dziennik*, the religious Zionism of *Dos yidishe vort*, or the orthodoxy of *Dos likht*.

Urbach admitted that the Orthodox themselves were divided over many issues and that these divisions hindered any attempt at Jewish unity; he recognized that internal splits 'weakened the strength of the Jewish community' while giving support to the community's opponents. To counter this division, Urbach established *Dos likht* in an effort to create an independent newspaper, as he stated in the very first issue, for all religious groups, 'to create a united, strong, effective force ... We hope that all Jews, without exception, all who have an interest in the strengthening of religious Judaism, who do not want their youth to go to foreign groups will help us in our important work ... ' Further, we hope that 'all Jewish Jews without distinction will support us in our fight for *yidishkayt*'. By calling on all 'Jewish Jews' to support the cause, the editor perhaps intentionally evoked the possibility of 'non-Jewish', presumably non-observant, Jews who would brobably not support the cause of *Dos likht*. While this group is not defined at all in the editorial, the terminology employed here implies that within the Jewish community, there was a range of religious observance that threatened the unity of the Jewish community. While the efforts of *Dos likht* to unite some of the Jewish community are well intentioned, one wonders how successful Urbach thought he was going to be. The secularization of the Jewish community had already begun well before the war, particularly in Cracow, and many religious Jews may have been reluctant to accept secular Jews as legitimate members of the community. Indeed, one wonders if Urbach even recognized the extent of the divisions within the Cracow Jewish community, ranging from linguistically assimilated Jews with their educations entirely in Polish to the Yiddish-speaking Orthodox he himself represented.

For Urbach, the divisions within the Jewish community physically threatened the Jews as much as another manifestation of change during the inter-war period, that of crime. While many of the incidents described in *Dos likht* did not take place in Cracow itself, their publication attests that they resonated within the Cracow Jewish community. According to *Dos likht*, an increased level of crime, with Jews as both perpetrators and victims, was one of the results of the secularization of the Jewish community, one of the reasons Urbach had grown so frustrated with the trends affecting Polish Jewish society. One writer in *Dos likht*, pondering crime within the community, asked the question, 'When one considers our current spiritual situation in light of the simple daily chronicle of our lives, one must wonder and ask how it has happened that we have come so far, but in such a short time have fallen so hard?'[21] The question itself is an admission that the modernization of the Jewish community had costs as well as benefits.

For example, a notice about a seventeen-year-old boy who had broken a window in a school in a town outside of Cracow became the focus of a longer article in which the unnamed author condemned the decline in the morality of the community and cited other chilling examples that help us to understand more precisely what provoked the Orthodox reaction. One tragic incident occurred in a Galician shtetl, where a Jewish student killed himself after being exposed to the anti-Semitism of a Polish teacher. In addition, the unnamed author was especially concerned with the crimes of Jews who victimized other Jews. In Zduńska Wola, a Jewish hooligan attacked an Orthodox member of the *kahal* council, a candidate in upcoming *kehilla* elections, knocking him unconscious with an iron. In Warsaw, within the space of one week, two separate murders had been committed where both the murderers and victims were Jews. A Jewish murder victim had also been pulled out of the water in Będrdzin (Bendin); four other Jews stood accused of the crime.

This increase in violence within the Jewish community, as viewed by *Dos likht*, was particularly troubling as evidence of violations of the higher morals of the Jewish community. The author of the article on Jewish crime wrote, 'for us, the belief in our chosenness was in no way chauvinistic, we never demanded any kind of payment for our chosenness – a higher position among the peoples, more rights, etc. But we demonstrated our chosenness with our higher morality.' In the view of *Dos likht*, this was no longer the case. The incidents cited in this article point to an increasingly troubled community.

How should the Jewish community address this increase in crime? *Dos likht* itself suggests that the 'fundamentalist' position of the Orthodox religious Jews was far from disappearing. The unnamed author defended traditional Jewish education, writing that 'the boys raised in the "dark" heders have always been strong in spirit. In the most difficult circumstances they have demonstrated that they are able to maintain the equilibrium to conquer the suffering.' In contrast to the characterization of the heders as withdrawn and even as vestiges of a medieval institution, *Dos likht* supported traditional Jewish education. The paper defended the heder as a way to stem the decline in traditional values as well as the recent increase in violence. The appearance of *Dos likht* points to the existence of a segment of the community ill at ease in the increasingly modern, and secular, Jewish community. The author concluded with a world-weary lament about the violence, '*Gevalt!* How can it get worse? It cannot be believed that this is only one page of the week's chronicle of Jewish events.'

While *Dos yidishe vort* was a newspaper of the Orthodox as well, it represented a secular political culture not present in *Dos likht*. The attitudes expressed towards Jewish education suggest the philosophical differences between these two papers. Probst was willing to support the Zionist Hebrew gymnasium, but Urbach was more firmly a supporter of the heders. *Dos likht, Di yidishe shtime* and *Dos yidishe vort* represented groups within Cracow Jewry very different from the polonized intellectuals reading *Nowy Dziennik* and the secularized Yiddish-speaking intellectuals of *Di post*. Yet even the more religious groups of Cracow Jewry were becoming increasingly modern, whether from choice or necessity.

Though Probst's work is itself evidence of the Jewish community's transformation to a self-consciously diverse and increasingly active and open society, Probst did not necessarily hail this change as positive. The three Yiddish titles with Orthodox Jews as their target audience arose from the need to defend Jewish religious life. In doing so, they helped to build a community that was in the process of significant change. For Probst, the change had come during the First World War, as a result of the influences of German Jews. Probst lamented that, though Orthodox Jews had taken seats in Poland's *Sejm*, no real advances protecting religious life had been made. Those who operated with the Shulhan Arukh at the foundation of their politics – the simple 'Ashkenazic Jew' – had no role in Jewish life.

At the core of the problem, for Probst, as well as others, was the lack of unity in any aspect of Jewish life. Probst identified the splits among various Orthodox groups, just as his comments often highlighted the at times conflicting goals of Cracow's Zionist factions. For Probst, the 'plague of division' within the Jewish community had real consequences, namely the removal of piety from Jewish life.[22] When the Zionists made Zionism a profession, they forgot to take off for the Sabbath and holiday; similarly, the professional socialist has become a man of the salon. Professional activists, whether Zionist or socialist, worsened the divisions within the Jewish community by creating even more opposition.

Yiddish newspaper editors may not necessarily qualify as professional activists, but they did respond to the visible proliferation of Jewish groups working to improve all aspects of Jewish life. Realizing that other Jewish groups were becoming leaders by establishing their own newspapers, political groups, schools, theatre societies and other groups, Orthodox Jews followed suit. Not only did they found their own institutions, Orthodox Jews, like Probst, even supported secular Jewish initiatives and the teaching of Polish among Jews. Such changes within the more Orthodox population confirm the transformation *Nowy Dziennik* represents – the Jewish community of inter-war Cracow was acculturating, taking a step towards assimilation without relinquishing a unique identity, however that identity might be expressed. Recognizing this, Jewish community leaders fought vigorously to maintain both traditional and secular notions of a separate Jewish community. While Probst, Geizhals and Urbach protected Jewish religion and tradition, others defended the most widely spoken Jewish language of the time, Yiddish.

YIDDISH IN CRACOW: *DER REFLEKTOR* AND *DI POST*

Moyshe Blekher, the editor of *Der reflektor* and, later, *Di post*, took a strong stand against the linguistic assimilation exhibited by the journalists of *Nowy Dziennik*. As Blekher saw it, the editors of *Nowy Dziennik* could not argue vehemently against polonization and write in Polish at the same time. Writing in Yiddish, Blekher was freer to criticize what he saw as the assimilationist trend within the city. The publication of *Der reflektor* in 1935 proves that while the Jewish community of Cracow was unique in being more acculturated than other Polish Jewish communities, there were enough Yiddish-speaking intellectuals to merit the publication of a Yiddish cultural periodical. It was also a turn towards cultivating Yiddish-speaking intellectuals and an attempt to persuade them not to use Polish.

Like other Jewish newspaper editors, Blekher saw *Der reflektor* as his effort to transform Jewish society, to reshape Jewish life, especially cultural life, according to his own conception of what that cultural life should be. Blekher saw *Der reflektor* as a bastion of Yiddish culture in an assimilated city, much as Urbach viewed *Dos likht* as a stronghold of Orthodoxy. Although it appeared that he wished to unite the community under the banner of Yiddish culture, Blekher had little tolerance for those who did not share his own views. He did not conceive of *Der reflektor* as an institution that could work with other Jewish organizations. Blekher's goal in *Der reflektor* was to develop an artistic centre (*kinstler-tsenter*) around which Yiddish writers, specifically writers supporting a progressive, socialist politics, would gather. Blekher did not define progressive, though articles calling for the proletarianization of Yiddish literature indicate that progressive meant generally leftist. Blekher wanted to attract Yiddish writers who wished to use their work to create a new type of Jew, a new type of man. He proposed nothing less than the creation of an identity rooted in a secular, intellectual and cultural viewpoint. Blekher saw literature and art as a way to respond to the difficult problems of contemporary Jewish life. He wished to 'use the pages of our tribune – with an eye turned towards the lives of the Jewish people, to the Jewish worker with his sufferings and joys, struggles and hopes – to reflect in word and picture the difficult, troublesome path of the Jew and provide an optimistic, hopeful view in better times'.[23] Blekher's editorial policy led him to publish articles expressing the opinions of proletarian writers, but he was more cultural than political. His journalistic activity may be seen as a response to the continuing, and increasing, anti-Semitism in Poland. His conception of a separate linguistic identity for the Jews would have assured a high level of ethnic cohesiveness, necessary to resist the political and cultural dominance of the majority and even violent attacks by individual Poles, such as those occurring at Polish universities in the late 1930s.

The publication of *Der reflektor* was Blekher's effort to introduce Yiddish culture to Cracow, just as *Dos yidishe vort* was Probst's effort to revitalize religious tradition within the city and *Nowy Dziennik* was the Zionists' effort to nationalize the Jewish community. Blekher's goals were laudable, but the relative weakness of any real efforts to organize Yiddish cultural life in Cracow before *Der reflektor* indicate that his task cannot have been an easy one. In addition, Blekher ignored issues important to the readers of the other, religiously oriented Yiddish newspapers, *Dos yidishe vort*, *Di yidishe shtime* and *Dos likht* (such as Zionist politics or an increase in crime), just as he ignored the very presence of another Yiddish newspaper in the city. Further, Blekher's insistence on his Yiddishist views was not combined with an awareness of local issues as in *Dos yidishe vort* or in *Nowy Dziennik*.

Commenting on the lack of Yiddish cultural activity in Cracow, Blekher wrote, 'One shouldn't wonder [about the lack of Yiddish culture] when Cracow, for example, doesn't have and doesn't want a Yiddish newspaper, or any kind of position within the Yiddish cultural community.'[24] Fighting for the cultural position of Yiddish creativity in Cracow was the goal of *Der reflektor*, an example of 'the rapid development of Yiddish towards a high-status language' in Eastern Europe.[25] Blekher feared a day when Yiddish culture would no longer be an integral part of Jewish life. Even allowing for exaggeration, Blekher's fears should at least be taken seriously as a warning against what he felt were the dangers of linguistic assimilation. While Berkelhammer and the other founders of *Nowy Dziennik* were comfortable expressing Jewish content in non-Jewish form as early as 1918, Blekher pointedly used a Jewish language to mark his involvement in the Jewish community.

As editor, Blekher focused on general Yiddish cultural issues. The first issue of *Der reflektor* included a reprint of an article previously published in Yiddish newspapers in Lwów and Warsaw, 'We and the Yiddish Language', by Moyshe Nadir. Blekher reprinted the article because Nadir took a 'healthy, proletarian approach' to Yiddish that was similar to his own and because it was especially 'timely and instructive for Cracow which is the centre of polonization and the assimilationist plague'.²⁶ Nadir's attitude towards the use of Yiddish was very practical, arguing against excessively grammatical approaches to the standardization of the language and advocating that writers write in the speech of the workers who speak the language. Nadir wrote, 'We renounce the "dizn-dozn" tendency [referring to ideas of Yiddish grammatical purity] to defer to the dominant language, as has been done by the assimilators of the different bourgeois newspapers. We allow Yiddish its freedoms, which arise out of an intimacy with others, out of living under one roof.' Significantly, Nadir admits that in accepting the use of foreign words in Yiddish, he is accepting the influence of non-Jewish cultures on the Jews. He even compares this acceptance to the publication of Jewish newspapers (by 'assimilators', *asimilatorn* in the original) in non-Jewish languages. Blekher's approach to Yiddish culture emphasized an insistence on the use of Yiddish among the Jewish community, as exemplified in Nadir's article. Like Nadir, however, Blekher did not exclude Polish influences. Blekher was open to other cultures as well, as the Yiddish translations of the poetry of the Romanian poet Mihai Eminescu, in *Der reflektor*, attest.

Der reflektor ceased publication the same year it began. More than a year passed after its demise before Blekher tried again to establish a successful Yiddish weekly newspaper in Cracow. Like *Der reflektor*, *Di post*, which was first published in 1937, included more serious literary articles than *Dos yidishe vort* and is of much greater cultural significance. In *Di post*, Blekher published the work of Yiddish writers such as Mordecai Gebirtig, I. M. Weissenberg, Ber Horowitz and Joseph Hillel Levy and addressed questions of Yiddish literary politics in much more depth than did *Dos yidishe vort*. Like the editors of other Jewish newspapers, Blekher wanted *Di post* to become the representative voice of the Jews of his city. Blekher, however, did not show an interest in the local activities of the many and varied Jewish groups within his own city. At the expense of Jewish organizations like the Hebrew gymnasium, Blekher focused almost exclusively on issues of secular Yiddish cultural life. In the first issue of *Di post*, Blekher, noting that other, smaller cities and towns with smaller populations had Yiddish newspapers, asked forthrightly, 'Is this situation not shameful for such a large

Jewish community as Cracow?'[27] His goals for *Di post* were very clear, and similar to those for the failed *Der reflektor*. In the first issue, he wrote that *Di post* would 'stand watch for the national honour of the Jews of Cracow and fight courageously against the plague of assimilation in all of its forms'. The vituperative nature of Blekher's rhetoric did not diminish over time. In an article highlighting the beginning of *Di post*'s second year of existence, Blekher reiterated the goal to rid Cracow of the 'stench of the assimilated' and to replace the stench with the 'beautiful traditions of the Jerusalem of Galicia, old Cracow'.[28] Presumably, Blekher meant simply the tendency to use Yiddish; he is otherwise the most indifferent of the Yiddish newspaper editors towards religious ideas.

Interestingly, Blekher recognized the need for a synthesis between opposing ideals, between the Yiddishists and the Hebraists, between partisans of Palestine and the Diaspora, and, in a specifically political sense, between humanity and socialist principles. His journalistic enterprises did foster a synthesis between these groups and ideals, but Blekher's often harsh rhetoric and unwillingness to support the efforts of others with different ideas mitigated his chances for success.

Blekher's voice in Cracow is an important one. It differs from that of other Yiddish cultural activists, most notably that of Mojżesz Kanfer. Kanfer's work to establish a residential Yiddish theatre troupe in the city was the only other comparable effort to establish some form of institutional Yiddish culture in Cracow. Blekher clearly stated that *Di post* would protect the national honour of the Jewish community, while Kanfer attempted to build a Yiddish theatre that would rival the city's established Polish theatre. Blekher assured the continuation of high Yiddish culture during a period of rapid linguistic assimilation towards the majority language in which Kanfer wrote. While *Nowy Dziennik* was already a much more established and successful enterprise when Blekher first published *Der reflektor*, *Di post* did manage to achieve some success. Only the beginning of the Second World War cut short its two years of publication.

That Blekher and Kanfer did not co-operate with each other in building a vibrant Yiddish cultural community in the city is not surprising given Blekher's attitude towards the 'so-called intelligentsia' of the city. Blekher was often outspoken in his condemnation of the city's Jewish intelligentsia, even insulting. His comments allow us to clarify the different groups within Cracow Jewry. Blekher argued that the problem of the titled intellectuals of the city, such as doctors, engineers, lawyers and those with academic degrees, was that they did not feel at home either among Jews or among *goyim*. These intellectuals paid for seats in the Tempel, the city's progressive synagogue, once a year on Yom Kippur, to hear the *kazania* (Blekher pejoratively used the Polish word for sermon in his Yiddish article).[29] Blekher wrote, 'Our intellectual with his academic titles sees Yiddish theatre, the Yiddish book, all of Yiddish culture, through the prism of his ... Tempel seat.' The city's Jewish intellectuals attended Jewish artistic events, such as the theatre, but, according to Blekher, only in the last month of the performance to show their token support. Blekher compared this behaviour to a retired person picking up his pension. He described the *tsdoke* (charity) cans as one of the symbols of the intelligentsia, 'in which the intelligentsia throw in *kapore-groshn* [literally, money for the scapegoat] for their national sins – and think that this frees them from their national obligations regarding our culture and literature, theatre and art'. Referring to the support of the city's so-called Jewish 'intelligentsia' for various Jewish causes, Blekher wrote further, 'Their national pride, their national uniqueness, culture, literature, art, politics – is enclosed in tin cans and other symbols in which we futilely look for their soul.'[30] That these intellectuals attended non-Jewish gatherings and receptions shocked and offended Blekher. He ominously asked, 'Which decrees still need to be born in the excited minds of modern Hamans so that our titled intelligentsia will finally understand that they are going down a slippery path?'[31]

Blekher reserved his sharpest criticism for the activities of the Cracow Yiddish Theatre Society.[32] In an article signed under the pseudonym T. Atral, Blekher admitted that the Yiddish theatre was the only real expression of Yiddish culture in the city, but he lamented the low number of Yiddish cultural activists, writing 'one can weigh the number of *Yiddish* [his emphasis] activists in Cracow on a drugstore scale and count them on the primitive abacus of a child'.[33] Simply presenting Yiddish culture in Cracow did not suffice for Blekher. He reproached Kanfer and the Yiddish Theatre Society for at least two reasons: first, because many in the society were not involved with the theatre on any professional basis and, second, because the language in which the members of the Theatre Society conducted their meetings, discussions and lectures was Polish, not Yiddish. Similarly, when Yiddish actors came to the 'assimilated city' of Cracow to present a Yiddish play, he described them as *polonizatorn*, or polonizers, because these same actors advertised their performances in Polish and traded on their reputations as stars in the Polish theatre in order to attract an audience to their Yiddish performances.[34] Posters advertising the Yiddish theatre only or primarily in Polish offended Blekher because, in his opinion, they did not do enough to spread Yiddish culture. Blekher did not tolerate the compromises made by the Polish-speaking Jewish intellectuals to promote Yiddish. When the Cracow Yiddish Theatre Society announced its intentions to build a new theatre building, Blekher expressed his disbelief that the proposed building would ever be used for its intended purposes. He described the Yiddish Theatre Society, rather unkindly, as *shlimazldikn* (unlucky or unfortunate, from the Yiddish *shlimazl*).[35] A letter to the editor supported Blekher's position on the Yiddish theatre and reflected his negative assessment of Yiddish cultural life in the city. The writer, Moyshe Buksboym, remarked that the task of the Cracow Yiddish Theatre Society would be rendered twice as difficult because of Cracow's less than hospitable atmosphere for Yiddish culture. Further, Buksboym complained that the director of the Yiddish theatre would not lower ticket prices, which drove audiences and actors to the Polish theatre where, he continues, they have the added benefit of not having to 'deal with the poverty of their own cultural world'.[36]

As the letters column of *Di post* indicates, there was a need for a Yiddish periodical in Cracow to counteract the Polish-language Jewish press. A letter to the editor published in *Di post* reflects Blekher's views and provides much information about the position of Yiddish culture in the city.[37] The author signed the letter '*a poylisher yid*' [a Polish Jew] and described him- or herself as a '*yid fun a gants yor*', or an everyday kind of Jew. The writer (who may very well have been Blekher himself) simply could not believe that something like *Di post* could come out of Cracow. After seeing the first issue of *Di post*, the author wrote,

'I do not possess the necessary amount of faith in the Cracow Jews of the Kazimierz district regarding something that comes out in Yiddish.' After seeing the second issue, the writer was ready to change his harsh opinion of Cracow's Jewish community for the better. Further, the writer maintained that Jews possessed three Jerusalems outside of the sacred city, namely Vilna, the Jerusalem of Lithuania; Varshe (Yiddish for Warsaw), the Jerusalem of Poland; and Kroke (Yiddish for Cracow), the Jerusalem of Galicia. The author conceded that Lemberg (Yiddish for Lwów) perhaps deserves the title more than Cracow, while the first two had earned the honour in the fullest sense. His remarks about the three Jerusalems in Poland are particularly apt. That Lemberg, or Lwów, rivalled Cracow in the letter writer's mind for the title of the 'Jerusalem of Galicia' says much about the extent of the latter's polonization. In spite of the many Jewish cultural organizations established during the inter-war period, Cracow, long an important city in Jewish history, was to this writer becoming less important as a centre of Jewish culture.

Growing tired of waiting for some form of Yiddish culture to appear in the city, the *poylisher yid* had nearly given in to despair as Vilna and Varshe (Warsaw) took the lead in developing aYiddish-language cultural life. For this writer, it was not too late. The *poylisher yid* addressed the Jews of Cracow: 'Do you not know that your grandparents blessed their dearest and most beloved children and grandchildren before the Kol Nidre of Yom Kippur only in Yiddish?!' The letter writer represents a very different attitude towards Yiddish than that expressed in the pages of *Nowy Dziennik*. If one accepts the letter writer's comments as a fair representation of reality, the Jews of inter-war Cracow had changed radically from the days of their parents and grandparents. Such transformations, in the opinion of the letter writer, were negative and reason to lament the future fate of Cracow Jewry.[38] The memoir literature confirms the changes of the younger generations. The literary critic Henryk Vogler describes his grandfather's strange habit (at least to Vogler) of attending the synagogue, and Leopold Infeld went from the *heder* to the university and fully adopted Polish culture.[39] The memoirs of Halina Nelken and Natan Gross also attest to the community's linguistic assimilation.[40]

Like Blekher himself, the *poylisher yid* advocated the Yiddish cause much more militantly than the editors of *Nowy Dziennik*, who founded a Yiddish theatre society and published articles on Yiddish writers but did not express equal dismay at the decline of the *mame-loshn* (mother tongue or, in this case, Yiddish). With the exception of Mojżesz Kanfer, the leading Jewish writers of Cracow encouraged the development of Jewish identity in a non-Jewish language. The author of this letter states that he waited a long time for the publication of a Yiddish periodical in Cracow that was worthy of the name.

Others writing in the paper also took note of Cracow's linguistic assimilation and praised *Di post* as a much-needed venue for Yiddish. Buksboym, also an ethnographic collector for YIVO, remarked upon the *daytshmerish*, or German, nature of the Yiddish spoken in Cracow and throughout Galicia.[41] Buksboym's criticism of non-standard Yiddish is not unusual. Though one might dismiss his comments as disrespectful of the very individuals he was studying, his remark about a poster announcing an evening of song and poetry from Palestine sponsored by the youth Zionist group Akiba is telling. The poster was in Polish, but Buksboym could not be certain what language would be used that evening – Yiddish, the language of the masses; Hebrew, the language of Palestine; or the 'language of assimilated Cracow, Polish'.

The Yiddish writer Yitzhok Shargel praised Blekher's efforts to combat the linguistic assimilation in Cracow, but he was not optimistic about any real chance for success. Shargel speculated that Blekher's *Di post* simply appeared too late for a *farpoylesht kroke*, or polonized Cracow. According to Shargel, Cracow was the model city of assimilation, where the nationalist Jewish youth spoke no language other than Polish.

Blekher's reaction to the linguistic assimilation he saw in Cracow was particularly active. But the publication of his periodicals does not attest so much to the strength of Yiddish culture in the city as to its weakness. Shargel was not necessarily right; it may not have been too late to advance the cause of Yiddish within Cracow. But Blekher's defensive posture indicates that *Nowy Dziennik* and the city's 'so-called' Jewish intelligentsia were certainly more prominent within the community. His unwillingness to co-operate with other Yiddish cultural activists in Cracow such as Kanfer no doubt hampered the development of Yiddish creativity in the city. *Der reflektor* and *Di post* did briefly provide a Yiddish alternative to the readers of Cracow's Jewish press. Blekher's argument for a return to Yiddish language and literature, expressed over the course of two years, was cut short only by the outbreak of war in 1939.

Blekher's criticism of the other Yiddish cultural institutions in Cracow can be taken in part as a manifestation of his disappointment that they were not more successful. But it was also part of his charges against the polonized Jewish intellectuals of *Nowy Dziennik*. As the publication of *Di post* attests, Blekher's own commitment to Yiddish culture was strong. It is not known which language he used on a daily basis. But from his articles in *Di post* we know that he would settle for nothing less than the exclusive use of Yiddish by Cracow's most important Jewish intellectuals. Polish culture was not entirely absent from the pages of Blekher's periodicals. He published Yiddish translations of the well-known Polish poets Leopold Staff and Bolesław Leśmian, for example. And Blekher's harsh criticism of Kanfer's Yiddish Theatre Society did not prevent him from participating in a literary evening with Irma Kanfer, a Polish-language poet and the daughter of Mojżesz Kanfer. The Polish culture present in Blekher's publications pales, however, against the Polish patriotism expressed in *Nowy Dziennik* and the frank acknowledgement of the editor of *Dos yidishe vort* that Jews should learn Polish. Blekher's rhetoric is equivalent to that in *Nowy Dziennik*, which judged other Jews as somehow less Jewish because of the positions taken on certain issues. The Jewish writers and community leaders who established these newspapers were promoting distinct types of Jewish identity and Jewish culture. They competed with each other in what was more or less a free market.

Blekher's goal – to transform Cracow into a cultural centre for Yiddish artists – was limited only to a certain part of the Jewish population. His concern for Jewish workers is notable but his emphasis on art and culture meant that he did not provide practical political solutions to the problems faced by Cracow Jewry. To that extent, the development of Yiddish culture in Cracow posed no threat to the local government or Polish state, or even to Jewish activists, like those associated with *Nowy*

Dziennik, who were much more pragmatic in suggesting ways to maintain Jewish identity in a changing world. Blekher's firm stance against the polonization of Cracow was perhaps understandable because that polonization was already so far advanced. *Nowy Dziennik* represented a response to assimilation that combined Jewish national identity with elements of Polish culture, most importantly, language. It was this concession towards the Polish language that so agitated Blekher and made plain the need, in his view, for a Yiddish-language newspaper in the city. The adoption of Polish by leaders of the Jewish community signalled that some boundaries between the majority and minority in Cracow were breaking down; Blekher's attempt to make Yiddish a language of high culture in the city was an effort to maintain the wall that had divided the communities.

Blekher, however, was in some ways similar to the polonized Jewish intellectuals he so often scorned. For example, he was no less secular than the Polish-language Jewish intellectuals he chastised so harshly. In fact, he was interested in many of the same issues, such as the development of a Jewish literature in Yiddish and Hebrew and the presentation of Polish culture to the Jewish population. Like the intellectuals of *Nowy Dziennik*, he did not claim to speak for religious Jewry. This task was left to others in the city who established newspapers that Blekher and other Jewish writers, including those of *Nowy Dziennik*, often overlooked. Blekher, rather, defended Yiddish, a language increasingly threatened by linguistic and cultural assimilation.

Various groups within the Cracow Jewish community espoused different types of identity based on cultural expression in Jewish and non-Jewish languages or on a traditional belief in the religious tenets of Judaism. The community's newspapers reflected these different approaches to defining Jewish identity. Some of these newspapers were more successful than others, with a greater circulation or a more established presence in the city, having been founded as early as 1918 (*Nowy Dziennik*) or 1925 (*Dos yidishe vort*). Others (*Der reflector* and *Di post, Di yidishe shtime, Dos likht*) presented views of the community that were not always included in the city's largest Jewish newspaper.

Each of these newspapers reflects the presence in Cracow of different Jewish subcultures, different groups of Jews expressing their Jewish identity in different ways. *Dos yidishe vort*, *Di yidishe shtime*, *Dos likht*, and Blekher's *Der reflektor* and *Di post* aimed to reach very different audiences. In *Dos yidishe vort*, *Di yidishe shtime* and *Dos likht*, Orthodox Jews found voices of concern for religious issues. Blekher's newspapers allowed the city's Yiddish secularists a forum to air their views. Probst's *Dos yidishe vort* attempted to bridge the divide between the religious and the secular, to work with other groups in the city towards a stronger Jewish community. Along with Berkelhammer of *Nowy Dziennik*, Probst reached out to other Jewish institutions and engaged the community in important, contentious issues.

That the city's Yiddish newspapers and cultural institutions did not co-operate with each other demonstrates the range of Jewish opinion regarding social and political issues and the contentiousness within the community. This lack of co-operation perhaps also points to the reason for the success of *Nowy Dziennik*. *Nowy Dziennik*, wishing to renew the Jewish community by educating both Jews and non-Jews and instilling Zionist ideals among the Jews, spoke to its readers more often in communal terms than the Orthodox or Yiddish secular titles. Blekher, especially, wished to convert as many as possible to his idea of Jewish identity, but neither he nor the editors of the religiously oriented Yiddish newspapers had the institutional backing *Nowy Dziennik* received from prominent Zionists and Zionist institutions.

For all their apparent differences, the publications discussed here do share one striking similarity. Responding to a perceived crisis within the Jewish community, each of the editors – Berkelhammer, Probst, Geizhals, Urbach and Blekher – intended to strengthen Jews' identification with Jewishness. The responses to this crisis, perceived differently by each, necessitated new methods of reaching the Jewish population, such as the use of Polish, the establishment of a newspaper by Orthodox Jews, or the promotion and development of a high Yiddish culture and Yiddish theatre. Certainly none of the methods the editors employed was meant to alienate their potential audiences, though some of them, such as the decision to publish *Nowy Dziennik* in Polish, were controversial within the community. *Dos yidishe vort*, *Di yidishe shtime* and *Dos likht* are of special significance as Orthodox responses to modern political culture.

The development of the different newspapers points to the varying needs of groups within the community and the abilities of those groups to meet those needs. The disparate groupings reflected in the city's Jewish press can also be seen in the city's Jewish educational institutions. More importantly, educational trends within Poland and the Jewish community point to the same phenomenon observed in the study of the press, namely, increasing linguistic and cultural assimilation that none the less allowed for the expression of a unique ethnic identity.

NOTES

1. For some background on Yiddish in Galicia, see Gabriele Kohlbauer-Fritz, 'Yiddish as an Expression of Jewish Cultural Identity in Galicia and Vienna', in *Polin: Focusing on Galicia: Jews, Poles, and Ukrainians 1772–1918*, 12 (1999), 164–76.
2. 'Tsum dershaynen fun ershten num. reflektor', *Der reflektor*, 1 June 1935, 1.
3. Most of the other titles of Cracow's Jewish press are readily available in Cracow's Jagiellonian University library. *Arbayter vort* can be found in the Central Zionist Archives, Jerusalem.
4. Brzoza, 'Bibliography of the Jewish Press in Cracow (1918–1939)', 107.
5. See the discussion on this topic in Chapter 2.
6. 'Tsu unzer leser!' *Dos yidishe vort*, 13 March 1925, 1.
7. 'Tsi tut men taki tshuve', *Dos yidishe vort*, 13 March 1925, 1.
8. *Dos yidishe vort*, 26 June 1925, 1.
9. 'A shturmisher farzamlung vegn a t't', *Dos yidishe vort*, 31 July 1925.
10. 'A por verter tsulib der bafarshtehender general farzamlung inem beyt seyfer ivri', *Dos yidishe vort*, 1 January 1926.
11. 'Di farzamlung in der hebreisher shule', *Dos yidishe vort*, 8 January 1926.
12. Tuition at the Hebrew gymnasium is discussed in Chapter 5.
13. 'Di general-farzamlung in der hebreisher shule', *Dos yidishe vort*, 12 February 1926; 'Vi azoy kenen mir unzere kinder far yuden makhn?' *Dos yidishe vort*, 26 February 1926.
14. 'Vi azoy kenen mir unzere kinder far yuden makhn?' *Dos yidishe vort*, 26 February 1926.
15. 'A por verter tsulib der fafarshtehender general-farzamlung inem "beyt sefer ivri"', *Dos yidishe vort*, 1 January 1926.
16. Brzoza cites 500-1,000 as the circulation for *Di yudishe shtime* and 1,200 as the circulation for *Dos likht*. See Brzoza, 'Bibliography of the Jewish Press in Cracow (1918–1939)', 91–2, 107.
17. D. R., 'Tsu iz noytig a ferayingter blok fun ale religieze yuden in Kroke?', *Di yidishe shtime*, 12 October 1928. D. R. most likely stands for Dawid Rozenfeld, the publisher of the newspaper.
18. 'Der yoyvl fun natsionaler bafrayung', *Di yidishe shtime*, 9 November 1928, 2.
19. 'Es muz opgeshtelt veren di khilel-shabes epidemie in kroke', *Di yidishe shtime*, 13 June 1929, 4.
20. 'A vendung tsu di lezer!' *Dos likht*, 16 January 1931, 1. *Nowy Dziennik* and *Dos yidishe vort* were in publication at this time, but apparently they were not sufficient to 'awaken' Cracow Jewry.
21. 'A bisele yidishe kronik un vos vayter?' *Dos likht*, 13 March 1931, 9, 2.

22. 'Di profesionale klal-tuer un kahal-farzorger', *Dos yidishe vort*, 29 June 1928, 1.

23. 'Tsum dershaynen fun ershtn numer "Reflektor"', *Der reflektor*, 1.

24. 'Kronik', *Der Reflektor*, July–August 1935, 29.

25. Holger Nath, 'Yiddish as the Emerging National Language of East European Jewry', *Sociolinguistica*, 6 (1992): 62.

26. Moyshe Nadir, 'Mir un di yidishe shprakh', *Der reflektor*, 1 June 1935, 2.

27. 'Tsum dershaynen fun ershtn numer!', *Di post*, 3 September 1937, 1.

28. 'Di post tret arayn in tsveytn kium-yor', 2 January 1938, 1.

29. 'Vi iz unzer azoygerufene "inteligents"?', *Di post*, 12 November 1937, 6.

30. Blekher's reference to tin cans used to collect money for charity, or *tsdoke*, is meant to insult those Jews who would support Jewish causes financially but never commit on a deeper level (such as by speaking Yiddish or emigrating to Palestine).

31. Haman is the name of the Persian official who plots to destroy the Jews in the Book of Esther.

32. This topic is discussed at length in Chapter 7.

33. 'On a maske (der emes vegn der higer teater-gezelshaft)', *Di post*, 19 November 1937, 6.

34. Moyshe Blekher, 'Lomir zogn dem emes vegn yidishn aktiorn (a bintl faktn, proyekten un sakh-hakhlen) … Aktior un aktriese als polonizatorn', *Di Post*, 14 August 1938, 3.

35. 'Unzer teater-ankiete', *Di post*, 12 November 1937, 6.

36. 'Fraye tribune (shmuesn tsvishn leyener un redaktor)', *Di post*, 1 October 1937, 6.

37. Letter to the editor of *Di post*, signed 'A Polish Jew', 17 September 1937, 7.

38. Both Lwów and Vilnius were also criticized for their lack of Yiddish culture. Vilnius came under attack for having lost its status as a centre of Jewish and Yiddish culture during the inter-war period in Wilhelm Mermelstein's article in *Opinja*, 'Wilno – bez różowych okularów', *Opinja*, 26 January 1936, 6. The writer and Jewish activist Ignacy Schiper lamented the lack of a school with Yiddish as a language of instruction in Lwów and the failure of Yiddish cultural organizers to sustain any kind of regular activity in 'Funem lemberger yidishn kultur-lebn', *Di post*, 22 October 1937, 4.

39. See Henryk Vogler, *Wyznanie mojżeszowe* and Leopold Infeld, *Quest: An Autobiography* (New York: Chelsea Publishing, 1980).

40. Natan Gross, *Kim pan jest, panie Grymek?* and Halina Nelken, *And Yet I am Here!*

41. Buksboym, 'A shpatsir iber yidisher drukerayin in kroke (yidish in goles bay … yidn)', *Di post*, 1 October 1937, 6–7.

4

Making Jews Polish: The Education of Jewish Children in Polish Schools

It was warm and clean in our elementary school. The parquet floors sparkled brightly. After entering, we took off our boots and put on felt slippers. The walls were very prettily decorated. I remember that on the landing General Dąbrowski smiled down at me from his portrait. His eyes told me that I should not be afraid.

Irena Bronner, *Cykady nad Wisła i Jordanem,* describing the public school she attended in Kazimierz, the Klementyna z Tańskich Hoffmanowa School Nr 15

First among the tasks of the post-war Polish state was the development of an educational system that unified the different educational traditions of the partitioning powers and that met the needs of a diverse population. Complicating matters was the fact that each of Poland's minorities was, collectively, in a different stage of national development. The multi-ethnic nature of Poland's population made it extremely difficult for the state to impose any level of cultural uniformity while at the same time providing an education for its national minorities. The need of the state to cultivate productive, loyal citizens did not coincide with the need of the national minorities to establish their own educational network with their own goals. An evaluation of the kinds of education Jewish children received from the state as well as from the Jewish community shows how the Jews of Cracow responded to a recognition of these conflicting needs. The study of the education of Jewish children in Cracow is further evidence of Jewish acculturation to Polish culture as well as of a significant effort on the part of many in the community to preserve Jewish identity.

MINORITY EDUCATION AND THE POLISH STATE

The question of state regulation of education is especially important as scholars of national movements have noted the relative importance of both primary schools and secondary and higher education in developing a national consciousness.[1] Schools were a significant part of the modernization process of the late nineteenth and early twentieth centuries and were used to transmit culture within a political unit. The Minorities Protection Treaty signed at Versailles in June 1919 gave religious and national minorities in Poland the right to establish their own social and religious institutions at their own expense (that is, without any monetary support from the government) along with the right to use their own language and practise their religion. It also required the government to finance minority public education in some areas. The contradictory and confusing nature of its language, however, left it open to abuse. In addition, guarantees incorporated into the constitutions of 1921 and 1935 were not always fulfilled. Significantly, the assurances in the Minorities Treaty and constitutions only required the state to support minority education in those situations where the 'minority' was in fact a majority. Most importantly, while the private schools of the national minorities were subject to state regulations, they did not receive any monetary support, even nominally, from the state.

Poland's educational policy during the inter-war period has been described as a policy of assimilation, though to what extent the Polish government forced assimilation is a matter of some debate. In addressing issues of minority education, the inter-war successor states essentially had two options: to aim for assimilation or to develop more liberal policies allowing some degree of cultural autonomy. The policies of the Habsburgs had allowed for freer use of minority languages and religions and the study of a minority's national past in Austrian Galicia, but these policies backfired by unintentionally encouraging an increase in nationalist activity.[2] As a state with a politically liberal constitution, Poland was bound to provide equal opportunities for its national minorities, a difficult task for a fledgling democratic republic attempting to unite different regions and different peoples. The newly independent state of

Poland accepted responsibility for unifying the different educational systems of the three partitioning powers, as well as a diverse society containing significant national minorities.

The regulations of the Polish state and at least theoretical constitutional guarantees that promised greater equality of opportunity transformed Jewish education in Poland after the First World War. While Polish would be the obligatory language of instruction in public schools, minorities had the right to education in their own language where there was 'a considerable proportion' of non-Poles. The relevant provisions of the Minorities Protection Treaty read as follows:

Excerpt from Article 2:

The government of Poland undertakes to grant to all its inhabitants without regard to place of birth, nationality, language, race or religion, full and complete protection of life and liberty.

All inhabitants of Poland will have the right to exercise, in public and in private, the practice of their religion and beliefs, to the extent that these do not conflict with public order and good mores.

Excerpt from Article 7:

There shall be no limitation on the free use by any citizen of Poland of any language, in private, in commerce, in religious matters, in the press and in publications of all kinds, as well as in public assembly.

Excerpt from Article 9:

In towns and districts where there reside considerable proportions of citizens speaking a language other than Polish, the Government of Poland will facilitate the public instruction for children of Polish citizens in their mother tongue. This will not hinder the Polish Government from making mandatory the teaching of the Polish language in these schools.

In localities and districts inhabited by a considerable population of Polish citizens belonging to ethnic, religious or language minorities, these minorities will be assured their rightful part in benefits and allocations from funds which the state, commune or other public body grants for educational, religious or charitable purposes.

Excerpt from Article 10:

School committees, appointed locally by the Jewish community, will assure, under the overall control of the state, the appropriate distribution of public funds for the benefit of Jewish schools, as specified in Article 9. The Committees will also oversee the organization and administration of these schools.[3]

According to the treaty, minorities were also to receive 'a fair share' of state and municipal grants.[4]

Though inconsistent, and existing alongside the educational initiatives of the national minorities, state guidelines provided a framework within which the national minorities were required to work. How Polish educators formed a new national educational system directly affected the experiences of Poland's ethnic groups, determining which types of schools were legal, which languages could be used for instruction, how many hours to devote to specific subjects, and other similar issues. In the late 1920s and early 1930s, Piłsudski and his associates promoted the idea of 'education for state citizenship' (*wychowanie obywatelsko państwowe*). The wording of the school reforms of 1932 stressed that education for state citizenship (*państwowe wychowanie*) did not contradict 'national education or the creation of humanitarian feeling'.[5] Thus, in the official view of the government, state education could coexist with national education; minority goals could coexist alongside the educational objectives of the majority. The 1932 reforms stressed respect for each part of society and advocated tolerance, but they did not entirely clear up the ambiguities of the definitions of 'nation' or 'national education'.[6]

Education for state citizenship was an important goal, but not without difficulties. Three of the four largest minorities in interwar Poland – the Jews, Germans and Ukrainians – presented particular problems for the government in that they developed their own educational agendas. Complicating matters for the Polish government was its unequal treatment of its different minorities. Zygmunt Ruta, a historian of Polish education, has asserted that there was no single policy regarding the national minorities; rather each minority was treated differently.[7] For example, the Łemkos, another ethnic minority group in southeast Poland, were the victims of a policy that aimed towards national assimilation, while the government allowed Germans much more scope for the development of German language and culture. Clearly, the Polish authorities were aware of the limitations the Minorities Treaty, in practice, imposed upon them. They knew that, for example, Germans would complain about any apparently unfair treatment.

In addition to distinctions between nations, Polish society was also divided along religious lines. Tellingly, there was no apparent disagreement over the issue of whether or not religious instruction should be provided in school. It was provided as a matter of course to both majority and minorities, though minority children had to make concessions in terms of scheduling.[8] By stressing religious distinctions, public schools reinforced national differences among students.

Educational policies favouring assimilation had their effects. Whether in public or private schools, Jewish children during the inter-war period were raised in a significantly different educational environment from that of their parents. Public, and to some extent private, education after 1918 stressed instruction in the Polish language and Polish history as well as the citizen's duties towards the Polish state. While this was certainly expected in public schools, private schools were also regulated by the state and conformed to state guidelines regarding the number of hours of instruction in Polish subjects. This conformity involved more than simple compliance with state regulations. Rather, it was the first step in accepting Polish national rule and in fitting into a new environment, a theoretically liberal state that offered the Jews the opportunity to develop their own national institutions as well as to become liberal citizens. The acculturation of Jewish life in Cracow was the result of the necessary accommodations to the Polish state as well as a natural desire to succeed economically and socially within Polish society. For many Jews, acculturation was qualified by an active involvement in both new and established Jewish national organizations. It is this space between the accommodation necessary to succeed economically and socially in a Polish context and the desire to maintain a distinct national identity that was a new feature of Jewish identity in inter-war Poland.

If Polish public schools were to some extent the instruments of both Polish nationalism and governmental necessity, Jewish children in these schools received a minimal Jewish religious education along with a Polish national education. More importantly, Jewish children in private Jewish schools did not escape education for state citizenship as government regulations ensured that they received a minimum level of instruction in Polish subjects. Religious and national differences were honoured while, at the same time, state laws were imposed. Minority children were learning how to function in two different, overlapping national environments.

As for the Jewish population, the Polish government did establish bilingual schools where necessary and allowed certain schools with a majority of Jewish children not to hold classes on Saturday (the *szabasówki*).[9] Polish school authorities did not always provide for instruction in Yiddish or assure that Jewish educators' concerns about the religious instruction of Jewish children were addressed. Lack of a consistent policy toward the national minorities in turn contributed to the minorities' unequal status. The Polish government's tendency to regard the Jews as a religious rather than as a national minority also complicated the issue. To be sure, the distinction between confession (*wyznania*) and nation (*naród*) also divided the Jewish community.

Before elementary school attendance was made mandatory by the state in 1919, heders had been the primary form of Jewish education in Poland. In essence, these were private Jewish schools, which were not always known for their high or even adequate standards. They were meant to provide Jewish children with a religious Jewish education. But Jewish education in Poland before 1918 depended to a great extent on the partitioning powers. In the German area of occupation, Jews attended local German public schools, and Jewish education was the responsibility of communal and synagogal authorities. Under the Russians, Jewish children attended heders that at different times in the nineteenth century were the target of Tsarist reforms.

In Austrian Galicia, the situation was quite different.

Ordinances of 1885 and 1889, according to the Jewish educator Shimon Frost, 'classified the hadarim as strictly religious institutions which did not exempt Jewish children from attending local public schools. The heder thus became a supplementary after-school educational institution.'[10] Thus, in Galicia, Jews experienced public education well before the establishment of an independent Poland.[11] A governmental decree of February 1919 took further the significant change in Jewish education that had begun in the 1880s.[12] The 1919 decree obligated Jewish children to go to secular schools, thus changing the function of the heders. In effect, this meant that the traditional schools that provided Jewish children with a religious education would supplement public elementary school education, unless of course Jewish parents could afford to send their children to private Jewish schools. As this was already the case in Galicia, this reform primarily affected the Jewish children in the former Russian Empire. But the reforms of the Polish Ministry of Religious Faiths and Public Enlightenment also affected the heders and other Jewish schools developed later in Cracow.[13] The reforms required the heders to have twelve hours of secular instruction along with between twenty-seven and thirty-seven hours of religious instruction.[14] Drawing conclusions from an inspection of schools in the city, a school inspector confirmed the general attitude that the heders symbolized a withdrawal from society. He wrote that the heders were more or less medieval in their educational outlook.[15]

As a minority community in inter-war Poland, the Jews did change their educational patterns, both religious and secular. Forced by the state to conform to newly promulgated laws, the community responded by complying with the regulations and providing their own educational alternatives. Just as community leaders founded different types of newspapers to reflect their own ideological perspectives, so, too, they founded schools with precisely defined goals, discussed in detail in the following chapter. The education Jewish children received in private and public schools of all kinds had lasting consequences, often affecting the development of their ethnic identity. Exposed to two cultures, Jewish children managed often conflicting demands by making individual choices about their school activities, religious beliefs and national identity.

Admittedly, Cracow cannot serve as a representative city for the purposes of examining Jewish education in Poland, but it can be used to point to some issues faced by both Jewish educators and children, most notably the conflict between Polish and Jewish educational goals. While Jewish children in Cracow had the opportunity to attend either public (Polish) or private Jewish schools, private Jewish schools were either Zionist (with Hebrew rather than Yiddish as the language of instruction) or Orthodox in nature. There was no Yiddish school in Cracow, perhaps due to the relatively early linguistic assimilation within the Jewish community. Jewish parents none the less had some options for their children, including public and private trade schools developed in the late 1920s and early 1930s. Each of the private schools confronted the conflicting demands of teaching the required Polish 'state education' as well as the desired Jewish studies and specialized curriculum. How Jewish educators faced these challenges, how they manoeuvred between their own ideals and those of the Polish state, is a significant part of the story of the transformation of Jewish national identity.

THE EDUCATION OF JEWISH CHILDREN IN A POLISH ENVIRONMENT

An examination of Jewish participation in the public school system in Poland reveals the extent to which Polish Jews were integrated into the educational life of the nation. Jews were finding their place within a multi-ethnic state that, while promising equality and civic rights, was also intent on erasing the boundaries between the different nations within the multi-ethnic state.[16] While it is widely recognized that the majority of Jewish students in inter-war Poland attended public schools, there has been little research on this topic.[17] Ruta states that 82.2 per cent of Jewish children in Poland attended public schools, while the percentage of Jewish children in private schools was only 17.8 per cent (this, in comparison to the significantly smaller percentage of non-Jewish children in private schools, 2.7 per cent).[18]

Roughly a third of the students in the public school system in Cracow were Jewish, with a slightly higher number of Jewish girls than Jewish boys, perhaps reflecting the tendency among Jews to provide sons with a religious education and daughters with a secular education.[19] Ruta's study of the Kielce and Cracow districts also confirms that the majority of private Jewish elementary schools were in the Kielce district and not in Cracow, which data tentatively suggest the greater degree of acculturation in the Cracow district.[20]

Much source material on the history of schools in Cracow has been lost, but that which remains can still provide a survey, though admittedly incomplete, of the different types of educational institutions in which Jewish children were placed. These included public schools, private Polish schools and private Jewish schools. Unfortunately, we have the least information for the public schools, which a majority of Jewish children attended. The *Kuratorium Okręg Szkolny Krakowski* (Trustees of the Cracow Area School District, or KOSK) regulated both public and private schools. Periodically, officials of this school agency visited each school for general inspections.[21] Officials visited both private and public Polish schools and private Jewish schools, including the Talmud Torah schools and heders. These inspection reports, along with the archival material and memoirs, allow for a study of the different types of schools and the children's experiences.

Jewish students made up a significant proportion of some public schools, especially in or around Kazimierz. They participated in the celebration of Polish national holidays along with Polish students and were involved in extracurricular activities that involved Polish children, such as the School Theatre programme. The ministry's 'policy of assimilation' reached far into the country's Jewish neighbourhoods. None of the public schools I examined was entirely Jewish, nor do they seem to have met the 'considerable portion' criterion necessary to receive instruction in a minority language, in spite of the numbers that show that often a third to a half of the students were Jewish. Jewish children were quickly being integrated into a Polish system.

During the inter-war period, there were between fifty-five and sixty public elementary schools and ten private elementary schools in Cracow, employing around 630 teachers, the majority of whom were women.[22] In her unpublished collected materials in Cracow's city museum, Zofia Wordliczek noted that Jews attended both public and private schools and listed the following public schools Jewish children attended: Kazimierz Wielki School, Nr 5; J. I. Kraszewski School, Nr 8; Mikołaj Rej School, Nr 14; Klementyna z Tańskich Hoffmanowa School, Nr 15; and Jan Długosz School, Nr 22.[23] Other schools not on Wordliczek's list also enrolled Jewish children, notably the following: Stanisław Konarski Elementary School, Nr 9; Jan Śniadecki Elementary School, Nr 16; and Józef Dietl Elementary School, Nr 11.[24] A focus on three of these schools in and around Kazimierz helps to determine the level of participation of Jews in Polish public schools.[25] Interestingly, the national or religious identification of the students is listed in the school registers. From the registers one can determine the number of Jewish students in one class at any given time, student grades, student status upon entering the class for a given year, as well as the addresses of the students and the professions of the fathers. The registers prove that Polish and Jewish children attended the same schools, that they had similar experiences, and were exposed to the same curriculum by the same teachers except for religious instruction.

Stanisław Konarski Elementary School Nr 9, a public girls' school on Bernardyńska Street, was established in 1877. In 1900/1901, the proportion of Jewish girls in the school was approximately 50 per cent. As the school's register is undated, there is no way to confirm this percentage for the inter-war period, but it is likely many Jewish children from the Stradom neighbourhood attended this school. Class size in this school was small, around twenty students in each class.[26] Directly across from the royal castle Wawel, the school was located near the playing field used by the Makkabi sports teams. In an account of her wartime experiences, Anna Zoga, a non-Jewish Pole, indicates she certainly knew of this sports field for the Jews during her years at the school, so there must have been some contact between young Poles and Jews.[27] A written history of the elementary school indicates that it offered a wide range of activities to its students, including participation in the city-wide School Theatre (*Teatr Szkolny*) programme and involvement in the commemorations of national holidays and the funerals of Juliusz Słowacki and Karol Szymanowski.[28] The students also participated in different activities such as theatre presentations and concerts to raise funds for a summer colony for poor students and the maintenance of the school. The efforts of the school were highly respected and the school was often used as a model for visiting representatives from teachers' seminaries in other cities.

Jan Śniadecki Elementary School Nr 16 was a boys' school established in 1892 and located on Dietla Street, a large thoroughfare separating the neighbourhood of Kazimierz from the city centre. In a newsletter of Cracow's first district (*Dzielnica Pierwsza*), the school librarian Teresa Anderle-Bilińska indicates that a significant number of students at school during the inter-war period were Jewish.[29] This is borne out by the school's registers, which show that Jews made up approximately 50 per cent of the school's population.[30]

Some inconsistencies in the registers of School Nr 16 may be of even greater significance. In 1929–30, the fourth grade was twice as large as any other class and divided along religious lines. One section of the grade was Roman Catholic, the other Jewish. There was, however, a small number of Catholics in the Jewish group and a small number of Jews in the Catholic group.[31] This segregation does not seem to have had any anti-Semitic motivation, as Jews and Catholics were in equal numbers in the other classes. Rather, it seems this may have been to make arrangements for religious instruction more convenient. As Teresa Anderle-Bilińska has related, in 1924, School Nr 16 was designated to be for Jews and School Nr 11 (on the corner of Starowiślna and Miodowa) for Catholics, for unexplained financial reasons. In addition, in the early 1930s, there seems to have been a noticeable decline in the number of Jewish students in the lower grades of School Nr 16. Similar low levels in the higher grades in the later 1930s confirm this decline. As Jews were still accepted in significant numbers and the class was not segregated in the following years, there does not seem to be an obvious explanation, such as anti-Semitism, for the admission of a smaller number of Jewish students. The tendency to divide students along religious lines is clear, whatever the reasons for the irregularities. Most likely, such seemingly inexplicable changes in enrolment may simply reflect the chaos accompanying the organizing of the school system in the early years after the war and then again in the early 1930s, during the period of educational reform. In the absence of similar evidence of segregation for other schools, it is difficult to draw any conclusions. What must be determined are the reasons for such segregation, whether out of anti-Semitism, financial reasons, or concerns regarding religious instruction.

Many Jewish children attended Józef Dietl Elementary School Nr 11 on the corner of Starowiślna and Miodowa, very near the oldest synagogues of Cracow and the Jewish cemetery. Many graduates of the school would later become prominent leaders, including the film director Roman Polański and an Israeli government minister of the early 1990s. Unfortunately, the school yearbooks (*kroniki*) from 1890 to 1939 perished during the war, though some registers of the school still exist. This seven-class boys' school offered scouting, field trips and the usual commemorations for the name days of Polish officials.[32] In general, Jewish children made up 50 per cent of each class in the 1930s (excepting the years 1932–34), though there are a few classes where there are only one or two Jews. This school was one of the two affected by the decision to segregate the students in 1924.

Evidence from one other public elementary school indicates further the extent of Jewish participation in Polish public schools. A unique document preserved in the archives of the Jewish Historical Institute tells of children's experiences in the public school Klementyna z Tańskich Hoffmanowa School Nr 15 for a period of several years.[33] This document is a scrapbook highlighting important occasions throughout the school year from 1933 to 1939. While I was unable to locate the class registers or any other archival documents related to this school, the contents of the scrapbook reveal the Jewish origins of many of its students. The scrapbook includes original student writings, newspaper clippings and drawings illustrating the events that happened at the school. Not surprisingly, the events receiving the most attention were holidays, including Purim and the name days of Polish leaders such as Piłsudski and Ignacy Mościcki. The work of several individual girls appears repeatedly throughout, as if a small group was in charge of keeping the class scrapbook or one girl was primarily responsible for recording important events. This scrapbook is over three hundred pages long. While the students did not write detailed descriptions of each event, the scrapbook none the less offers a rare look at the experience of Jewish children in a Polish public school. The brief text of each entry is accompanied by drawings, pictures of Piłsudski or other Polish officials, and news clippings of special events, such as the 3 May Constitution Day and 11 November independence day holiday.

In her memoir about growing up in Cracow, Irena Bronner described the students of the school, located in Kazimierz on Miodowa Street, as coming from middle-class and poor families. According to Bronner, who attended the school in the early 1930s, there was only one non-Jew in her class, a Seventh Day Adventist, who came to the school from a neighbourhood somewhat distant from Kazimierz. Bronner describes her school years positively, mentioning her feeling of security at the school and the copy of Adam Mickiewicz's *Pan Tadeusz* she won as an award upon graduation.[34]

The girls at the Klementyna z Tańskich Hoffmanowa School wrote about participating in the celebrations of national holidays, meeting visitors at the school, and taking part in school trips, such as those to Las Wolski, a park and forest on the outskirts of Cracow. The descriptions of these seemingly mundane events reveal the ways in which Jewish youth were being taught to respond to life in Poland. One commemorative celebration was held in honour of the 250th anniversary of the victory of King Jan Sobieski over the Turks near Vienna. Regina Holländer wrote, 'Our king Jan Sobieski brought us this victory. It is a joyful moment not only for Poles, but for all nations.'[35] After the celebration for the fifteenth anniversary of Polish independence, Ida Schlesinger wrote on behalf of her classmates, 'We resolved to study well. In our Poland each child must be strong and brave.'[36]

The focus on political and civic life is natural for a school; in Cracow's public schools, it may also have reflected the values in Jewish homes. For example, Bronner describes the cult of Piłsudski that dominated in her home, how children naturally loved Piłsudski but that their parents actually believed in him as a political leader. She relates that his death was seen as a heavy blow to the family.[37] Bronner attended a memorial evening for Piłsudski at the Hebrew gymnasium and, like so many others in

Cracow, was at the service for Piłsudski at Wawel. Students in the school participated in Piłsudski's funeral procession in Cracow, and, naturally, wrote about it in their scrapbook.

The school hosted a number of impressive visitors in the mid- to late 1930s, including Minister Wacław Jędrzejewicz and former American President Herbert Hoover. But they also hosted a visit from a *góral* (mountaineer, highlander, from the Tatra mountains south of Cracow). The *góral* played the *kobza* (bagpipes) and awed the children with the strength he used to produce the songs they liked so much.[38]

Anniversaries, commemorative celebrations and other civic functions marking important local events were held both at school and in the synagogue. For example, a ceremony dedicating the school banner was held at the synagogue with a reception following on the playground of the school.[39] The girls prepared special speeches and songs for the occasion. On another occasion, Cracow's Rabbi Schmelkes spoke about Piłsudski as the architect of a reborn Poland.[40] Classroom activities also address a connection to Poles and the Polish state. After a special report commemorating the Day of Poles Abroad, the girls took up a collection for the building of Polish schools abroad. On an anniversary marking the joining of the sea to Poland, the girls sang a hymn to the Baltic and listened to a special radio programme. The students also corresponded as pen pals with children in a school from Podlesie, a distant region to the east.

Without more evidence from the students themselves, it is difficult to gauge the cumulative effect of such activity. The holding of commemorative events in the synagogue countered to some extent the emphasis on Poland and Polish political and civic life. Further, the girls noted the school celebrations of Purim.[41] One student, Mala Kupferberg, remarked upon the dancing and singing and described the celebration as very cheerful. At this Purim celebration, the girls collected money to buy a watch for their teacher.

The evidence of the connections between the students in the school and the majority community is particularly intriguing. Jewish children in public schools mourned the death of a pope in one of the city's synagogues. To mourn the death of Pope Pius

XI the students walked with the school banner to the synagogue for a memorial service. The entry in the scrapbook mentioned that a speaker (a Dr Pfeffer) spoke of the special merits and achievements of the deceased pontiff. After the choir performed, those gathered sang the Polish hymn 'Boże coś Polskę' along with a Jewish hymn.

The scrapbook of the Klementyna z Tańskich Hoffmanowa school confirms the range of experiences of Jewish children in public schools. While one cannot conclude that these children considered themselves Poles from this slim evidence, the girls' diary entries confirm that public education exposed Jewish children to Polish patriotic ideals and ensured their participation in activities with Polish children. More importantly, the descriptions of Purim as celebrated by the students in the school indicate that public education did not entirely efface Jewish identity. Indeed, the synagogue services indicate that there was a degree of accommodation made for Jewish students. Public schools worked with leaders and officials in the Jewish community to serve Jewish students. While public schools may not have met all the needs of the Jewish community, they did provide an education that placed Jews squarely within a Polish cultural context, in ways that did not always work directly against Jewish identity.

The memoirs of Jews from Cracow can tell us much about how individual children experienced the schools during the inter-war period. Writing about her mother's family, the art historian from Cracow, Halina Nelken, relates that her aunts went to the private Saint Scholastica School. Nelken herself was educated in public and private Polish schools. She first went to the public Dąbrowki Elementary School and then to the public Adam Mickiewicz Gymnasium on Starowiślna, located rather far from her home in Podgórze. She then transferred to the private Kołłątaj Gymnasium.[42] Nelken was well aware of the reason for the change in schools. An anti-Semitic incident had occurred at the Mickiewicz Gymnasium which led her parents to move their daughter to another school. As Nelken describes this incident, three Jewish girls discovered that Stars of David had been etched into the newly purchased coats of the required school uniforms. Though Nelken herself had not been singled out, her father withdrew from participation in the parents' committee of this school after confronting the school principal about this incident and informing her of his plans to transfer his daughter to another school. During her years at the private Kołłątaj Gymnasium, Nelken was educated in Polish culture, taking part in local celebrations and dressing in traditional Polish costumes. Also at that time she began a diary that she would continue in hiding during the war. Years later, after the war, Nelken returned to the Mickiewicz Gymnasium, where the anti-Semitic incident had occurred. There she met the principal who remembered Nelken's father's good work on the parents' committee and expressed her appreciation. Nevertheless, this woman had done nothing to protect the Jewish students in her school at the time of the incident. Ironically, even tragically, Nelken finished her education at the Mickiewicz Gymnasium after the war.

Nelken's reminiscences reveal an aspect of Polish Jewish life historians do not often recognize. Though Jewish, Nelken was educated in Polish culture and her background and professional career reflect this. As a child and teenager, Nelken was aware of her Jewishness, but she would have identified her family as *Polacy wyznania mojżeszowego* (Poles of the Mosaic faith).[43] She did not receive the same education as Jewish students in private Jewish schools. In the first year of the war, Nelken attended the Hebrew gymnasium when Jews were not allowed by the Germans to go to public school. She writes that she felt 'foreign' there.[44] In short, Nelken and others like her, more than other Jews who received exclusively Jewish educations, straddled two worlds and identified with two different cultures. As the anti-Semitic incident at the Mickiewicz Gymnasium indicates, this could be painful. Her Jewish identity did not preclude her from receiving a Polish education.

The example of Frydka, a young Jewish girl writing in *Ceirim* [*Youth*] (the title of the publication of the Zionist youth organization Akiba); *ceirim* is the Polish transliteration of the Hebrew for youth) in 1935 shows that Jews in public schools did not necessarily forsake identification with the Jewish nation for a Polish identity.[45] Sitting in class in a Polish school, the young girl listened to her geography teacher's lecture on the nationalities of Poland. The teacher said there were 3 million Jews in Poland according to the last census, but only 25 per cent of them were Jews by nationality, as 75 per cent of the Jews declared a nationality other than Jewish (presumably Polish).[46] Frydka describes a great sense of shame at learning that three-quarters of the Jewish population would not admit to Jewish nationality. She was not able to conceive how this could have been possible and simply expresses the hope that some day these Jews would 'return to their nation' and 'accept the magic of the Jewish street'. The effect of the lecture was to increase her identification with the Jewish people. Though the numbers the geography teacher gave were exaggerated, Frydka understood that other Jews were readily admitting a national affiliation with another group. While this in itself is not particularly surprising for a stateless minority, it does show that there was an additional affiliation that, for those like Nelken, was being strengthened not least by attendance in Polish schools. Frydka, however, reacted differently from Nelken, explicitly taking pride in her Jewish identity by taking an active role in a Zionist youth movement. The experiences of both young women illustrate the changes occurring simultaneously within Polish Jewry – namely, an increase in national awareness and greater integration into the majority community.

RELIGIOUS INSTRUCTION IN PUBLIC SCHOOLS

The Jewish community kept close track of the number of Jewish pupils in the public schools (though the records are at best fragmentary), as they were concerned with providing Jewish religious education for these children. Religious distinctions still played a tremendous role, not necessarily because of discrimination but simply because both Poles and Jews desired religious instruction in the schools. This had to be organized efficiently to accommodate the needs of both Jewish and non-Jewish children. Records from the official Jewish community of Cracow indicate the number, roughly ten to twelve, of Jewish religious instructors in Polish schools (and, by extrapolation, the number of students). Each teacher, during the course of a week, would visit as many as four different schools.[47] Instruction varied from half an hour to an hour for each class; instructors often complained that they needed more time because students did not remember lessons from the previous year.[48] Such efforts were not the Jewish community's preferred method of educating young Jews, but the lessons none the less kept alive the religious and national distinctions between the minority and majority peoples.

M. Jakob, a censor and translator for the Austrians, developed a curriculum for Jewish religious instruction in the public schools. Jakob himself was one of these religious instructors. This curriculum was detailed, including a presentation of the material in Hebrew and in Polish translation. Lessons focused on Jewish history and literature, religion and ethics.[49] The goals of the curriculum included improving the reading of Hebrew, mastering short blessings, morning prayers, and imparting a general knowledge of scripture and the holidays and rituals. In the first three classes of secondary school, students were expected to be fluent in reading with Sephardic pronunciation. The next five classes of the secondary school introduced the students to post-Biblical literature.

It is difficult to tell how much the weekly religious instruction contributed to a student's sense of Jewish ethnic identity. Memoirs of Jews schooled in inter-war Cracow say little about the religious instruction.[50] While the part-time Jewish teachers worked to instil knowledge of Jewish tradition, Polish authorities ruled that a lack of knowledge of Hebrew on the part of a student could not be used to keep that student from progressing to the next class.[51] Polish authorities provided for Jewish religious instruction in the public schools, but they also worked to keep that instruction from being academically meaningful for the student. The government's refusal to enforce standards in Jewish religious instruction demonstrated that the subject was unimportant to the state. Nevertheless, the efforts made by the Jewish community to reach those Jews most in danger of leaving the community, that is, those Jewish children in Polish public schools, helped ensure that they would maintain some sense of ethnic identity.

The leaders of the *kehillah* saw Jewish religious education in the public schools as a community priority and expressed different concerns about state regulations and the level of instruction. Cracow's Jewish leaders objected to the regulation that required teachers of the Catholic religion in the public schools to be approved by the ecclesiastical authorities, because this implied that teachers of other religions did not have to be approved by that group's authorities.[52] In 1923, the *kehillah* formed a commission made up of both Orthodox and more progressive members of the *kehillah* to examine Hebrew language teachers.[53] The community also handled requests to evaluate teachers of Jewish subjects in public schools for their knowledge of Hebrew. Regarding another issue brought to the attention of the *kehillah*, one letter found in the community archives concerned a request to the military that teachers of Jewish religion in the army be treated the same as priests, yet another example of the importance of religious distinctions.[54] The writer's request merited a brief, vague response from a government official indicating that qualification for Jewish religious teachers had already been normalized in Polish law.

Employment records and correspondence in the community archives indicate that the part-time religion teachers were often highly educated, had university degrees and even doctorates.[55] The religion teachers worked part-time, around twenty to thirty hours per week. The compensation the *kehillah* offered them did not match their education level, however. At a meeting on 17 April 1919, religion teachers in the public elementary schools decided they wanted more money because of inflation and were hoping for some kind of subvention. Another letter indicates that teachers in Podgórze received 100 zlotys less than teachers on the other side of the river for doing the same job.[56] Thus community leaders addressed many different aspects of religious education in the public schools and made this one of the priorities of the *kehillah*. With nearly 90 per cent of Jewish children in Cracow in public schools (though surely many of these received some form of private Jewish education as well), it is even somewhat surprising that there were not more teachers or greater involvement on the part of the official Jewish community in the public schools.

The teaching of Jewish religion in the public schools of inter-war Lwów provides an important example of how the private *kehillah* interacted with Polish governmental authorities, reflecting Jewish involvement in Cracow in making sure Jewish students received Jewish religious instruction. As several public schools held classes on Saturday, Jewish children in the public schools were not able to attend synagogue services on the Sabbath. Recognizing attendance on the Sabbath as an integral part of Jewish religious instruction, *kehillah* leaders planned a programme in 1930 that would periodically allow Jewish students in secondary school to be excused from classes early on the Sabbath in order to attend services.[57] This was a complicated task, involving the administrations and teachers of religion at ten different schools. The plan involved careful consideration of the sensitivities of Orthodox Jews, who objected because the Jewish students might come dressed inappropriately and, carrying all their materials for school, might not act respectfully. Issues of timing and transportation were also a concern. Students could not attend in the late afternoon because winter afternoons were too short. In many cases, the children lived too far away from the synagogue, a difficulty because they could not use transportation on Saturday. Eventually, a plan was devised for the Jewish students of ten secondary schools to attend synagogue services every third Saturday. While some Jewish leaders objected to the programme as much too modest to meet the real need of Jewish religious instruction, the *kehillah* presented the plan to the city school authorities. While there was some protest because the programme would require the early dismissal of some Jewish students from classes each Saturday, the authorities eventually approved the programme. Jewish leaders even succeeded in gaining an important concession. While the teacher of Jewish religion accompanied the students, the *kehillah* requested and received permission in schools where most students were Jewish for a teacher of a secular subject to be freed for this activity as well. The second teacher released from teaching responsibilities for that period of time may or may not have been Jewish. The *kehillah* leaders argued that releasing the teacher of a secular subject was necessary in order to impress upon the students the importance of this activity.

The presence of Jewish religious instruction in Polish public schools, along with the experiences of Frydka and Nelken, suggests that Jewish students in Polish public schools could form a type of Jewish identity, however vague this might have been. But Nelken's unequivocal description of herself as a Pole in her memoir also proves the influence of Polish education among Jews. Nelken lived in the middle of a *Polish* Jewish community. Only later during the war did she encounter what she described as 'a real Jewish community' for the first time. After entering Bełz during her initial flight from Cracow in November 1939, Nelken wrote in her diary, 'For the first time, I came in contact with a real Jewish community, quite different from Kazimierz in Cracow.'[58] Still, in transferring her to a private school, Nelken's father made certain she would become aware of her Jewish identity and of the responsibility of solidarity with other Jews. This may also have been an attempt to ensure that her Jewish awareness would be positive and not a result of anti-Semitism. Not all Jewish youth accepted identification with the majority society so easily, however. In contrast, Frydka experienced a strong Jewish identity as a result of her public school experiences. Certainly each individual Jewish student left the Polish public school system with distinct impressions, many of which most likely involved the anti-Semitism expressed by other pupils and teachers. But as the examples of Nelken and Frydka relate, attendance at a Polish public school was no certain indicator of later ethnic identification.

JEWISH PARTICIPATION IN PRIVATE POLISH SCHOOLS

A preliminary study of Cracow private schools shows that Jewish children did, in some cases, make up as much as 50 per cent of a non-Jewish private school's population. Private Jewish alternatives (other than the heders) did not exist before the 1920s. Thus Jewish leaders may have felt acutely the need for future Jewish leaders to receive a Jewish education. In the view of some Jewish educational leaders, Jewish attendance at private Polish schools placed the Jewish community at risk, because an education in Polish culture distanced Jews from a Jewish culture that was still primarily religious. Still, private Polish schools were not as great a threat as the public education system that enrolled many more Jewish students. But private Polish schools did provide an alternative that challenged the Jewish community to find its own ways to educate Jewish children.

To take only one example, 28 per cent of the students attending the Queen Jadwiga Private Gymnasium for Girls in

1937 were Jewish.[59] In the school year 1922–23, thirty-five of fifty-nine students in the second grade were Jewish; twenty-one of thirty-one students in the seventh grade were Jewish; and ten of twenty-two students in the eighth grade. Similar ratios hold for all the classes throughout the 1920s and into the late 1930s. Located right on the main market square, the Jadwiga Gymnasium enjoyed an exceptionally good reputation by any standards. The faculty employed modern teaching methods that promoted independent learning and offered many extra-curricular classes in diction, singing, drawing, stenography and foreign languages. In addition, the school presented a theatre performance in the Słowacki Theatre, and students even received a stipend for summer vacation. The school did not seem to have any real financial problems, paid close attention to students, and provided a lively intellectual environment.

Jewish students in this school were clearly being educated in a non-Jewish environment, indicating some breakdown of the separation between the Polish and Jewish communities. The school was not in Kazimierz, but in the literal centre of the city. It was not an unknown school, but an impressive educational institution that educated many of Poland's most prominent women, including Wanda Wasilewska, the writer and later Communist leader and daughter of Leon Wasilewski. Jewish participation in such an institution indicates a degree of assimilation. Nearly 30 per cent of the children at the Jadwiga Gymnasium in the late 1930s were Jewish, at a time when other private alternatives existed. At the very least, such participation suggests the necessity of a Polish education for professional success in the modern world.

While the subsequent careers of the Jewish girls who attended this school are not known, not all of them abandoned the organized Jewish community. Nella Thon, the daughter of Ozjasz Thon, was a graduate of this school. Significantly, Thon went on to become perhaps the foremost advocate of Jewish education in Cracow throughout the late 1930s, though she herself received her formal education in Polish. Thon used this education in a Polish private school to make private *Jewish* education an alternative for Jewish families (at least for those who could afford it).[60] Like Frydka, the young Jewish girl in the public school who was encouraged to become more involved in

1. Flag bearers of the Hebrew High School on a school march in Cracow, Poland, 1938 (Beth Hatefusoth Photo Archive, Tel Aviv).

2. Members of the YMCA, Cracovia and Makkabi swimming teams, winter tournament in Cracow, 1937 (Muzeum m. Krakowa)

3. Ping-pong players of the Ha-Gibor sports club, 1936 (Muzeum m. Krakowa)

4. The Hebrew Gymnasium Principal, Hirsch Shrer, receiving the school flag from the Gymnasium President, Dr Hayim Hilpstein, Cracow, Poland, 1929 (Beth Hatefusoth Photo Archive, Tel Aviv, courtesy of Natan Gross, Israel).

5. Teachers at the Hebrew High School in Cracow, Poland, *c.* 1935. From right to left: Waldman, N. Mifelew, Mordecai Gebirtig and Sperber (Beth Hatefutshoth Photo Archive, Tel Aviv, courtesy of Nahum Manor, Israel).

6. Hanukkah play performed at the Hebrew Gymnasium in Cracow, Poland, 1930 (Beth Hatefusoth Photo Archive, Tel Aviv, courtesy of Natan Gross, Israel).

7. Members of the Hebrew School Orchestra during the Lag Ba'Omer celebration in the Makkabi playing field, Cracow, Poland, 1935 (Beth Hatefusoth Photo Archive, Tel Aviv, courtesy of Natan Gross, Israel).

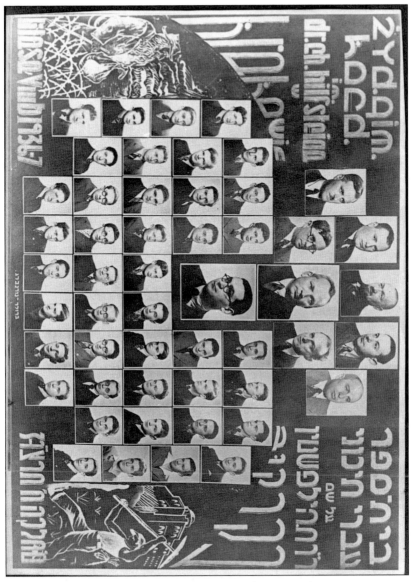

8. Graduation photo of students of Dr Hayim Hilpstein Hebrew
Gymnasium in Cracow, Poland, 1936/37 (Beth Hatefusoth Photo Archive,
Tel Aviv, courtesy of Nathan Gross, Israel).

9. The Temple synagogue, Miodowa Street, around 1925 (Muzeum m. Krakowa)

10. The Temple synagogue, Miodowa Street, around 1925 (Muzeum m. Krakowa)

11. The Old Synagogue / Alta Shul / Stara Synagoga, interior, 1925 (Muzeum m. Krakowa)

her Jewish identity because of education within a non-Jewish environment, Nella Thon functioned both within Polish and Jewish culture. Just as her father's participation in parliamentary politics indicated the entry of the Jews on to the modern political scene in ways to which Orthodox Jews violently objected, her own education at Queen Jadwiga indicates an assimilation towards modern ideas of education. Perhaps Nella Thon's active involvement in Jewish life is not so surprising given her father's position in Jewish religious life and politics. Having attained an education under the auspices of educators from another nation, Nella Thon worked to improve Jewish education.

The memoir of Henryk Ritterman-Abir provides one of the finest sources of information regarding Jewish students in Polish private schools. He attended one of the most prestigious private gymnasiums in the city, the Jan Sobieski Private School (*Prywatna Szkoła im. Jana Sobieskiego*). Ritterman-Abir (he adopted the name Abir after moving to Israel) came from a relatively prosperous Jewish family that had the means to send him to school in Vienna during the years of the First World War. Before he left for Vienna, he went to a school on Dietla (most likely School Nr 70), but upon his return he went to Sobieski because of the school's justified reputation for academic excellence.

Ritterman-Abir provides an interesting description of how the Jewish community's religious instructors taught Hebrew in the city's private Polish schools. According to Ritterman-Abir, David Rosenmann, his Hebrew teacher, was rather ineffective. Apparently, he focused too heavily on Hebrew grammar. When Ritterman-Abir went to Israel after the war he found that he could speak other foreign languages much better than he could Hebrew.[61] This may not have been Rosenmann's fault, as it is logical to assume that Ritterman-Abir had more instruction in foreign languages other than Hebrew. Ritterman-Abir is simply making the assumption that, as a Polish-speaking Jewish child, Hebrew should have been his best second language, though this was clearly not the case. Ritterman-Abir's memoir attests to the fact that Hebrew was taught to Jewish children in Polish private schools, and that other languages were often better taught or better learned, no doubt for all kinds of reasons. In short, Ritterman-Abir was learning as much or more about Polish and

other European cultures as he was about Jewish culture and
Jewish life. Again, like Frydka, Nelken and Thon, Ritterman-
Abir was learning how to function in a society that encompassed
much more than Jewish tradition. While the heders prepared
Jewish children for a traditional Jewish life, more modern public
and private schools trained young Jews for the secular world.

Ritterman-Abir's love for the theatre, imparted to him during
his years as a student at Sobieski, illustrates further the effects of
a Polish education. As a student at Sobieski, Ritterman-Abir had
the opportunity to participate in school drama productions. He
even had a small part in an Eduard Rostand play at the Słowacki
Theatre, and this involvement began his lifelong interest in the
theatre. When the well-known Yiddish-speaking theatre troupe
from Vilnius, the Vilner Trupe, came to perform at the Yiddish
theatre on Bocheńska Street, Ritterman-Abir attended the
production and was impressed with the actors' performances.
The troupe had been denied the right to perform in the larger
Bagatela Theatre nearer the city centre, and Ritterman-Abir, in a
youthful attempt to make up for this discrimination by adults,
decided to invite these artists to his own performance at the
Słowacki Theatre.[62] In a private conference, the school principal
reprimanded Ritterman-Abir for inviting Jews to the theatre. To
his credit, Ritterman-Abir pointed out the obvious to the
principal: that he himself, and many other students in the
school, were Jewish. Ritterman-Abir simply stated that he did
not know how this could be a problem. Faced with his student's
apparent naivety, the principal dropped the matter.[63]

This example of direct conflict with the school authorities
illustrates the difficulties Ritterman-Abir faced as a minority
student in the private Polish schools. In inviting the Vilner Trupe
to his performance at the Słowacki Theatre, Ritterman-Abir was
attempting to integrate two different aspects of his life that came
together in his interest in the theatre. As the incident with the
principal suggests, such integration was not looked upon
favourably. The principal made a distinction between Ritterman-
Abir and the Yiddish-speaking actors of Vilner Trupe, a
distinction that Ritterman-Abir himself did not make.
Ritterman-Abir was, however, aware of the distinction between
himself and his principal. That Ritterman-Abir thought he *could*
invite the Jewish actors to the Słowacki Theatre suggests the

school's anti-Semitism was not obvious, but the principal's reaction led him to recognize that he *did* live in two different worlds. He himself was bringing these separate worlds closer together. Ritterman-Abir challenged the principal to acknowledge the differences among the school's students.

Ritterman-Abir describes the teachers at the gymnasium in great detail, and his anecdotes are revealing. His memoir is especially useful because he points out who was and who was not Jewish in his world. Writing of his teacher Franciszek Fuchs, he regrets that this teacher was not Jewish – he liked him so much he wanted to claim him as Jewish.[64] Ritterman-Abir's experiences affirm that there was participation in the majority society by the minorities. He recalled with some disdain how another teacher, Dr Władysław Bogatyński (Reicher), though Jewish, celebrated all the Polish national holidays more enthusiastically than anyone else, presumably in an effort to prove his loyalty to Poland and the Polish state. For Ritterman-Abir, Bogatyński's actions were clearly a charade.

The Jewish students and teachers in Sobieski lived in two different worlds, with two separate identities and with two different cultures. It was perhaps the confidence gained in these elite Polish schools that gave some of these more acculturated Jews the resources to challenge societal restrictions limiting movement between different communities. The very presence of Jewish students and teachers in the most elite of private Polish schools indicates a degree of success in adapting to the majority culture, while Ritterman-Abir's invitation to the Yiddish actors points to emerging efforts to transform Jewish culture from a newly gained perspective.

Public and private education in Polish, even in the most elite of the city's schools, did not prevent an awareness, and at times even an acceptance, of Jewish identity. The weekly religious instruction maintained the difference between Jewish students and those of other faiths, and Jewish children were also able to participate in Jewish activities outside of the public schools, in the types of cultural organizations discussed in Chapter 6. Nevertheless, the public schools hastened the linguistic assimilation of the community and ensured that more Jewish children would be able to enter the majority society. Private schools trained students in an educational atmosphere that was much superior to that of the public schools. While Jewish students in the private Polish schools were trained to enter elite Polish society, they were still aware of their Jewish origins. Nella Thon, as the daughter of a public figure, is perhaps too exceptional to serve as an example of this. But Ritterman-Abir's memoir confirms that the Jewish student in the elite private Polish school did not necessarily abandon organized Jewish culture in favour of Polish. Private Polish schools, like the public schools, did not make an identification with the Jewish community an impossibility. They did, however, ensure an identification with the larger Polish community.

While public and private Polish schools did not efface Jewish identity, they did not offer the Jewish education many parents wanted for their children. In private Jewish schools, Jewish community leaders offered an extensive Jewish education that included much more than the weekly Jewish religious instruction in the public and private Jewish schools. Though only a small percentage of Jewish children in Cracow attended the private Jewish schools, examining these schools will reveal how Jewish educational leaders maintained and nurtured a separate civil society.

NOTES

1. See *The Formation of National Elites*, Comparative Studies on Governments and Non-Dominant Ethnic Groups in Europe, 1850–1940, Vol. VI, ed. Andreas Kappeler (New York: New York University Press, 1992) and Irina Livezeanu, *Cultural Politics in Greater Romania: Regionalism, Nation Building, and Ethnic Struggle, 1918–1930* (Ithaca, NY: Cornell University Press, 1995) and 'Inter-war Poland and Romania: The Nationalization of Elites, the Vanishing Middle, and the Problem of Intellectuals'.
2. See 'Governments and the Education of Non-Dominant Ethnic Groups in Comparative Perspective', by Knut Eriksen, Andreas Kazamias, Robin Okey and Janusz Tomiak, in *The Formation of National Elites*, 389–417.
3. Quoted in Shimon Frost, *Schooling as a Socio-political Expression*, 20–1. See also Michał Ringel, 'Prawa zasadnicze mniejszości żydowskiej w Polsce i ich dzieje', in *Żydzi w odrodzonej Polsce*, ed. Ignacy Schiper et al. (Warsaw, 1933).
4. J. J. Tomiak, 'Education of the Non-Dominant Ethnic Groups in the Polish Republic, 1918–1939', in *Schooling, Educational Policy, and Ethnic Identity*, ed. J. J. Tomiak, et al. (New York: New York University Press, 1991), 190.
5. Zygmunt Ruta, *Szkolnictwo powszechne w okręgu szkolnym krakowskim w latach 1918–1939* (Wrocław: Zakład Narodowy im. Ossolińskich, 1980), 158.
6. Ruta wrote that after 1936 there was an evolution of *wychowanie państwowe* (state

education) in the direction of *wychowanie obywatelskie* (citizenship education). Given the instability of inter-war Polish politics, it is risky to speak of a uniform policy in any one area. Ruta's assertion points to a government that changed over time, but without a clear definition of 'national education', it is difficult to determine if there was any real change in attitudes towards minority education in 1932 and in 1936.

7. Zygmunt Ruta, *Szkolnictwo powszechne w okręgu szkolnym krakowskim*, 168–9.

8. Attesting to the importance of the religious distinctions, a student's religion was duly noted in the school register, allowing the researcher to determine the ethnic background and other individual characteristics of each student.

9. On the *szabosówki*, see Shimon Frost, *Schooling as a Socio-political Expression: Jewish Education in Interwar Poland* (Jerusalem: Magnes Press, Hebrew University, 1998), 30–33.

10. Shimon Frost, *Schooling as a Socio-political Expression*, 29.

11. See Żbikowski, *Żydzi krakowscy*, 'Szkolnictwo i życie kulturalne', for an extended treatment of the history of Jewish education in Cracow in the mid- to late nineteenth century.

12. Magdalena Woźniak, 'Żydowskie szkoły w II Rzeczypospolitej: zarys problematyki', *Studia o Szkolnictwie i oświacie mniejszości narodowych w XIX i XX wieku*, 91–104.

13. This is the most literal translation of the Polish Ministerstwo Wyznań Religijnych i Oświecenia Publicznego. This branch of government functioned as a ministry of education, though specifically religious concerns were also within its purview.

14. Woźniak, 'Żydowskie szkoły', 97.

15. Ibid.

16. For an excellent discussion of the demands of liberal citizenship in multi-ethnic states, see Jeff Spinner, *The Boundaries of Citizenship*.

17. The lack of sources has made this one of the more difficult topics to research, and any conclusions about Jews and public education in Cracow are based on a limited source base. The information here can be based only on the records of three public schools operating in Kazimierz before, during, and after the inter-war period, the archives of KOSK, the local governing authority for education, and the limited amount of memoir material that addresses this issue. Unfortunately, the files of the Ministry of Education did not prove to be especially helpful when it came to local education.

18. Ruta, *Szkolnictwo powszechne w okręgu szkolnym krakowskim*, 90.

19. 'Szkolnictwo powszechne w Krakowie', *Nowy Dziennik*, 28 May 1924, 6.

20. Ruta, *Szkolnictwo powszechne*, 114–15.

21. Because the records of KOSK are fragmentary at best, I do not have a set of complete inspection reports for any school in inter-war Cracow. Considering the origin of these sources, they seem remarkably even-handed.

22. 'Szkolnictwo powszechne w Krakowie', *Nowy Dziennik*, 28 May 1924, 6; Żydowski Instytut Historyczny, Gmina Wyznania Żydowskiego w Krakowie (Jewish Historical Institute, Jewish Community in Cracow; hereafter ŻIH GWŻK), File 626.

23. Following are the schools' Polish names and addresses: Szkoła N 5 im. Kazimierza Wielkiego przy ul. Wąskiej 3/5, Szkoła Nr 8 im. J. I. Kraszewskiego przy ul Miodowej 36, Szkoła Nr 14 im Mikołaja Reja przy ul. Dietla 2, Szkoła Nr 15 im. Klementyny z Tańskich Hoffmanowej (zlokalizowana była przy ul. Miodowej 36a) and Szkoła Nr 22 im. Jana Długosza przy ul. Wąskiej 7.

24. The registers of these schools' archives confirm the attendance of Jewish children. These three schools are discussed in greater detail below.

25, At least one of the public schools in or near Kazimierz, Nr 14, in the heart of Cracow's Jewish neighbourhood on Wąska Street, had no surviving records from the period. Only fragmentary material remained from the other schools, but fortunately this material provides some evidence of Jewish participation in these schools. Little has been written about the experiences of minorities in the Polish educational system that extends beyond the statistics. Information was taken from the listings of class members, or class registers (*katalog klasowy*), and the *Kronika* (yearbook) of the school, if it existed.

26. Estimates taken from *Księga Wizytacyjna*, Szkoła Podstawowa Nr 9 im. Stanisława Konarskiego.
27. Anna Zoga, *Wspomnienia*, unpublished material in the archives of Szkoła Podstawowa Nr 9 im. Stanisława Konarskiego.
28. *Historia Szkoły Podstawowej Nr 9*, Szkoła Podstawowa Nr 9 im. Stanisława Konarskiego. From the school's private archives.
29. Teresa Anderle-Bilińska, 'Krótka historia Szkoły Podstawowej Nr 16 w Krakowie', *Dzielnica Pierwsza*, April 1996, 8.
30. *Katalog klasowy, 1919–1940*, Szkoła Podstawowa Nr 16. As mentioned above, the student's religious and national affiliations were noted in the school's registers.
31. *Katalog Klasowy, Rok szkolny 1929/1930*, Szkoła Podstawowa Nr 16.
32. *110 lat Szkoły Podstawowej im. Józefa Dietla w Krakowie 1886–1996* (Cracow: Patria, 1996).
33. Kronika Szkoły im. Klementyny z Tańskich Hoffmanowej w Krakowie, Żydowski Instytut Historyczny, Pamiętniki Żydów, sygn. 302/293.
34. Bronner, *Cykady nad Wisłą i Jordanem*, 118. Bronner also describes her transition to the private Hebrew gymnasium, discussed further in the next chapter.
35. Kronika Szkoły im. Klementyny z Tańskich Hoffmanowej, 12 September 1933.
36. Kronika Szkoły im. Klementyny z Tańskich Hoffmanowej, 11 November 1933.
37. Bronner, *Cykady nad Wisłą i Jordanem*, 48.
38. Kronika Szkoły im. Klementyny z Tańskich Hoffmanowej, 11 April 1935.
39. Kronika Szkoły im. Klementyny z Tańskich Hoffmanowej, 15 June 1937 and 22 June 1937. These entries concern the formal dedication of the standard of the school and list important visiting officials, along with the stamps and signatures of individuals who bought the stamps to support the making of the standard. One of these individuals was Laura Tignerowa, the president of the parents' committee of Cracow's Hebrew gymnasium.
40. Kronika Szkoły im. Klementyny z Tańskich Hoffmanowej, 3 November 1938.
41. Celebrations of Purim by Jewish students in public schools were not limited to Cracow. For a colourful description of a Purim celebration in Lwów, see Cynicus, 'Karnawal ghetta', *Ze szkolnej ławy*, January–February 1934, 18–9. *Ze szkolnej ławy* [*From the School Bench*] was the publication of the W. Bogusławski Drama Circle of Gymnasium Nr 9 in Lwów.
42. Nelken, *Pamiętnik*, 63–4.
43. Nelken, personal communication, 12 February 2000.
44. Nelken, *Pamiętnik*, 83.
45. 'Czy tak być powinno', *Ceirim*, 1 January 1935, 48.
46. Whatever the exact numbers were, the teacher was wrong. The 1931 census did not ask about nationality, only mother tongue. Most Jews then either identified a Jewish language, Yiddish or Hebrew, reflecting their linguistic reality or an ideological position. According to the 1931 census, 41.3 per cent of Cracow Jews gave Yiddish as their mother tongue, while 39.8 per cent gave Hebrew. The high number for Hebrew reflects the success of a campaign led by *Nowy Dziennik*. The newspaper encouraged its Jewish readers to identify Hebrew as their mother tongue rather than another language (such as Polish) in an effort to ensure that Jews would be counted as Jews. The numbers from 1931 are as follows. Of the total of 56,515 Jews in the city, for native tongue (*język ojczysty*): Yiddish – 23,316; Hebrew – 22,487; Polish – 10,517.

These numbers reflect a positive sentiment for Hebrew rather than an accurate linguistic reality. See 'Di shprakhn bay yidn in umophengikn poyln: an analiz loyt der folkstseylung fun 1931', Jacob Lestchinsky, *YIVO Bleter*, November–December, 1943, XXII, No. 2.

47. ŻIH GWŻK 747.
48. ŻIH GWŻK 750.
49. ŻIH GWŻK 756 *Sekcja naukowa*.
50. The religious instruction and memoir literature will be discussed further below.
51. ŻIH GWŻK 749 *Sekcja naukowa II*; according to *Dziennik Urzędowy*, Kuratorium Okręg Szkolny Krakowskie (hereafter KOSK), 16 March 1931.
52. ŻIH GWŻK 748 *Sekcja naukowa*. This appeared in a letter to the *kehillah* from *Sejm* delegate Rabbi Aron Lewin, handwritten draft.
53. ŻIH GWŻK 584, 1911–28.
54. ŻIH GWŻK 750 *Sekcja naukowa II Sprawy szkolne*.
55. ŻIH GWŻK 753.
56. ŻIH GWŻK 747 *Sekcja naukowe* 1919–22 r.
57. 'Protokoly konferencji', Fond 701, Opis 3, Sprava 1121, Central State Historical Archives, L'viv.
58. Nelken, *Pamiętnik*, 81; English quote from Alicia Nitecki's translation, *And Yet I am Here!*, 54.
59. KOSK 33, File 11, Sprawozdanie z wizytacji prywatnego gimnazjum żeńskiego im. Kr. Jadwigi Towarzystwa prywatnego gimnazjum żeńskiego im. Kr. Jadwigi w Krakowie. Dates of inspection: 27 February, 1 March, 2 March 1937. This high percentage confirms my own count of Jewish students at the Queen Jadwiga girls' school in the 1920s.
60. Unfortunately, Nella Thon's published writings are limited to memories of her father. Her views on public and private education would offer a unique perspective that would greatly enhance a further study of private Jewish education. For her assessment of her father's life and work, see her self-published memoir of her father published in English as *Jehoshua Thon: Preacher, Thinker, Politician* (Montevideo, 1966).
61. Henryk Ritterman-Abir, *Nie od razu Kraków zapomniano* (Tel Aviv: Związek Żydów Krakowiań w Izraelu, 1984), 51–2.
62. The exact date is unclear in Ritterman-Abir's memoir, but it is most likely in the mid-1920s.
63. Ritterman-Abir, *Nie od razu Kraków zapomniano*, 80–1.
64. Ritterman-Abir's anecdotes also reveal the difficulties of making assumptions about whether or not people are anti-Semitic. For example, Ritterman-Abir tells the story of his Latin teacher, Rozmarynowicz. Rozmarynowicz (Ritterman-Abir does not describe him as Jewish) made a sarcastic remark about Ritterman-Abir's older brother. Ritterman-Abir wondered if this comment stemmed from anti-Semitism. Years later, practising as a lawyer in Cracow, Ritterman-Abir encountered Dr Bolesław Rozmarynowicz, his former teacher's brother, in the courtroom, assuming him to be anti-Semitic because of his links with the Chadecja, the Christian Democratic movement. Fifteen years later, Ritterman-Abir learned that both Rozmarynowicz brothers had saved Jews during the war. Ritterman-Abir, *Nie od razu Kraków zapomniano*, 49–51.

5
Maintaining Community: Jewish Participation in Private Jewish Schools

How was a Hebrew school different from a Polish school? In a Polish school the Jew had to be a good student, perhaps even better than others, but a Hebrew school allowed one to be a bad student, to neglect lessons and disregard teachers, to misbehave as much as your spirit wished, to cut school. This was an oasis, an island isolated from the Polish reality, though Poland and Polishness in all its manifestations were here in our Hebrew school, represented and transmitted better than Jewishness ... [1]

Natan Gross, *Kim pan jest, Panie Grymek?*
(Cracow: Wydawnictwo Literackie, 1991)

When Irena Bronner transferred from the public Klementyna z Tańskich Hoffmanowa School to the private Hebrew gymnasium, she worried about how she would fit in. Bronner did not want to go to the Hebrew school. Hebrew was too liturgical, not a language for reading and writing, she thought. But her mother insisted, even obtaining a substantial discount on the tuition from the school's director, making it financially possible for Bronner to attend. Irena resisted, as she describes, because she was not yet confident enough to attend the Hebrew school.[2] Bronner came to appreciate her mother's insistence, because, after an initially difficult period adjusting to the school, her experiences there were quite positive.

If Jewish leaders deemed public and private Polish schools threatening to the Jewish community, then private Jewish schools were the way Jews could ensure that their children received a Jewish education and remained a vital part of the community, even after an elementary education in a public Polish school. The establishment of private Jewish schools in inter-war Cracow marked the beginning of a more self-conscious Jewish national identity in the city, a period when the Jews themselves were assessing and reconceiving their educational needs. Mandatory laws obligating public school attendance resulted in even greater contact with the non-Jewish community. Private Jewish schools were perhaps the most important way that Jews reinforced their separate identity. At the same time, private Jewish schools in Cracow reflected the various ideological and religious viewpoints of different sectors of the community. An examination of the private Jewish schools of the city reveals the type of education the potential future leaders of the community received, but it also shows that even here there was no escaping the influence of the majority culture. The accommodations Jewish leaders made to the government of the majority introduced Jewish children to the Polish language, Polish culture and the responsibilities and demands (though not necessarily the benefits) of Polish citizenship. Jewish education itself had to adapt to the requirements of life in Poland's Second Republic and provide an education necessary for the modern world.

Jewish educators recognized early on the difficulties of educating a minority population in a theoretically liberal multi-ethnic state. Maks Bienenstock, a Jewish educator and Zionist senator in the *Sejm*, wrote in *Nowy Dziennik* that establishing a Jewish school in Palestine would be 'normal', but that here in Poland a good Jew should be a citizen of Poland who recognized his obligations as a result of the rights imparted to him.[3] Thus Bienenstock recognized that the Polish Jew, because he or she lived in Poland, had to meet certain obligations to receive the benefits of the state, namely, civil rights. This was the dilemma faced by Jews in inter-war Poland: how to fulfil the obligations of a liberal citizen while maintaining their ethnic identity.

While unable to wield any significant influence over the school system, Polish Jews nevertheless established their own schools which were meant to instil Jewish national conscious-ness in Jewish children and, more generally, to preserve the distinctiveness of the Jewish community. There were at least two reasons for the founding of separate Jewish schools: the growth of anti-Semitism and Jewish national rebirth.[4] In 1936, the Jewish educator Henryka Fromowicz-Stillerowa outlined the need for Jewish education by describing the problems Jewish children encountered in public schools.[5] Jewish children were often taunted by students and teachers and faced dilemmas about what to do for the Jewish holidays.[6] Recommending that Jewish parents of children in public schools set up committees to deal with these issues, Fromowicz-Stillerowa argued passionately for Jewish education for Jewish children. The best situation for a Jewish child, according to her, was in a Jewish school. According to Fromowicz-Stillerowa, teachers in public schools simply did not know how to treat Jewish children. Private Jewish schools could not, however, hope to reach all Jewish children. The problem Jewish educators faced was how to integrate their own efforts with the Polish campaign to modernize the state. This tension between Polish goals and Jewish national aspirations was evident not only in public schools, but also in private Jewish schools as well.

Jewish educational leaders could not always agree on what types of schools to establish. Some favoured religious education; others promoted secular training. Still others supported schools founded to advance the ideals of Zionism or socialism. Some endorsed schools with instruction only in Hebrew, or Yiddish, or Polish. Like the various elements of the Jewish press, the different schools represented a range of options for Jewish parents. If parents were financially able and so desired, they could place their children in schools that promoted secular Zionism or religious Orthodoxy. As one of the components of national identity, language became an important issue in debates on the education of national minorities and was especially important for Jews. In one debate, M. Braude, a Zionist senator in the *Sejm* and the leader of the Union of Social Associations for the Maintenance of Jewish Secondary Schools in Poland, a national network of Jewish schools, took issue with the statement of another Zionist senator, Yakov Wygodzki.[7] Wygodzki claimed that Jewish schools with Polish as the language of instruction were Polish schools, not Jewish schools. Braude disagreed, supporting the use of Polish among Jewish elementary and secondary school students. Noting that 80 per cent of Jewish children spoke Polish and had not had the benefit of a Jewish education, Braude affirmed the Jewish ethnic identity of these students in spite of their use of a non-Jewish language. He was an important national voice legitimizing the use of Polish among Jews.

For Braude, language was not necessarily the determining factor of ethnic distinctiveness or national identity. Braude still recognized the need to establish private Jewish schools. He did not dismiss Polish-speaking Jewish children as the offspring of assimilationists; rather, he aimed to provide them with a Jewish education. These schools were an important indicator of the growth of Jewish national identity and the success of Jewish efforts to maintain a high level of ethnic cohesion. Jews in Poland were beginning to found institutions that used the non-Jewish majority language but were clearly a part of the Jewish community. Linguistic assimilation did not necessarily hinder the growth of Jewish ethnic and national identity, even on an institutional level.

Divisions among the private Jewish schools went along lines other than language as well. Writing in Polish in 1919, Bienenstock distinguished between two different types of Jewish schools, confessional (*wyznaniowy*) schools and national (*narodowy*) schools.[8] According to Bienenstock, confessional schools separated Jews from everyone else, like the Great Wall of China. National schools did not. Further, in Bienenstock's view, national schools promoted a new conception of education and did not have anything in common with confessional schools, which taught the precepts of the Jewish religion. For Bienenstock, national identity did *not* separate. He anticipated that some Jewish leaders would be concerned that Jewish national schools would raise another Chinese wall. He declared that national schools (for Jews) placed them on an equal footing with non-Jews and fostered an entirely different kind of relationship between Jews and non-Jews.[9] Just as Poles, Germans or Ukrainians promoted their own brand of national identity, so did the Jews.

Bienenstock declared that this national education would not lead to further separation between Jews and non-Jews. In short, according to Bienenstock, separate schools of a national minority could exist alongside the schools of the majority without any damage to the relationship between Jews and non-Jews. He dismissed any possible effects of segregation. Private Jewish schools, by inventing and reinforcing a Jewish national identity, would produce students who would have a different relationship with the majority culture because of their extensive

Jewish education in Polish. Further, as the Polish government insisted that private schools adhere to state curriculum guidelines, these students would have a different conception of Polishness as well. Consequently, separate Jewish schools would not yield a Jewish population that would identify solely with Jewish national life. Bienenstock argues, realistically, that given the situation of minority education, separate schools would not lead to further separation but simply to a changed relationship between the minority and majority. Implicitly, this would change the minority community itself as well.

A series of articles on the need for private Jewish schools that appeared in Lwów's Polish-language Jewish daily *Chwila* highlighted the change that these schools might effect.[10] Jewish children taught previously in Austrian and Polish schools had been separated from the traditions and religion of their fathers. Private Jewish schools, as run by the Zionists, could do nothing less than create a new type of 'Jew-citizen' (*Żyd-obywatel*). The wording in Polish was as new and awkward as the concept. The Polish press claimed that such educational initiatives were a step towards the separation of Jews from Poles. The bilingual Polish-Hebrew gymnasium in Lwów was described as an 'anti-civic experiment' by one of the city's Polish newspapers.[11] Zionists themselves argued just the opposite. Private Jewish schools were not meant to be separatist. As one Jewish leader put it at a meeting of Jewish professionals in education, 'In one word: a national Jewish education will raise good Jews, good people and good Poles, in a civic sense, ready to defend their fatherland.'[12] Jewish educational leaders recognized that, if Jewish schools received any kind of state funding, that they would have to submit to state power. This was not perceived negatively, since, as leaders at the meeting indicated, private Jewish schools would lead to greater Polish–Jewish understanding. Private Jewish schools would actually create both Jews and citizens by educating children in both religious traditions and civic life. The timing of the opening of the schools worked to foster the thinking in the Polish press that the schools were 'anti-civic experiments'. The opening of the schools coincided with the first days of the newly declared independent state and attacks on Jews in Lwów and throughout Galicia in November 1918. The anti-Semitic violence immediately following the First World War was not the reason for the establishment of private Jewish schools; associations to found the schools had been established, as in the case of Cracow, over a decade earlier. The violence, however, did increase many Jews' desire to send their children to private schools.[13]

Bienenstock, whom Polish educators respected both as an educator and writer, called the failure of Polish–Jewish relations to improve his greatest disappointment shortly before his death in 1923.[14] Writing over a decade later, Fromowicz-Stillerowa reiterated the need for separate Jewish education but with significantly less enthusiasm. Bienenstock had asserted that private Jewish schools were necessary to sustain a high level of ethnic cohesiveness and protect Jews from anti-Semitism, but he also suggested that separate Jewish education would also change for the better the relationship of Jews to Poles. By the time Fromowicz-Stillerowa wrote in 1936, she must have concluded that that was impossible. Bienenstock's work helped the Jewish community to maintain a minimum level of cohesiveness within a majority population. Fromowicz-Stillerowa continued this work as increasing anti-Semitism in Cracow in the mid- to late 1930s threatened Jews in the city's public schools and university.

In addition to the debate over the types of schools to be established, the Jewish educator Alexander Koller noted further difficulties the Jews faced in developing Jewish education. According to Koller, even Jewish teachers in Jewish schools were assimilated or uninvolved in the Jewish community.[15] For Koller, the efforts of Cracow's Jewish nationalists to provide a Jewish education for Jewish children were not enough. While Koller's complaints about the level of Jewish identification of Jewish teachers may have been justified, each Jewish organization defined this level differently. Each Jewish school taught students Jewishness in different ways, placing varying amounts of emphasis on secular learning, religious tradition and the teaching of Jewish languages.

Understandably, Koller explains, the private Jewish schools scrambled after Polish public rights, or the government accreditation allowing the school's students access to the next educational level. A school with full public rights satisfied all the various educational requirements of the government. Only private schools granted full public rights could offer the necessary *matura*, or university entrance examination, to Jewish students. To solve what he viewed as the problem of accommodation to the Polish state, Koller suggested a solution that lay in a *synthesis* between Jewish schools, national education and new pedagogical ideas.[16] It is unclear how new pedagogical ideas would appease Polish officials looking for some guarantee that its citizens would be educated for membership in the state. His suggestion shows that the conflict between governmental priorities and minority goals was a significant problem for the Jewish community and had to be addressed if Jewish children were to function within both Polish and Jewish cultures. Koller's suggested synthesis aimed to modernize Jewish education at a moment when Jews were increasingly aware of the advantages of participation in the majority culture.

The leaders of organizations formed to establish private Jewish schools faced great obstacles. One fundamental issue was the question of organization. The writer of an article in *Nowy Dziennik* in 1921 pointed out that organizers of Jewish schools had to contend with the apathy of the Jews themselves. In addition, the writer felt the organizers would have a better chance of success if they stayed away from religious matters, which alone indicates that religious education was a divisive issue in the community. The implication is also that the new private Jewish schools established after the war were very different from the heders. On top of these organizational obstacles, the Jewish leaders were also in dire need of direct financial help.[17] Another issue to be considered when examining the private Jewish schools in Cracow is their accessibility to the average Jew. Tuition for private schools, whether Polish or Jewish, was high and often parents made great sacrifices on behalf of their children. Not all Jewish parents were able to send their children to private Jewish schools. The schools themselves, as well as other charitable organizations, provided whatever financial support they could, but private Jewish education was still possible for only a small number within the Jewish community.[18]

Determining the number of Jewish students in private Jewish schools is particularly important since it gives an indication of the number of Jewish youth who received a secondary education and who were likely to remain involved within the Jewish community. A leader of the Professional Union of Secondary School Teachers in Poland, A. Wolfowicz, cited a relatively high number of Jewish children attending private Polish schools. According to this article, 50 per cent of Jewish youth attended private Polish schools in Poland, much higher than Ruta's nationwide estimation of 17.8 per cent.[19] The concern expressed in this article was that the 'better' Jewish society (wealthier), were sending their children to Polish schools instead of Jewish ones. Such an attitude towards private Jewish schools was termed 'snobism'. Given the latter comment, it is likely that the figure of 50 per cent is artificially high in order to support Wolfowicz's point. Nevertheless, data from Cracow lends at least some support to Wolfowicz's point. Nearly a third of the students at the private Queen Jadwiga Gymnasium as late as the late 1930s were Jewish; private Polish schools did not lose their attraction for Jewish parents even after significant development in the private Jewish school sector.[20]

The wide range of private Jewish education includes the traditionally oriented Talmud Torah schools and the more modern secondary schools. Each one of the private Jewish schools during the inter-war years experienced a period of remarkable growth, especially the Hebrew gymnasium and Sore Shenirer's Beys Yakov schools and teachers' seminary. While Polish schools also went through a transformative experience after the regaining of Polish independence, the Jewish schools, in most cases, began from nothing. In the Hebrew gymnasium, enrolment grew from only fifteen students in 1918 to nearly 750 students in the 1930s. In the early 1930s, the gymnasium authorities opened additional schools for the special needs of the community. Sore Shenirer's Beys Yakov school for Orthodox girls, founded in 1916, grew into a large network of schools worldwide. This growth is indicative of an increasingly active, self-aware, able Jewish community focusing on its own goals and needs. These and other schools should be examined for what they tell us about how Jews perceived their goals and needs and, most significantly, how they accommodated these to the demands of the Polish state.

In the absence of schools in Cracow sponsored by Yiddishist organizations like the Bund or the Central Yiddish School Organization (Tsisho, according to its Yiddish acronym), Zionists dominated the Jewish education of the city's youth. Jewish education was moving towards greater use of Hebrew as a national language of the community at the expense of the cultural acceptance of Yiddish, further curtailing the extent of Yiddish culture in the polonized Jewish community of Cracow. While the association to support the Hebrew gymnasium was attached to a more political Zionist perspective and was the leader among the private Jewish schools, the more religious schools were also an important factor of Jewish life in the city. Yiddish was used as an instructional language in the more religious schools (discussed below), but the languages of instruction in the Hebrew gymnasium were Hebrew and Polish. Even without Yiddish schools, Jewish education in the city was diverse. The parents of students with specific needs and interests could choose from a variety of educational institutions, each geared towards the development of a specific aspect of Jewish culture.

FROM HEDER TO ELEMENTARY SCHOOL

Cracow's progressive Jewish community leaders had contended with the Orthodox over the issue of education since the 1860s. Progressive leaders supported the city's Polish public schools and supported the polonization of Jewish children. Largely because of their greater financial resources, they were able to ensure that a Jewish school sponsored by the *kehillah* held instruction in Polish.[21] Moreover, progressive leaders were opposed to the traditional heders. Already by the 1870s, both Jewish and Polish community leaders regarded the heders in Cracow as 'symbolic of the universally held view that the Jewish masses are withdrawn' from the rest of society.[22] The conditions that led to this view persisted until the inter-war period. In his writings on his life in Cracow, Rafael F. Scharf described one of the city's heders:

> On the ground floor, in the courtyard, there was a 'cheder', a Jewish elementary school for boys, where reading the Bible was taught. Boys from the neighbouring houses were brought there by a 'belfer', often by force, against their will. All day long, through the half-closed windows, the

courtyard was filled with a rhythmic sing-song, children repeating after the teacher, the 'melamed', verses from the Scriptures. Now and again there was a shriek, some kid being beaten by the 'melamed' with a belt or a whip – the traditional teaching method.

I went to 'cheder' once only; my Father considered this to be my (or rather his) duty, although my Mother protested. I did not like it – and refused to go again.[23]

In 1885, there was a total of 1,808 boys and 1,816 girls of school age in Cracow. Of these, 719 boys and 1816 girls went to public schools; 482 boys and 118 girls went to heders, of which there were 22 in the city. Thus, even as early as 1885, a majority of Jewish children in the city[24] were attending public schools. Efforts to provide secular Jewish education did not begin until the early years of the 1900s and were not successful until the inter-war period. An undated file in the Cracow collection of the Jewish Historical Institute lists the addresses of students, number of students, status of the teachers, number of girls in the heders, if any, the rate of the students' participation in public schools, the age of students, and the number of assistants.[25] A total of forty heders are listed. The heders provided only religious instruction until the government's educational reforms during the inter-war period. The total number of students in these heders was 1,141; approximately 500 attended public schools as well (necessitating afternoon instruction in Jewish subjects for these students).[26] The numbers must be approximate because for some schools the exact number is not given (only an adjective like 'majority' or 'a few'). Interestingly, the questionnaire asked about the number of girls in the schools and whether or not girls and boys studied together, but there were no girls in any of the schools.[27]

Some of the larger heders had three or four rooms; most just had one or two. Most of the responses state that the rooms were reserved for the exclusive use of the heder. Most, perhaps even all, of the directors of the heders stated that they were not otherwise employed, and most had one assistant, unless they were very small. Heders with fifty or sixty students had three or four assistants. Boys in these heders ranged in age from three to fifteen. Students usually received six hours of instruction in the morning and afternoon. (The times of instruction were usually from around nine to twelve in the morning and three to six in the afternoon, with some variation.) Subjects taught included the reading of Hebrew and translation of Torah, the Bible, Talmud and the Prophets. More importantly, though, it should be recognized that many, perhaps even most, students in the heders, attended public schools in the morning and early afternoon as well, even if this was only in deference to state law. Given that nearly 90 per cent of Jewish children in Cracow attended public schools, the heders no longer served as the only way to educate Jewish children. Rather, they served as, often, the only way for children to receive a Jewish education that was completely in the hands of Jews. The statistics make it clear that education in the public schools had superseded a traditional heder education. To date I have not found any information indicating the number of heder students who went on to private Jewish education, though it is likely that at least some of them continued in the Cheder Iwri (Hebrew School) schools, the more traditional private Jewish school alternative, while others may well have continued in other less traditional secondary schools, including trade schools.[28]

The government's reforms of the heders were a part of Polish attempts to modernize the newly independent Polish state. The 1919 reform was overwhelmingly successful. By 1929, 82 per cent of Jewish children across Poland attended Polish public schools. The percentage in Cracow was slightly higher, 89.9 per cent.[29] The Polish educational reforms, Polish anti-Semitism, the national ideals of the Jewish community itself, and the fact that a majority of Jewish children attended Polish public schools all combined to make real the need for private Jewish schools. Private Jewish schools such as those established in Cracow during the inter-war period aimed to train Jews to live within Jewish and Polish culture, the latter if only as a necessity for an economically successful life. Such schools by definition represented a response of the Jewish community to modernization, which not only had made school attendance mandatory but also increasingly valued a secondary education.

An official school inspection report for one of Cracow's Talmud Torah schools in 1938 reveals a school in dire need of major improvements to meet contemporary educational standards. The Talmud Torah school, for children of pre-school age, was located in a building with two floors on Ester Street. The courtyard was connected to a house of prayer. The building itself was described as virtually destroyed, without any kind of renovation or preservation.[30] Approximately 1,200 boys attended this one school in 1937–38.[31] In the eyes of the Polish school inspectors, remodelling was the most important priority and the list of improvements needed gives some idea of the desperate conditions in which young Jews found themselves. These included damaged concrete steps and floors, problems with plumbing and iron stoves, and puddles of water on wooden steps. Books and old rags were found on the same shelves in old cabinets. Bathroom sinks lacked soap and towels. In general, the conditions were unhygienic. This same report urged the immediate correction of the lack of signs for the bathrooms in Polish. The inspector was also concerned that the general public passing by on Ester Street also used the toilets and this contributed to the primitive conditions of the facilities in general. The courtyard and building were dirty and poorly maintained. In addition, sweets and other foods were sold to the children in the narrow hallways. The inspectors described the lack of electricity and the signs on the bathroom doors as problems that the school should resolve 'without delay, not later than the thirtieth of August 1938, under the penalty of the closing of the cheder if found not in compliance'.[32]

Classes were overcrowded; the benches were not suited for the size of the students; and the students themselves, their clothes, their notebooks, were also dirty. The teachers taught as they liked, and many were not prepared for their lessons. There were too few hours of study for certain subjects, and no courses in drawing, music or physical education were offered. The report also singled out the afternoon study period, when students were tired from the day's earlier classes, as the cause of poor student results. City school authorities recommended in 1938 that the entire school be cleaned, teaching methods be improved, with greater attention paid to the level of writing and pronunciation, more hours of instruction in general, including field trips. Significantly, the report also recommended that the school purchase new portraits of Polish leaders and Polish state seals for the school hallways.

During his visit to Cracow in 1924, the German Jewish writer Alfred Döblin visited a Talmud Torah on Ester Street, most probably the one described above by the Polish school inspectors. Döblin wrote the following about his observation of a class at the school:

> The teacher is on a platform again, a boy with a book next to him: an eager repartee between them. Meanwhile, the forty other boys, between eight and twelve years old, sit around at their desks, behind books swaying their upper bodies lightly or intensely, some quite wildly, whispering, speaking, singing, prattling. 'They are learning,' says the red-faced old man from above. [The Yiddish verb *lernen* means 'to study a holy book'.] They all wear lovely black round skullcaps; they're all squeaky clean; their earlocks are long. They stand up, class is over, they run past us to the door. Some walk gently and earnestly. What a black, melancholy glow in their eyes. And a new class, older boys studying a passage from the Talmud. The rooms are separated only by wood; the purring, the confused talking, the chanted learning resound from right and left. Over nine hundred pupils in this huge old house. I've never seen a school like this.[33]

Inspectors also criticized another Jewish elementary school, the Jesodej Hatora (The Basics of the Torah) school. A total of 243 students attended this school in 1938, all listed as of Polish nationality but Mosaic confession.[34] The inspector criticized the elderly director of the school, Henryk Teufel, a retired teacher, for leading an inefficient staff and for not taking the initiative necessary to make needed changes. According to the report, teachers obviously did not clean their classrooms and did not work very hard. Students worked for twelve hours without a break, from six in the morning to six in the evening, with Jewish subjects in the first part of the day. A 1936 report stated that there was only one square metre of space for each of the 226 students.[35] The inspector wrote, 'In these conditions, it is difficult to speak about education – it simply does not exist.'[36] Perhaps the real issue was the fact that 'state education' (*wychowanie państwowe*) was 'barely evident', and then only during official inspections, and that a sort of Jewish nationalism was felt 'at every step'.[37]

The report also criticized the school for holding only 120 hours of instruction in secular subjects rather than the required 172. At the same time, the school devoted 184 hours of instruction to Jewish subjects. In comparison with public schools, this school just did not fulfil its task, and Polish school authorities refused accreditation. Accreditation would have allowed students unhindered access to secondary education. Students who attended elementary and secondary schools with public rights were more easily admitted to the next educational level and so the issue of public rights was important to parents.

One of the reports for Jesodej Hatora indicates more specifically the nature of the school's educational efforts in Polish language and culture.[38] Curriculum guides included many educational objectives for Polish language and Polish history, notably the telling of common fairy tales in Polish, such as 'Jaś i Małgosia' (similar to Hansel and Gretel) and 'Kopciuszek' (Cinderella) and the royal history of Poland, including accounts of the battle at Grunwald, the events depicted in Jan Matejko's historical paintings and, of course, the exploits of Józef Piłsudski. Indicating the extent to which these Jewish educators mollified official Polish authorities, the curriculum guide lists the pictures the school hung on the wall – images of *górale*, fishermen, traditional dress from the Cracow region, modern Polish industry and trains, in addition to the usual illustrations of plants and animals, health and hygiene, and symbols for maths and geometry. The pictures of Polish industry may have been mere decoration in a school in which Jewish religious education was the primary goal. But interestingly, students in the fifth, sixth and seventh grades of this school could participate in science classes with Public School Nr 5 in Kazimierz. Nevertheless, the co-operation with Public School Nr 5 suggests accommodation to a multi-ethnic environment, a way in which students in a private Jewish school encountered Polish students and secular learning.

THE HEBREW GYMNASIUM

Jewish youth were often in the forefront of battles for the definition of the Jewish community in inter-war Poland. The

Zionist youth organizations, so important in Cracow and throughout Poland, attest to the changes young Jews were bringing to the Polish community, just as the development of private Jewish schools indicates the importance Jewish leaders placed on educating those who would eventually replace them. The nature of the institutions formed for the benefit of Jewish youth was often in dispute. While few would argue that youth is naive and that individual youths need role models, as Moyshe Blekher suggested in an article in *Di post*, Blekher's further assertions were more controversial. According to Blekher, the most pressing problem facing Jewish youth was that 90 per cent of the Jewish teachers in the private Jewish schools were thoroughly assimilated. They pledged their allegiance to a 'foreign state and a foreign culture'.[39] Blekher claimed that students transferring from public schools to private Jewish schools were going from one 'gehenna' to another. Blekher's harsh criticism is in line with his often derogatory remarks about the city's polonized Jewish leadership and his support of Yiddish culture. But Blekher ignored the complexity of the Jewish reality and dismissed the efforts of Jewish leaders to establish schools in line with particular beliefs, whether religious or Zionist. By the late 1930s, the city's Hebrew gymnasium had served as a model Jewish institution for twenty years, providing an education in Jewish subjects and in the language, literature and history of Poland, a 'foreign state and a foreign culture'. But as the memoirs of Jews from Cracow who had been students at the Hebrew gymnasium attest, Poland and Polish were perhaps not as foreign to them as Blekher claimed.

The most important private Jewish school in the city was the Hebrew gymnasium. As one graduate described his alma mater, 'The school was a sort of oasis where pupils could maintain an illusion that the world was and would remain a benevolent place.'[40] A forerunner of the gymnasium had been founded before the outbreak of the First World War, thanks to the efforts of Shlomo Leser, the leader of the school in its early years. The original intent of Leser and other early leaders of the gymnasium was to teach young Jews Hebrew in preparation for emigration to Palestine. The school opened in 1908 and later became a gymnasium, eventually receiving full accreditation from the Polish government in 1924, enabling its students to take the *matura* and enter the university. In the 1930s a trade school was established in co-operation with the gymnasium. The Hebrew gymnasium (its full name: Żydowskie Gimnazjum Koedukacyjnego, or Jewish Coeducational Gymnasium) arose out of the efforts of the Association of the Jewish Elementary and Middle School, founded by Jewish leaders in 1902 to form a private Jewish school. By the late 1930s, the efforts of the society had resulted in three different schools addressing the educational needs of the Jewish community. An elementary school opened in 1908–09 and grew to over one hundred students by 1912. The gymnasium was founded in 1918 with only fifteen students. A coeducational institution, it had more than 750 students by 1937. Because of this tremendous growth, a third school grew out of the gymnasium, a lyceum with three departments: humanities, mathematics-physics and natural sciences. In 1933–34, the association opened a three-year trade school that graduated its first apprentices in 1936. This was certainly an important achievement of the Jewish community. Private Jewish education could no longer be associated merely with the heders. The movement for private Jewish education in Poland had adopted modern pedagogical ideas and educational success.

Shlomo Leser, a descendant of the original founder and a previous student at the gymnasium, outlined the changes of the school in a short history. According to Leser, the goals the association set for the school in 1913 were 'to raise Jews for God, for people, for Israel and for the world of deeds'.[41] These goals were modified over the years. In 1921 the goals were enumerated in order of importance:

1. General education and Hebrew education comprising all of the Hebrew culture
2. Hebrew education in the spirit of absolute attachment and commitment to his people and to his people's striving for a cultural and political renaissance in Erets Yisrael
3. Good citizenship
4. Educational process focusing on the foundations of the moral principles of Judaism and of humanity
5. Physical education and love for work.

By 1936, those same goals were more succinctly stated, most likely, Leser suggests, for the benefit of a political state that could grant or withhold the public rights that entitled students of the school to be considered for admission to Polish universities. The aim in the late 1930s was 'to create a good citizen, a Jew conscious (of his Jewishness) and a human being of value'.

Inspection reports of the school address some minor areas for improvement, but were in general rather positive.[42] The detailed nature of these reports, including comments on the placement of chairs next to the radiators, lends credence to the criticisms and overall positive evaluation. The students in the school came from the professional intelligentsia and merchant families, and a rather high number of parents, around 70 to 80 per cent, took part in the parents' organization.[43] Attesting to the popularity of the school and this type of education, the younger grades often had more than fifty students in each class, as the school accepted more students than normal year after year. The inspector expressed concern at the increased class size. The school employed thirty-three teachers, some of whom worked in the public schools as well. The inspector suggested that the teaching of Polish history and knowledge of Poland should apply greater emphasis to contemporary issues and problem solving. The minor criticisms (*bolączki*, in the Polish of the inspection report) included an admonition to the students to take better care of their uniforms. The report also criticized the organization of laboratories as not demanding enough of the students and encouraged the development of a geography lab.

Regarding the general atmosphere at the school, the inspector wrote, 'The academic level of the students is high. They are interested in their lessons, they are lively, gladly participate in class discussions, and conduct independent work. Written work in Polish is at the normal level. All the teachers pay close attention to the written work, to making corrections as well as to the students' notebooks.'[44] Overall, though, the reports of the level of the students were very good, and the inspector was pleased with the degree of student involvement in the learning process. The report was highly favourable.

Significantly, the inspectors noted that the school trained its students in the 'Jewish national spirit' as well, indicating the dual task faced by Jewish educators in Poland. 'Along with the education of the youth as citizens of the state, work in the national (Jewish) spirit is conducted in all sincerity and also without agitation.'[45] An earlier report from 1935 described the leaders of the school as Zionists, but not particularly vocal. The inspector at that time wrote,

> The Jewish Coeducational Gymnasium in Cracow is led by a Jewish society composed of Zionists. The same can be said of the director and the teachers of the school; none of these persons, though, are particularly vocal, which means that they take every opportunity to stress the citizen's relationship to Poland. The teaching of Polish language, history and geography is at a proper level from the moment students will benefit from an education in citizenship.[46]

The inspector's remarks were perhaps the highest compliments the inspector could have given the school. The Hebrew gymnasium had been successful in integrating a programme geared towards developing Jewish national identity into a rigorous school curriculum that met the requirements set forth by the Polish educational authorities. That Jews could study alongside other Jews in an environment free of anti-Semitism was the unique factor of the school. The importance of such an experience should not be underestimated.

This was perhaps the reason so many were attracted to the school. Certainly the excellent education and shared Jewish national ideals were also factors. Discussing the background of the student body, Natan Gross, a student at the school, divided the student population into three categories: students like himself who were more assimilated (*zasymilowany*), the more religious students who came to the gymnasium after some initial study at the Tachkemoni school (another secondary school in the city, discussed further below), and the students who described themselves politically as Zionist Revisionists (followers of the militant Zionism of Vladmir Jabotinsky). Gross's categorization reflects the distinctions within the Jewish community. These diverse groups, seemingly so different in outlook, none the less met in the Hebrew gymnasium, making an education there a singular experience.

This singular experience, however, was limited to those who could afford it or those fortunate enough to receive financial aid.

Irena Bronner described the students at the Hebrew gymnasium as wealthy or rich, a step up from the middle-class families whose children were her classmates at the public Klementyna z Tańskich Hoffmanowa School. Tuition fees were especially important, because 72 per cent of the school's budget came from tuition and only 5 per cent from the *kehillah*.[47] Children from poorer families or middle-class families who needed financial help to send their children to a private school, like Bronner, often received a 50 per cent discount. Still, even wealthier families occasionally had a difficult time paying the school's relatively high tuition on time. Bronner recalled that those late with the tuition were sometimes asked to leave class immediately. The high tuition fees of the Hebrew gymnasium were an issue in the Yiddish press as well. *Dos yidishe vort*, for example, criticized the high fees of the Hebrew gymnasium whenever the cost of tuition was raised. In his brief study of the Hebrew gymnasium, Shlomo Leser explains how students had to produce a pass in order to enter the building; the pass indicated whether students' parents had paid the required tuition. If not, the student was sent home. Leser termed this practice drastic and pedagogically worrisome. The method adopted later in place of the pass does not seem like one that would have alleviated any individual embarrassment. The names of students whose tuition had not been paid were read out in the classroom and only then were the students sent home.[48]

Rafael Scharf's writings on Cracow challenge these criticisms of the school's high tuition. According to Scharf, 'Fees were modest, most pupils had them reduced, nobody was barred from admission for lack of funds.'[49] Scharf tells a story high-lighting the democratic nature of the school. Recalling a familiar beggar on the streets of Kazimierz, a man with no legs, Scharf remembers,

> One day it came to my knowledge that this beggar had offspring. I was startled out of my wits – how does he do it? I found out about this because he applied for his son to be admitted to our school – my Father was on the committee adjudicating exemptions from fees. This became the subject of a heated argument over the dinner table. My Father thought such ambition arrogant and presumptuous, whereas my brother and I argued that the beggar's son had

an entitlement equal to ours, if not better. Better?! – my Father nearly had an apoplectic fit, fearing that he had fathered a couple of imbeciles.[50]

Students who were able to attend the school received what has been described as a first-rate education. Some of the teachers were especially popular, especially the Hebrew teacher Nakhman Mifelew and, perhaps the most beloved of all, the Polish literature professor Juliusz Feldhorn. Both were involved in many extracurricular activities and well-known for their achievements in their fields outside of the gymnasium. Mifelew continually promoted the use of Hebrew within the Jewish community even as his stories and articles appeared in the Jewish children's magazine published in Cracow, *Okienko na Świat*. Feldhorn was known for preparing students excellently for future study of the Polish language and literature, sometimes at Cracow's Jagiellonian University.[51]

As Feldhorn's literature classes indicate, the linguistic assimilation of Cracow's Jewish community can also be seen in the Hebrew gymnasium. Though the school was established to impart to Jewish students a Jewish national identity and knowledge of Hebrew, Gross asserts that Polish was the language that dominated the school. Hebrew was used only in classes dealing with Jewish subjects. Gross further clarified the issue of language use in the school:

> Yiddish was not heard in the hallways. It is true, too, that one did not hear Hebrew either, unless a student spoke with a teacher of one of the Hebrew subjects. Because at our school – not like in the schools of the Tarbut network, where the language of instruction was Hebrew and mathematics, biology, history, etc. were also taught in the sacred language – only four subjects were taught in the language of our ancestors: Hebrew (language and literature), Bible, religion and Jewish history. All others – in Polish.[52]

Gross describes a school where Hebrew held the most important position among foreign languages, implying, of course, that Hebrew was taught only as a foreign language and that Polish was the *de facto* language of the school. Gross himself wrote that he was not happy with his Hebrew teachers. 'Did it come to me easily?' he writes. 'Well, not Hebrew, which I regret to this day … But perhaps this was not so much me, as it was the teachers.'[53] According to Gross, they knew Hebrew, but they were poor teachers. Like Ritterman-Abir, Gross considered Hebrew the weakest of his foreign languages when he found himself in Israel after the war. Gross himself is convinced that he could have been a good Hebraist, had he only had better instruction in the Hebrew gymnasium.

Jewish leaders in Cracow did address the difficulties of learning Hebrew. As early as 1921, the society that founded the Hebrew gymnasium was already undertaking efforts to expose teachers of Hebrew to new pedagogical ideas.[54] The cultural section of the central Hebrew school commission, part of the Zionist organization in Cracow, sponsored a course on pedagogy held in the Hebrew gymnasium. Cracow was one of the last large cities in Poland where such courses were established. Teachers of Hebrew learned new pedagogical methods. The writer Felicja Infeld-Stendigowa pointed out that mothers faced great difficulty as their children learned much more about Jewish national culture and Hebrew than they knew themselves.[55] Stendigowa called for special Hebrew courses for Jewish women so they could co-operate more fully with the Jewish national school in their children's education. In one case, a grandfather took advantage of the opportunity to learn Hebrew along with his granddaughter, indicating that the family had acculturated to the Polish language from Yiddish a generation earlier.[56]

Though students knew Polish better than they knew Hebrew, the significance of a Jewish school with Hebrew as the language of instruction is difficult to overestimate. A Hebrew gymnasium was a new kind of school in Poland, and perhaps its importance lies more in the fact that it provided a safe haven for young Jews than in its promotion of Hebrew. Gross explains,

> How was a Hebrew school different than a Polish school? In a Polish school the Jew had to be a good student, perhaps even better than others, but a Hebrew school allowed one to be a bad student, to neglect lessons and disregard teachers, to misbehave as much as the spirit wished, to cut school.

This was an oasis, an island isolated from the Polish reality, though Poland and Polishness in all its manifestations was here in our Hebrew school, represented and transmitted better than Jewishness...[57]

The school was instrumental in returning Jews to an identification with Jewish culture, even as it built an educational environment in both Polish and Hebrew.

As the Hebrew gymnasium grew, it even attracted the attention of parents who had already moved beyond the Jewish neighbourhood of Kazimierz, leaving their Jewish heritage behind. In 1936, L. Kahanowa described this phenomenon in a short description of the gymnasium in *Ogniwa*:

Parents who not long ago would have cringed at the thought of sending their children to school 'in Kazimierz' now try diligently to get their children accepted to the school of this society, quickly teaching them Hebrew, as required for acceptance. We are witnesses to an interesting phenomenon. These children from nearly completely assimilated families are bringing national feeling, an attachment to Jewish tradition and a deep love of Palestine, which they absorb in school, into their homes and families. What a wonderful thing.[58]

This startling evidence is one of the few indications that there was an almost completely assimilated sphere of Jewish families that would not think of being associated with Kazimierz. Further, it is evidence that the efforts of the founders of the association reached parts of the Jewish community that one might have thought lost to assimilation. At least some Jewish parents were choosing the Hebrew gymnasium over private Polish schools. In short, the Jewish nationalists of Cracow were extending their influence within the Jewish community. Thus, those Jews who reconsidered their decision not to send their children to school in Kazimierz became more, rather than less, affiliated with the Jewish community during the inter-war period. One can assume that this reverse assimilation went only so far. It is not likely that these families stopped identifying with Polish culture once they had found a way to identify with Jewish culture that was comfortable to them. They more probably maintained their ties to the Polish community while nurturing a newly intensified connection to the Jewish community. Education not only provided a path to accommodation with the Polish majority but also a path for assimilated Jews back to Jewish culture.

The Hebrew gymnasium did indeed introduce a new culture to Jewish youth; it served as a place where young Jews could assert their Jewish identity without fear of confrontation or conflict. Shlomo Leser recalled that during the school year 1936–37 an army official directed exercises in the school for a statewide military training programme once a week.[59] The official's relations with the students were fairly good, though formal. Once, however, he crossed an unspoken and undefined boundary, perhaps, as Leser suggests, because he wanted to get closer to the students. Standing in line, the students heard him call out unexpectedly 'Whoever is of Polish nationality, step forward.' Nobody did. The official knew that the school was a Zionist institution but, according to Leser, he did not know enough to not ask such a question, even in a way that Leser describes as not threatening or racist.

The transition for those students transferring from other schools involved a real adjustment to another type of atmosphere. Neither the atmosphere in the public schools nor the environment of the private Jewish school was necessarily the gehenna Blekher described. Irena Bronner, who argued with her mother about going to the Hebrew gymnasium, was eventually grateful for her mother's insistence that she attend the school.[60] Yet, in spite of her real love and affection for the school's faculty and her classmates, she wrote, 'In spite of its many positive qualities, the Hebrew gymnasium was a little stuffy, a little "like the ghetto". I was interested in other matters, other people and I placed my hopes in a country building itself anew.'[61] Though Halina Nelken first attended the gymnasium under drastically different circumstances, when the Germans forbade Jews to attend other schools after their occupation of Poland in 1939, her comments reflect Bronner's:

> School is forbidden to Jews, unless it is the Hebrew school. Papa has already enrolled me, but I don't know how I will

manage there because so many subjects are strange to me. I don't know Hebrew and Hebrew literature, and I hardly remember the history of the Jews.

It's all over with the Hebrew gimnazium. The Germans have closed it. There were searches in Kazimierz, they beat the Jews, plundered the Temple and the synagogues. The Torah and books were thrown out into the mud and trampled, the old Jews were pulled by their beards and shaved. They are rounding up the Jews on the streets for the most humiliating work – so how could they allow us to get an education? Well anyway, I do not miss this school, I felt alien there. It was not my gimnazium.[62]

The Hebrew gymnasium ranks high as an important Jewish institution during the inter-war period because of its substantial growth from its beginnings immediately after the war and, not least, because of its place in the memories of Jews from Cracow in Israel. It is important to remember, though, that its achievements represent only one of the many Jewish subcultures within inter-war Cracow. While the school had grown into one of the city's most important Jewish institutions by the 1930s, the gymnasium did not provide an education for all Jewish children in Cracow. New educational ventures of the association working on behalf of the school, such as the trade school, indicate that Cracow's Jewish leaders were introducing innovative developments that might have ultimately transformed the city's Jewish community. While Bronner pointed out that some children were publicly embarrassed because of their parents' inability to pay tuition on time, she also suggested that class distinctions within the gymnasium did not necessarily affect students' progress. According to Bronner, even poorer students could do well at the gymnasium.[63] Still, though, other schools for poorer Jewish children remained a necessity, just as ways to reach Jewish children in public schools would become increasingly more important as the process of linguistic assimilation continued.

The local Jewish community and parents' organizations supported the Hebrew gymnasium as much as possible. The community in general encouraged a kind of Jewish education that emphasized Hebrew language and literature but which also recognized the need for its students to be trained to enter the university; this entailed a thorough education in Polish culture as well. *Dos yidishe vort* simultaneously praised the efforts of the gymnasium while also criticizing it in an effort to encourage it to provide the best traditional education for its students. More concerned about the religious education the students received, *Dos yidishe vort* was consistently more critical of the school than *Nowy Dziennik*. Still, the Yiddish paper enthusiastically championed the efforts of the educators who founded the Hebrew gymnasium and offered suggestions for improvement. That such different groups came together in at least one Jewish institution indicates that some Jewish community leaders appealed successfully to the larger community.

While the school's efforts to resurrect Hebrew as a spoken language met with some success, however limited, the original goal, to prepare students for emigration to Palestine, was not met. Jewish students at the gymnasium did receive a solid education in Hebrew language and culture (along with Polish, as required by the state), but students did not go to Palestine upon graduation in record numbers.[64] They remained largely in Poland, and it is important to ask why they stayed and how these students, trained in a more Jewish environment than their peers, affected Jewish, and Polish, community life. As war intervened, the students who survived did make significant contributions to the Jewish community, but in Israel rather than in Poland. When Chaim Hilfstein, the last director of the Hebrew gymnasium, arrived in Israel in 1946 after surviving the Holocaust, former faculty and students of the gymnasium already there welcomed him warmly. Shortly thereafter, the graduates of the gymnasium formed an Association of Former Students of the Hebrew Gymnasium in Cracow.[65] Many of its members came to prominence in politics, the arts or academia. The organization included two Knesset members and government ministers, Elimelech Rimalt and Chaim Landau. Natan Gross became a prominent journalist writing in Hebrew and in Polish, and Miriam Akavia wrote novels in Hebrew, some of which she based on her family's experiences in Cracow. Like Gross, the poet and historian Meir Bosak wrote for the Israeli press in both Hebrew and Polish. Moshe Landau and Emanuel Meltzer became historians of the Jewish experience in Poland and developed the study of East European Jewish history in Israeli universities.

Not all former faculty and alumni of the gymnasium lived in Israel after the war, however. Seeing little chance of pursuing his chosen field of law because of anti-Semitism, and fearing for his future in Poland, Rafael F. Scharf left for London in 1938, where he was a correspondent for *Nowy Dziennik*. He later became an important voice in Jewish journalism with his work on the *Jewish Quarterly*, published in London. His recent collection of writings attests to a deeply felt connection to the city of his birth.[66] Others remained active in Polish culture, notably faculty members Chaim Löw, Maksymilian Boruchowicz and Artur Sandauer. Löw, who taught Polish language and literature at the gymnasium, was known before the war for his translations into Yiddish of Homer's *Iliad* and *Odyssey*. After surviving the war in the Soviet Union, he returned to Poland and, under the name Leon Przemski, became a prolific writer of historical novels, biographies and popular works on linguistics.[67] Maksymilian Boruchowicz, writing under the name Michał Borwicz, published memoirs of his time at the university in Cracow and edited a Polish-language anthology of literature from the concentration camps.[68] Sandauer became one of Poland's most important literary critics.[69] The continued affiliation with Poland of these former Hebrew gymnasium students and faculty suggests that attending or working for the Hebrew gymnasium did not guarantee that the student or faculty member would always privilege his or her Jewish identity.

COMBINING RELIGIOUS AND SECULAR STUDY

The Hebrew gymnasium was successful in educating students who, in terms of their intellectual abilities and cultural interests, were comfortable in both Polish and Jewish culture. Not all private Jewish education aimed at such a well-rounded secular experience. The founders of Cheder Iwri took another approach to private Jewish primary and secondary education. They founded the school with 'the thought that it was possible to combine in the same educational establishment Jewish learning in a strictly religious and traditional sense with the secular education according to the programme of the government schools'.[70] Cheder Iwri was founded in 1921 as a three-class elementary school but grew to the extent that the addition of a gymnasium, the later Tachkemoni school, was necessary in 1931. A new three-floor building erected at Miodowa 26 held both the Cheder Iwri elementary school and Tachkemoni, the boys' gymnasium. Wordliczek asserts that the Tachkemoni gymnasium was the only one of its type in Poland, combining general knowledge with Jewish subjects.[71] In 1936/37, the Cheder Iwri Association expanded its activities even further, establishing a one-year vocational school for thirteen- to eighteen-year-old boys who had already completed an elementary school education. This school combined instruction in general subjects with both a professional and Judaic education.

The Cheder Iwri organization clearly did not have the same extensive resources as the Hebrew gymnasium. Still, when parents did not have the money for tuition, the association granted discounts and allowed many students to attend for free. Established in 1921–22 with only three classes, the Cheder Iwri elementary school grew to seven grades in 1925 with 193 students and fifteen teachers (seven instructing in Hebrew, eight in Polish). In the first four grades, the majority of time was spent on Jewish subjects. In the first grade, eighteen hours of weekly classroom instruction went to Jewish subjects and twelve to secular subjects. The second grade increased the number of hours spent studying Jewish subjects to twenty-four while secular studies still were the focus of twelve hours of instruction. In the third and fourth grades, students spent the same amount of time on Jewish studies, but increased their hours in secular studies to eighteen. In the sixth and seventh grades, they continued this level of secular study, while increasing the hours spent in Jewish subjects to thirty.

In the words of an official school inspector, the Cheder Iwri schools served their purpose. Orthodox parents would be unlikely to send their kids to any public school if it were not Orthodox in character. The inspector wrote: 'In this way youth receive a general education and are educated not only in a religious spirit, but also in a spirit of state citizenship (*obywatelsko-państwowym*). Moreover, the school will not hinder its students on their road to eventual higher studies.'[72] At the very least, from the inspector's point of view, the children received some type of education and this was, if not sufficient, at least acceptable. Most importantly from the point of view of the state, the school did not hinder its students from going further in their education. In other words, the school did no harm and, in providing an education in citizenship, did some real good. Rather than viewing such schools negatively, the Polish authorities liked the idea of these private schools because they ensured that the law regarding public education would be obeyed and they gave the state yet another venue to promote its version of civic education. The school authorities also expressed the desire for Jews to continue their education as far as possible. Both Poles and Jews still viewed education as the best solution to the poverty of their societies. While the Polish government appreciated the opportunity to educate its citizens in the apparent virtues of the Polish state, Jews maintained their identity by educating their own people in their own way. Yet, at the same time, Orthodox Jewish educational leaders and teachers adapted to the reality of Polish government.

Next to the Hebrew gymnasium, the Tachkemoni school in Cracow was one of the most important private Jewish secondary schools. Developed from courses that had already begun in 1926–27 with classes sponsored by the Cheder Iwri Association, the gymnasium itself was founded in 1931.[73] The Tachkemoni gymnasium was not nearly as sophisticated pedagogically as the Hebrew gymnasium. In an official report, the inspector recommended that teaching methods be developed and applied. In spite of relatively poor pedagogical standards, the gymnasium sponsored many different academic organizations for its students covering all kinds of interests. The students none the less participated in musical radio auditions and the citywide school theatre programme. According to the inspector, they came from conservative religious and Orthodox families, or middle-class artisan and merchant families from Cracow and neighbouring communities.[74] Forty-seven parents, roughly half, participated in the school's parents' organization. Inspectors' recommendations for the school focused on enlarging the physical facilities, the labs, and getting its own gym. In the late 1930s, the school usually employed eight to nine teachers for around sixty-five to eighty students. A majority of the teachers were fully qualified, with state certification and a university degree. About ten of the students lived at the school.

Inspection reports from the school from 1935 and 1936 identified its educational objectives as 'specifically Orthodox-religious' and 'preparing students for the rabbinate'.[75] A year later, in 1937, these objectives were expressed differently. The orientation of the school had changed to one where, according to school officials, the goal was to produce a 'faithful Jew, a citizen of Poland'.[76] Here school officials stated their dual task explicitly. This may have been due to fear of government officials or the pressure to meet state guidelines that required a minimal level of Polish education in the schools. Even so, this shift in stated educational objectives is itself an accommodation to Polish culture. The 1937 report on the school in the *Almanac of Jewish Education* further illustrates how the school stood on both sides of the fence, between humanism and the Torah, science and faith, belief in the self and belief in humanity. The educator Meir Korzennik described how the school's philosophy fostered both religious and secular learning:

> Often in Polish language lessons one encounters words from the Bible and the Prophets. Study from the Talmud facilitates learning in the hard sciences. History or biology lessons not only illustrate examples of citizenship or general humanity but also call forth praise in the honour of God ... Science through belief ... belief through science! This is the way one may formulate the essence, and actual scientific and educational results, of this Jewish middle school, the only one of its type in Poland.[77]

The leaders of this school were willing to see themselves as Polish citizens as long as they were able to remain faithful Jews. Admittedly, they had no real choice, but none the less they did conform to the standard of Polish citizenship that was expected of them and, at the same time, promote the practice and maintenance of Jewish traditions.[78]

The Private Coeducational Gymnasium of the Jewish Social School Association (*Prywatne Gimnazjum Koedukacyjne Towarzystwo Żydowskiej Szkoły Społecznej*) opened in 1937, and took yet another approach to Jewish education.[79] The school was not located in Kazimierz or the nearby neighbourhood of Podgórze, but directly on the market square, at Rynek Główny

17.[80] Children aged twelve to sixteen attended this four-class, coeducational school where the language of instruction was Polish. A KOSK inspector's report of the facilities is generally fair, though the inspector notes there is no gym or biology lab, largely because there were so few students.[81] More importantly, the inspector remarked that the teachers were qualified but uninterested, that the school needed some pedagogical platform, and that the classes still had to be structured according to a real curriculum. The inspector recommended some course improvements for the autumn if and when enrolment grew. A later inspection from November 1938 repeated some of the same criticisms, but recommended that the school look for a new location in which it could develop further.[82] While the inspector's report was critical in some ways, it also made helpful recommendations. This school was neither explicitly religious nor nationalist; moreover, its location on the main market square (rather than in Kazimierz) suggests that it may have tried to serve a segment of the Jewish population that was not satisfied with either the Hebrew gymnasium or the Cheder Iwri and Tachkemoni schools. Its founding in 1937 suggests that it may have been a reaction to the increased anti-Semitism of the late 1930s. The establishment of the school is certainly evidence of a community providing for its own educational needs until the very outbreak of war.

THE EDUCATION OF JEWISH GIRLS

While coeducational schools grew and developed during the inter-war period, those who wished Jewish girls to receive a separate education could turn to the Beys Yakov schools, founded in Cracow. Some Jewish girls did attend heders even before the inter-war period, but it is unclear what type of education they received there; generally speaking, traditional religious education was closed to Jewish girls, a fact which accounts for the high number of Jewish girls in secular schools in Eastern Europe. During the inter-war period, the distinction between the education of Jewish boys and girls was blurring, as both Jewish boys and girls attended the secular public schools in overwhelming numbers. Still, though, the Cheder Iwri and

Tachkemoni schools, for example, enrolled only Jewish boys, and girls had fewer private Jewish alternatives.

Sore Shenirer began the most influential educational trend to emerge from Jewish Cracow. In November 1917, Shenirer began to realize her dream of providing a religious education for Jewish girls by opening a small one-room school on Katarzyna Street in Kazimierz. After the war, Agudes yisroel and the Jewish Senator to the Polish *Sejm* from Cracow, Mojżesz Deutscher, supported Shenirer's efforts, which led to the development of the Beys Yakov schools for girls.[83] Such schools were founded all across Poland and the educational movement had spread to many foreign countries by the 1930s. Beys Yakov schools comprised many different types of educational facilities, including an elementary school, trade schools and religious courses, which were after-school religious classes for Jewish girls who attended public school. Most important, a teachers' college to train teachers for the Beys Yakov schools was founded in Cracow. A total of 120 young women participated in this school in 1937.[84]

By the time of Shenirer's death in 1935, over 200 Beys Yakov schools had been founded worldwide with over 20,000 students. Shenirer's efforts to teach Jewish girls the basics of their religion no doubt transformed Jewish society in ways that may not yet be recognized. Shenirer serves as an example of the importance of Jewish Orthodoxy to the Jews of Cracow, despite their reputation as an acculturated community. Shenirer was born in Cracow into a Hasidic family in 1883. Attracted to religious study, she found herself in a non-traditional position for a religious Jewish woman. Seeking an outlet, Shenirer even attended at least one meeting of Christian women, but because of the strictures of religious orthodoxy, she was not able to fulfil her dreams of a higher religious education for herself. Instead she worked as a seamstress and dreamed of providing 'spiritual raiment' for the same girls for whom she was making clothing.[85] It was in Vienna during the First World War that she came under the influence of Rabbi Dr Flesch, whose lectures on the history of the Jews and Jewish Orthodoxy in the Austrian capital's Stumpfergasse synagogue inspired her to realize her dream of starting a Jewish school for girls.[86]

For Shenirer, according to the Yiddish scholar Irena Klepfisz's reading of Shenirer's *Gezamlte Shriftn* [*Collected Writings*], 'language was the dress of the soul'. Klepfisz argues that Shenirer was something of an activist on behalf of Yiddish, desiring that her girls learn and speak in Yiddish. Some concessions were made, however, as the journal of the Beys Yakov educational movement, the *Bejs Yakov zhurnal*, appeared in both Polish and Yiddish in its initial issues. Many of Shenirer's young students made the argument that they could live fully Jewish lives in Polish as well as in Yiddish, but she disagreed, promoting the language politics of the Yiddish linguist Shloyme Birnboym and calling for signs to be put up around the schools saying, 'Speak only in Yiddish'. These anecdotes demonstrate that linguistic assimilation had already taken place, even among the Orthodox supporters of Agudes yisroel, those who would have been most likely to send their Jewish daughters to Shenirer's network of schools. In short, Shenirer had begun the fight for the survival of Yiddish. This is not meant to imply that Yiddish was dying, but it does show that individual Jewish students made conscious choices about which language to speak – and they did not always choose a Jewish language. The students' view that they could live Jewish lives in Polish as well as in Yiddish confirms that Jewish identity, even for a more religious population in Cracow, was changing, and suggests the girls' belief that their Jewish identity could withstand a degree of linguistic assimilation. It is ironic that this opinion came from the students at one of the more traditional Jewish schools in Cracow because it is so similar to Irena Klepfisz's own formulation of Jewish secular identity in the late twentieth century.[87]

Language use in the Beys Yakov school was a particularly difficult issue. While Yiddish was the preferred language of instruction in the Beys Yakov schools, it seems that the faculty had difficulty suppressing the use of Polish among the students.[88] From an excerpt from a Beys Yakov publication, we learn that Shenirer had to advocate the use of Yiddish by her students. Shenirer recognized that the faculty and students in the Beys Yakov schools were using Polish more often than Yiddish. At a nationwide conference, the school director J. L. Orlean had called on the faculty, the educational leaders themselves, to speak only Yiddish for a period of three months, so that they would learn to use Yiddish out of habit. Shenirer called on the students as well to speak Yiddish and explicitly rejected the attitude that Polish could be spoken as long as Yiddish was spoken at other times. Orlean's appeal to the faculty and Shenirer's remarks suggest that there was a significant degree of linguistic assimilation even among those attracted to private Jewish education. While this is impossible to quantify, it is important to note that Orlean and Shenirer recognized a need to make such comments in defence of Yiddish.

Shenirer's influence remains discernible today, as can be seen in the work of Beys Yakov schools in the United States and the many publications of Orthodox groups. Shenirer was an important figure in the history of Jewish women as well as in the history of Jewish education. The scholar Deborah Weissman includes Shenirer in a line of feminist developments in Jewish religious life because Shenirer's efforts succeeded in getting women outside of the home by providing them with more education.[89] Shenirer herself seems to have faded somewhat into the background once the men of Agudes yisroel took over her school and used it as the model for the group's women's educational programme.

By the late 1930s, secular education exclusively for Jewish girls was growing as well. Bronia Infeld founded *Our School* or *Nasza Szkoła*, located near the main market square, in 1937. The founding of a secular school for Jewish girls was likely a response to both the increased anti-Semitism of the late 1930s and the need for a different type of Jewish education not found in the Hebrew gymnasium, the Cheder Iwri and Tachkemoni schools, or the Beys Yakov schools. Nasza Szkoła serviced a population whose needs were not addressed by the religious school and perhaps not emphasized enough by the Hebrew gymnasium.

Leopold Infeld, the theoretical physicist and Bronia's brother, wrote about his sister's educational activities in his memoir *Szkice z przeszłości* [*Sketches from the Past*].[90] According to her brother, Bronia Infeld established Nasza Szkoła as a progressive alternative to the Hebrew gymnasium, which he described as 'rather reactionary'. The school was established as a co-operative; those who wanted to teach in the school were to invest in it one thousand zlotys. According to Leopold Infeld, the school did provide some competition for the Hebrew gymnasium. As the school was not founded until 1937, it is impossible to say whether or not it would have grown into a larger school that would have rivalled the Hebrew gymnasium. Its founding, though, is evidence that a part of the city's Jewish intelligentsia did not look favourably on the Hebrew gymnasium. Significantly, this also suggests the stratification of the Jewish community. The Hebrew gymnasium was explicitly Zionist, and this position concerned Infeld and those with whom she established the school. Bronia Infeld established a private Jewish school because she recognized the need for separate Jewish education. Infeld's effort is also notable because it occurred so late during the inter-war period. More than anything, educational efforts such as Infeld's indicate the tenacity of Jewish community leaders.

The establishment of the school was most likely the expression of a need for another form of Jewish education and a response to anti-Semitism. Celia Heller has documented how increasing anti-Semitism affected the number of Jewish students in private Polish and Jewish schools over the course of the inter-war period. She notes a drop of 28 per cent in the number of Jewish students in private Polish schools from 1925 to 1935.[91] Heller rightly attributes this decline to anti-Semitism, but it is important to remember that private Jewish schools were also a positive expression of Jewish identity, not simply a defensive reaction. Infeld's Nasza Szkoła shows that Polish Jews realized they needed a protected environment in which to educate their children but also that they were committed to improving their community and educating their children for their future as Polish citizens. The school was a refuge as well as an institution of cultural development. Jewish parents could have sent their children to the Jewish schools already established. The education provided in Nasza Szkoła was in Polish and the school represents a perhaps naive faith in Polish citizenship despite growing anti-Semitism. Infeld's task was a challenging one: to form a secular Jewish identity for people who may well have already assumed that a separate Jewish identity could not be sustained in a liberal Polish state.

The school opened in June 1937, and city inspectors visited the school for the first time on 29 October 1937.[92] Nasza Szkoła was located on the third floor in a rented building in the centre of town, at Starowiślna Nr 1. The school building had thirteen rooms, a biology lab, two sewing machines, a recreational hall, as well as rooms for teachers and administration. In the first year of its existence, the school was still developing its curriculum and raising money. By the second year, sixty students attended the school, twenty in the first grade, forty in the second.[93] Students came from the homes of the intelligentsia and, according to inspectors, 'spoke a correct and pure Polish'. The school's objectives 'set forth plans oriented towards both education in state citizenship and religious morals'.[94]

The remarks of the official inspectors indicate that the school was making considerable progress in its first year.[95] This was perhaps due in part to parental involvement. Parents were actively engaged in the life of the school, organizing a summer colony in Rabka and donating a piano to the school. In addition, the school organized its own musical auditions. Parent education was also an important aspect of the school's life, and, as in other private Jewish schools, the administration sponsored talks on different aspects of education.

Secular education exclusively for Jewish women, such as Bronia Infeld advocated, lagged far behind the developments of Shenirer's Beys Yakov schools. As Jewish girls had already been attending public and private Polish schools since the nineteenth century, this is perhaps not so surprising. Parents who accepted a secular education for their girls could simply send them to public or private Polish schools; they had several alternatives. In a school that placed little emphasis on religion, Infeld faced the task of making a secular education Jewish, while Shenirer aimed to provide a traditional religious education for a population she felt was in danger of assimilation. The education of Jewish girls in Cracow illustrates the diversity of the institutions Jews founded to develop their community. Whether single-sex, religious or secular, the private schools met specific needs of different parts of the population.

JEWISH VOCATIONAL EDUCATION

While educational leaders recognized the need for Jewish

vocational education, Jews interested in a more practical education for their people faced two obstacles: the tendency of Jews to prefer a more usual academic education and, once the schools were founded, how to integrate Jewish content into the vocational curriculum. The goal of the Private Jewish Coeducational Middle School for Trade of the Association of Jewish Graduates of the Higher Trade School in Cracow was to provide another alternative for Jewish children.[96] The founders of this school recognized that the education of Jewish students in either religious or secular topics with the sole intent of advanced study only served a minority group in the community. In their view, equally, if not more, important was the opportunity to obtain practical skills, a trade, necessary if Jews wished to make a living in the increasingly difficult economic times of the 1930s. They understood that even parents who realized their children would be working in a trade preferred an educational programme that concentrated on academic studies, but they established the school out of the need for practical training.

Samuel Stendig, the director of the school, opened the Middle School for Trade in August 1933. With slightly over a hundred students in three grades, the school grew to four hundred students in less than four years.[97] The school's curriculum aimed to provide a traditional education in the humanities with an emphasis on practical skills and trade courses. Languages of instruction included Polish and Hebrew but also English and German. The curriculum guide does not suggest that the goal of the school was to prepare its students to go to Palestine, but there was a special course on Palestine and the Near East. This course focused especially on economic aspects of the Near East and economic relations between Poland and Palestine.[98] It was most likely the presence of this course in the curriculum that led one newspaper writer to praise the special emphasis that the school placed on *both* civic education and Judaic subjects.[99]

The curriculum guide provides further evidence of the type of education the children in this school received. The school also offered arithmetic, bookkeeping, economics, geography, typing and two hours of religion and two hours of history and social studies (*nauka o państwie*, 'knowledge of the state'). In addition, the third grade had a one-hour class on contemporary Poland. This course included such topics as ethnic relations. Course descriptions for the language classes suggest that more attention was paid to the teaching of Polish than Hebrew. A high knowledge of Hebrew was the instructional aim, but the curriculum tasks simply prepared students for correspondence in Hebrew. In contrast, the guidelines for the Polish language classes included an additional emphasis on Polish literature.[100] Students in the school also participated in a range of different activities, including literary evenings, visits to the theatre, museums and exhibitions.

Additional courses were held in the school building of the Middle School for Trade for girls over seventeen and boys over eighteen who had finished elementary school,[101] and were intended for those 'of the Jewish faith, of Polish and Jewish nationality'.[102] The wording here is noteworthy. Even if one assumes that the phrase 'of the Jewish faith' or 'Jewish confession' was used merely to placate the Polish authorities who would be reading the statute, the organizers of the school who wrote the statute still described their prospective students as of both Polish and Jewish nationality. Private educational efforts entailed a degree of participation in the majority culture, even if this meant simply submitting such statutes, that they simply could not avoid. Further, the wording indicates that Jews themselves adopted a form of Polish nationality, recognizing the reality of their minority status.

The leaders of another school, the Private Jewish Coeducational Gymnasium of Cracow Merchants, saw a real need to train Jews to be able to conduct trade between Poland and Palestine and the Near East, while also stressing knowledge of Jewish subjects.[103] Owned by the Society of Merchants in Cracow, this school provided a three-year course for children aged thirteen to seventeen years, meant to prepare students for economic life through practical training.[104] Students were to have finished a six-class elementary school or a two-class general-interest gymnasium before entering.

Jewish girls were not entirely left out of the trend to develop Jewish vocational schools. The Girls' Vocational School of the *Ognisko Pracy* [Centre of Work] Association in Cracow opened in 1923, thanks to funds from the American Jewish Joint Distribution Committee and the Fränkel family. The school offered courses in dressmaking and tailoring, linen manufacturing, embroidery, knitting and home economics. Funds from the Fränkel family enabled the school to expand over the years and to build its own premises in Kazimierz, opened in 1935. The opening of the building marked a new era in the growth of the school.[105]

Specialized private Jewish schools did not only focus on vocational education. The Jewish Music Society founded a music school in Cracow in 1932.[106] Though little is known about the school, 150 students attended the school in the 1935–36 school year. Róża Arnoldówna directed the school, located at Żyblikiewicz Street 5. The curriculum included Jewish folk and art music as well as the work of famous Jewish composers. Addressing different levels of musical education, the school conducted the only *kurs mistrzowski* (maestro course) in the city as well as an exemplary pre-school. Henryk Apte, the music critic for *Nowy Dziennik*, was the president of the Jewish Music Society for many years, and it is most likely he was directly involved in the efforts of the music school. This topic requires more research into direct questions about musical life in inter-war Cracow and later.[107]

PRIVATE JEWISH SCHOOLS AND PARTICIPATION IN POLISH CULTURE

Just as Jewish leaders developed original approaches to the teaching of religion in public school settings during the inter-war period, so too did Jewish students participate in new efforts of the Polish school authorities to enhance the academic life of the country's children and youth. Perhaps the most innovative programme was the School Theatre programme, *Teatr Szkolny*. The educational efforts of Juliusz Osterwa, the director of the Słowacki Theatre in Cracow in the 1930s, enriched the cultural life of all Cracow school children. His programme deserves special mention since it affected children in both private Jewish and public Polish schools. Osterwa developed a *Teatr Szkolny* [School Theatre] for Cracow schoolchildren, which presented plays, usually dress rehearsals of full-scale productions at the Słowacki Theatre, for student audiences during school hours. According to a collection of articles about the programme published in 1936, the School Theatre was established in 1932 and had performed twenty-five plays a year for approximately 7,000 schoolchildren each year. National and local school officials supported the programme because the plays performed were the most important in Polish literature and expressed ideals particularly worthy of presentation to children. All Polish and Jewish children of school age, whether in private or public schools, participated in this programme. This includes the overwhelming majority of Jewish children in the Polish public schools as well as Jewish children in private Jewish schools such as the Hebrew gymnasium, the *Szkoła Handlowa* [Middle School for Trade] and *Ognisko Pracy*, a vocational school for Jewish girls. Thus, even private Jewish schools were not completely isolated from the Polish educational institutional culture.

School Theatre programmes were established in other cities as well, such as Lwów and Vilnius. Though Lwów had been the capital of Austrian Galicia, which allowed Poles more freedom in cultural expression, the programme in Vilnius was better developed.[108] Archival evidence in Vilnius indicates that the School Theatre programme functioned for most of the 1930s, from 1934 on. Hundreds of Jewish students in public and private Jewish schools attended performances by such playwrights as Molière, Shakespeare, Aeschylus and Żeromski.[109] The School Theatre programme did not begin in Lwów until 1935, the year of the arrival of a new director of Lwów's City Theatre, Jan Budzyński, who was sympathetic to the idea. As one young reporter for a school newspaper reported, Jewish youth (and likely many others) had tired of seeing Polish theatre classics, Słowacki's *Kordian* and Fredro's *Zemsta*.[110] Left to seek cultural entertainment on their own, young Jews were likely to drift to the increasingly popular cinema or to local revues.[111] The School Theatre programme provided first-rate entertainment and educated children. In its first year, the programme proved a success. The School Theatre mixed Polish standards like Wyspiański's *Wyzwolenie* with more contemporary dramas like Henrik Ibsen's *Peer Gynt* or Schiller's *Pastorałka* or Nowaczyński's *Wielki Fryderyk*. When Budzyński left Lwów and a new theatre director arrived, the programme changed for the worse, and students were no longer encouraged to make the theatre part of their regular academic life. As the available evidence on the School Theatre programme shows, Jewish children in private Jewish schools throughout Poland enjoyed the same opportunity to see the best in Polish drama alongside their Jewish and non-Jewish counterparts in public schools.

Young Jews often defended the School Theatre programme from charges that the performances were poor. M. Bornstein wrote that Jewish students appreciated the special theatre productions for school audiences more than parents, since student audiences recognized the performances as 'real art' with first-rate actors.[112] Because the students attended only the rehearsals, the well-known essayist Zygmunt Nowakowski contended that the students did not see the actors in their top form during the evening performances. Still, Manuel Boner enthusiastically defended the School Theatre, arguing that younger audiences demanded truer portrayals of characters on stage and that they would be less likely than adult audiences to accept artistic mediocrity.[113] Not only does this point to possible involvement between private Jewish schools and public schools in Poland, but it is also further evidence of how Polish culture was presented to Jewish youth. Even those in private Jewish schools simply could not avoid it.

Jewish community leaders established private Jewish schools of all types. These included separate institutions for secular or religious instruction, for boys and girls, and for special interests of all kinds. This level of activity was a response to the predominance of the majority culture, to growing anti-Semitism, the increasingly influential ideas of Jewish nationalism, and the new freedoms of the inter-war period. The many different private schools reflect the urgent need for private Jewish education. Hilfstein, Shenirer, Teufel, Infeld and other educational leaders founded these schools to promote their own versions of Jewish religious, national or secular identity.

Nevertheless, none of these schools, not even the most traditional, was immune to the influence of the larger Polish community. Each school confronted this influence in its own way. Just as the members of the Jewish community founded various newspapers to serve a diverse community, so, too, educators provided the community with many options in which to express Jewish identity in Cracow's multi-ethnic environment. Some schools, like Sore Shenirer's Beys Yakov schools, fought Polish influence in an effort to stem acculturation. Others, like the Hebrew gymnasium and Infeld's Nasza Szkoła, furthered the education of Jews in Polish while providing a separate Jewish environment. Acculturated leaders of Jewish organizations besides schools did the same. They provided a number of ways Jews could participate in a larger Jewish community. None of these, from sports clubs to theatre societies, was isolated from participation in the majority culture around them.

NOTES

1. Gross, *Kim pan jest, panie Grymek?*, 96.
2. Bronner, *Cykady nad Wisłą i Jordanem*, 118–9.
3. Maks Bienenstock, 'Problem szkoły żydowskiej', *Nowy Dziennik*, 6 June 1921, 4.
4. 'Przegląd spraw szkolnych i wychowawczych', *Nowe Życie*, June–August 1924, 440–50.
5. Henryka Fromowicz-Stillecowa, 'Problemy narodowe i religijne w wychowaniu dziecka żydowskiego', *Nasza Opinja*, 7 June 1936, 8.
6. Halina Nelken describes this most eloquently in her diary and memoir. The anti-Semitism Nelken experienced is discussed further below.
7. Markus Braude, 'Język wykładowy, a narodowy charakter szkoły żydowskiej', *Nowy Dziennik*, 15 February 1926, 9.
8. Bienenstock, 'Pierwiastek narodowy w żydowskiej szkole średniej', *Nowy Dziennik*, 12 November 1919, 3.
9. Ibid.
10. 'Dla szkoły żydowskiej', *Chwila*, 14 February 1919, 1; 'O narodową szkołę żydowską', *Chilwa* 19 February 1919, 2; 'W obronie rodzimej kultury', *Chwila*, 27 February 1919, 1.
11. Michal Brandstätter, 'O żydowskiej szkole we Lwowie', *Chwila*, 14 July 1919, 2–4. The article describing the private Jewish school as an anti-civic experiment appeared in *Kurjer Lwowski*.
12. b.h., 'O żydowską szkołę narodowę', *Chilwa* 5 June 1919, Nr 141, 3–4.
13. 'W obronie szkoły żydowskiej', *Chwila*, 1 May 1919, 1.
14. Abraham Insler, 'Maks Bienenstock, W rocznicę zgonu', *Chilwa* 9 April 1924, 3–4.
15. Alexander Koller, 'O zdrową podstawę szkoły żydowskiej', *Nowy Dziennik*, 20 February 1921, 4.
16. Ibid.
17. 'O zorganizowanie szkół zawodowych', *Nowy Dziennik*, 8 October 1921, 4–5.
18. For an extended discussion on the intersection between class and educational options for Jews, see Celia Heller, *On the Edge of Destruction*, 215, 225–32.
19. 'Sytuacja nauczycielstwa żydowskiego, Rozmowa z prof. A. Wolfowiczem, prezesem Zarządu Głównego Związku Zawodowego Nauczycieli Szkół Śr. w Polsce', *Opinja*, Nr 24 (72), 8.
20. *Katalog główny, 1920–1938*, Gimnazjum żeńskiej Królowe Jadwigi. WAPKr.

21. Andrzej Żbikowski, *Żydzi krakowscy*, 241–3. Żbikowski does not identify this school as public or private, and it is unclear precisely what role the school played within the Jewish community.
22. Ibid., 247.
23. Rafael F. Scharf, *Poland, What Have I to Do with Thee* ... : *Essays without Prejudice*, 9–10.
24. Żbikowski, *Żydzi krakowscy*, 249.
25. ŻIH GWŻK 755, *Statystyka chajderów w Krakowie*. No date given, *rok?* (year?) written in pencil in a corner of the front page. Unfortunately, it is not clear who prepared the questionnaire, whether the city, state or Jewish community. Given its position among other files, the document is most likely from the early years of the inter-war period.
26. It is not clear why the others did not attend public school; either their parents were in violation of the civil law, or, more likely, they were simply underage for the public schools.
27. This is a change from the 1885 statistics showing that 118 girls attended the heders. The file does not offer any explanation.
28. The Cheder Iwri schools are discussed further below.
29. 'Powszechne nauczanie wśród ludności żydowskiej w Polsce w świetle cyfr', *Sprawy narodowościowe* 2 (1929), 297.
30. KOSK 70, Protokól spisany w dniu 14 lutego 1938 z powodu komisyjnego badania stanu pomieszczeń szkoły wyznaniowej – cheder – Talmud Tora I przy ul. Estery L. 6 w związku z pismem Inspekt. Szkoln. Krak. Miejskiego w Krakowie z dn. 20.X.1937 L. 2635/37.
31. Ibid.
32. Ibid. There is no later inspection report that confirms the compliance with these recommendations or the closing of the school.
33. Alfred Döblin, *Journey to Poland* (New York: Paragon House Publishers, 1991) trans. Joachim Neugroschel, 199–200.
34. KOSK 70, L. 233/38, Sprawa: przyznanie praw szkół publicznych szkołe 'Jesodej Hatora', dnia 28 stycznia 1938.
35. KOSK 70, Odpis, Protokól spisany dnia 16. kwietnia 1936 r. w sprawie zbadania przydatności lokalu szkolnego 7-mio klasowej Prywatnej Ortod. Żydowskiej szkoły powszechnej 'Jesodej Hatora' w Krakowie.
36. KOSK 70, L. 233/38, Sprawa: przyznanie praw szkół publicznych szkóle 'Jesodej Hatora', dnia 28 stycznia 1938.
37. Ibid.
38. KOSK 70, Spis pomocy naukowych, znajdujących się w pryw. ortodoks. żyd. szk. powsz. Nr 57. 'Jesodej Hatora' w Krakowie.
39. Moyshe Blekher, 'Di tragedie fun der yiddisher yugnt', May 15, 1938, p.2.
40. Rafael F. Scharf, *Poland, What Have I to Do with Thee* ... , 24.
41. Shlomo Leser, *The Hebrew School in Cracow, 1908–1939: A Historical Study of a Bilingual Polish-Hebrew School* (Haifa: Vaadat Hahantsakha shel Yotsey Krakov be haifa, 1990), XV–XVI.
42. KOSK 33, File 19. Inspection reports for 1937 and 1938.
43. KOSK 33, File 17, *Sprawozdanie z wizytacji Gimnazjum Żydowskiego Tow. Szkoły Ludowej w Krakowie w dniach 25–27 stycznia i 22 lutego 1937 r.*
44. Ibid.
45. KOSK 33, File 17, *Sprawozdanie z wizytacji, odbytej w dniach 4, 5 i 6 grudnia 1935 r. w Krakowie.*
46. Ibid. Gross attributes the high level of Polish language teaching to Juliusz Feldhorn, a well-known critic and novelist in the Polish language. Feldhorn is an extremely

interesting example of a Jewish intellectual active in Polish. He published one of his novels, *Cienia nad kołyska,* under the pseudonym of Jan Las. The anti-Semitic National Democratic press reviewed the novel favourably, not knowing Feldhorn was the real author. Feldhorn planned but presumably never published two later volumes of this novel, which was to trace the story of a young man who found out he was Jewish. Natan Gross, *Kim pan jest, panie Grymek?* (Cracow: Wydawnictwo Literackie, 1991), 112–20.

47. Shlomo Leser, *The Hebrew School in Cracow,* IV.
48. Ibid.
49. Scharf, *Poland, What Have I to Do with Thee* ... , 65.
50. Ibid., 69–70.
51. Bronner, *Cykady nad Wisłą i Jordanem,* 132–3. Also see Meir Bosak, 'Juliusz Feldhorn', in Natan Gross, ed., *Zeh hayah bayt-ha-sefer ha-ivri-ba-krakov* (Tel Aviv: Wydawnictwo Ekked, 1989), 32–5.
52. Gross, *Kim pan jest, panie Grymek?,* 96.
53. Ibid., 98.
54. 'Otwarcie hebrajskich kursów nauczycielskich w Krakowie', *Nowy Dziennik,* 25 July 1921, 4–5.
55. Felicja Infeld-Stendigowa, 'Czy matka żydowska spełnia swe zadanie wychowawcze?' *Ogniwa,* October 1936, 5–8.
56. Ibid.
57. Gross, *Kim pan jest, panie Grymek?,* 96.
58. L. Kahanowa, 'Z zagadnień wychowawczych, Wędrówka po żydowskich szkołach Krakowa', *Ogniwa,* October 1936, 2.
59. Shlomo Leser, *Poems and Sketches in English and in Polish,* preliminary edn, Haifa 1993.
60. Bronner, *Cykady nad Wisłą i Jordanem,* 119.
61. Ibid., 169.
62. Nelken, *And Yet, I am Here!,* 56.
63. Bronner, *Cykady nad Wisłą i Jordanem,* 128–9.
64. Shlomo Leser, *The Hebrew School in Cracow, 1908–1939,* XVII.
65. Natan Gross, 'Semper Fidelis (o Związku b. uczniów Hebrajskiego Gimnazjum w Krakowie),' in *Zeh hayah bayt-ha-sefer ha-ivri-ba-krakov.*
66. Rafael F. Scharf, *Poland, What Have I to Do with Thee* ... , 29–30.
67. 'Nauczyciele piszą,' *Zeh hayah bayt-ha-sefer ha-ivri-ba-krakov,* 41.
68. Michał Borwicz, *Ludzie, Książki, Spory* (Paris: Księgarnia Polska, 1980).
69. For biographical information about Artur Sandauer, see *'Śnil mi się Artur Sandauer' Rozmowy i wspomnienia,* ed. Józef Baran (Cracow: Centrum Kultury Żydowskiej na Kazimierzu, 1992).
70. ŻIH GWŻK 753. Letter of 16 December 1925 to presidium of gmina from Cheder Iwri school official.
71. Zofia Wordliczek, 'Szkolnictwo Żydowskie na terenie miasta Krakowa w okresie II Rzeczypospolitej Polskiej', 1. Unpublished material, Muzeum miasta Krakowa, Stara Synagoga. Wordliczek writes, 'There was only one boys' middle school in Poland combining general knowledge and a modern state education with Jewish studies in spiritual belief and tradition.' This claim seems somewhat overstated, but inspection reports confirm the school's efforts to combine a strong religious training with secular studies.
72. KOSK 33, Nr 19, Prywatne Gimnazjum Męskie 'Tachkemoni' w Krakowie, sprawozdanie z wizytacji odbytej dnia 26 lutego 1937 r.
73. KOSK 33, Nr 19, Odpis, Prywatne Gimnazjum Męskie Stowarzyszenia 'Cheder Iwri' i 'Tachkemoni' w Krakowie, Rok szkolny 1938/39, Sprawozdanie z wizytacji

odbytej dnia 15 i 16 grudnia 1938 r.

74. Ibid.
75. Ibid.
76. KOSK 33, Nr 19, Odpis, Prywatne Gimnazjum męskie 'Tachkemoni', Stowarzyszenia 'Heder Iwri' w Krakowie, Rok szkolny 1937/38, Sprawozdanie z wizytacji odbytej dnia 23 i 24 march 1938 r. Inspekcja odbyła się 29 pazdżiernika 1937 r.
77. Meir Korzennik, 'Gimnazjum męskie "Tachkemoni",' in *Almanach szkolnictwa żydowskiego w Polsce* (Warsaw: Wydawnictwo 'Renesans', 1937), 104–5.
78. Ibid.
79. KOSK 33, Nr 17, Odpis, Sprawozdanie z wizytacji Prywatnego Gimnazjum Koedukacyjnego Towarzystwa Żydowskiej Szkoły Społecznej w Krakowie.
80. KOSK 88, Statut Prywatnego Gimnazjum Koedukacyjnego Towarzystwa Żydowskiej Szkoły Społecznej w Krakowie.
81. KOSK 33, Nr 17, Sprawozdanie z wizytacji Prywatnego Gimnazjum Koedukacyjnego Towarzystwa Żydowskiej Szkoły Społecznej w Krakowie.
82. KOSK 33, Nr 17, Sprawozdanie z wizytacji dokonanej w dniach 28 i 29 listopada 1938 r. w Prywatnym Gimnazjum Koedukacyjnym Towarzystwa Żydowskiej Szkoły Społecznej w Krakowie.
83. J. Z-n., 'Sara Szenirer', *Almanach Szkolnictwa Żydowskiego w Polsce* , 56–7.
84. B. Frydman, 'Wyższe kursy nauczycielskie "Bajs Jakow" (seminarium) w Krakowie', *Almanach Szkolnictwa Żydowskiego*, 140.
85. Deborah Weissman, 'Bais Yaakov: A Historical Model for Jewish Feminists', in *The Jewish Woman*, ed. Elizabeth Koltun (New York: Schocken Books, 1976), 141. See also Irena Klepfisz, 'Di mames, dos loshn: The mothers, the language: Feminism, Yidishkayt, and the Politics of Memory', *Bridges*, Vol. 4, No. 1 (Winter/Spring 1993), 12–47.
86. J. Z-n., 'Sara Szenirer', *Almanach Szkolnictwa Żydowskiego*, 55.
87. Klepfisz, 'Di mames, zos loshn/The Mothers, the Language: Feminism, Yidishkayt, and the Politics of Memory'.
88. Sore Shenirer, 'Yidishkayt un yidish', in *Never Say Die*, ed. Joshua Fishman (The Hague: Mouton, 1981), 173–6. Originally printed in *Beys yakov*, 1931, 71–2.
89. Deborah Weissman, 'Bais Ya'akov as an Innovation in Jewish Women's Education: A Contribution to the Study of Education and Social Change', *Studies in Jewish Education*, Vol. VII (1995): 278–99.
90. Leopold Infeld, *Szkice z przeszłości* (Warsaw: Państwowy Instytut Wydawniczy, 1964), 37–46. Infeld's memoir was subsequently published in English as *Why I Left Canada: Reflections on Science and Politics*, ed. Lewis Pyerson and translated by Helen Infeld (Montreal: McGill-Queen's University Press, 1978).
91. Heller, *On the Edge of Destruction*, 230. My own numbers for the private Queen Jadwiga Gymnasium do not seem to indicate such a drastic decline.
92. KOSK 33, Nr 17, Odpis, Prywatne Żydowskie Gimnazjum Żeńskie Towarzystwa Oświatowego 'Nasza Szkoła' w Krakowie, Rok szkolny 1937/38, Sprawozdanie z wizytacji odbytej dnia 18 lutego 1938 r. Inspekcja odbyła się dnia 29 października 1937 r.
93. KOSK 33, Nr 17, Odpis, Nasza Szkoła.
94. Ibid.
95. Ibid.
96. J. Z., 'Prywatna Żydowska Koedukacyjna Średnia Szkoła Handlowa Stow. Żyd. Abs. W. S. H. w Krakowie', *Almanach Szkolnictwa Żydowskiego*, 73–4.
97. KOSK 113, Program Nauczania, Prywatnej Żydowskiej Koedukacyjnej Średniej Szkoły Handlowej Stow. Żydowskich Absolwentów Wyższego Studjum

Handlowego w Krakowie.
98. Ibid.
99. 'W żydowskiej średniej szkole handlowej w Krakowie', *Nasza Opinja*, 20 September 1936, 5.
100. KOSK 113, Program Nauczania, Prywatnej Żydowskiej Koedukacyjnej Średniej Szkoły Handlowej Stow. Żydowskich Absolwentów Wyższego Studjum Handlowego w Krakowie.
101. Ibid.
102. Ibid.
103. Statut Prywatnego Żydowskiego Koedukacyjnego Gimnazjum Kupieckiego Krakowskiego Stowarzyszenie Kupców w Krakowie.
104. Ibid.
105. 'Szkoła Zawodowa Żeńska Towarzystwa Ogniska Pracy w Krakowie', *Rocznik Jubileuszowy, Związku dla szerzenia wykształcenia zawodowego wśród Żydów w Małopolsce 'WUZET' oraz Kalendarz na rok 1937–5697* (Lwów: Nakładem Związku, 1938), 110–12. Included in this publication are profiles of similar vocational schools in Lwów.
106. L. Kahanowa, 'Wedrówka', *Ogniwa*, October 1936, 4.
107. Wordliczek also mentions a couple of other schools for which I was unable to find other documentation detailing the school's orientation and development. These include the following specialized schools: Prywatne Seminarium dla Dziewcząt z programmem religijno-gospodarczym przy ul. Paulińskiej (Private Seminary for Girls with a religious and economic programme on Paulińska Street), Prywatna Szkoła Rytmiki i Plastyki prowadzona przez P. Berger i L. Plater (Private School of Music and Sculpture led by P. Berger and L. Plater), and Szkoła Specjalna dla umysłowo upośledzonych przy ul. Wąskiej 7 (Special School for the Mentally Disabled on 7 Wąska Street). Wordliczek, 'Szkolnictwo Żydowskie na terenie miasta Krakowa w okresie II Rzeczypospolitej Polskiej', 4.
108. Cynicus, 'O teatr szkolny we Lwowie', *Ze szkolnej ławy*, September–October 1935, 41–3.
109. Lithuanian Central State Archives in Vilnius, Kuratorium Okręgu Szkolnego Wileńskiego, Fond 172, Apyrašo 1, Tom 4399.
110. Cynicus, 'O teatr szkolny we Lwowie', *Ze szkolnej ławy*, September–October 1935, 41–3.
111. Leon Rappel, 'Lwowski teatr szkolny', *Opinja*, 8 March 1936, 9.
112. M. Bornstein, 'O teatrze szkolnym', *Opinja*, 5 August 1933, 9.
113. Manuel Boner, 'Zamiast kroniki krakowskiej, Teatr na czczo, czy po kolacji?' *Nasza Opinja*, 12 January 1936, 1936, 11.

6
Voluntary Associations and the Varieties of Cultural Life

My father spoke about the Jewish theatre public of Cracow with sarcasm: assimilated snobs for whom the Jewish language was a type of jargon and for whom real theatre is – Polish theatre.

Irene Kanfer, 'Słów kilka o teatrze żydowskim w Krakowie', in *Teatr Żydowski w Krakowie*, 207

In his writings on the Yiddish theatre, Sholem Freund noted in 1927 that the 'Jewishness' of Cracow changed in 1904 with Jewish immigration to Cracow from Eastern Galicia. Freund wrote, 'It was these immigrants who taught us about the other side of the border,' where Galician Jews pursued all kinds of specifically Jewish political and cultural activities. These immigrants 'opened new perspectives and horizons' by introducing the Jews of Cracow to 'new sources of Jewishness'.[1] Freund does not define these 'new sources of Jewishness', but it is clear he is referring to higher levels of specifically Jewish cultural activity. Freund suggests waves of Jewish immigration changed the nature of Jewish life in Cracow, just as the *Ostjuden* did in other Central European cities, most notably Berlin and Vienna. This change contributed to the Jewish political, social and cultural life of Cracow, enriching it by increasing the need for a variety of associations to serve an increasingly diverse population. The Cracow Jewish community underwent further change when the devastation of the First World War resulted in the founding of organizations and schools established to meet the needs of orphaned children and youth. Before the inter-war period, Jews who declared themselves assimilated and independent dominated the Jewish community politically. After 1918, Jews in inter-war Cracow participated increasingly in secular organizations that promoted various forms of Jewish cultural identity that did not necessarily require them to forfeit participation in Polish cultural life.

A study of the most important Jewish cultural organizations in Cracow, besides the press and the schools, can help to determine the concerns of the community and the relative importance of different forms of culture in its daily life. The Jews of inter-war Cracow could no longer simply be divided into the 'assimilated' and the 'Orthodox'. Indeed, by the 1930s, the Zionist presence in Cracow was keenly felt in all areas of Jewish life. In addition, Jewish cultural institutions such as the Cracow Yiddish Theatre Society and the Association of Jewish Artists illustrate that in between traditional Jewish religious life and complete assimilation into Polish society lay an alternative, a way for Jews to be involved in Jewish life without having to subscribe to religious ideals or melt into Polish culture. Participation in these organizations tied the Jews of Cracow even further to life in the Diaspora, allowing them different ways to express Jewish identity while remaining citizens of the country in which they lived.

By establishing separate cultural institutions of all kinds, Cracow Jews exhibited the same phenomenon observed in the development of Jewish education. Jews participating in public and private schooling, as well as in other cultural institutions, expressed a strong desire to remain a separate ethnic group while participating in the majority Polish culture. Jewish organizations were dedicated to raising the general cultural level of their members but at times focused on more specific goals. The institutions discussed in this chapter include sports teams, reading rooms, associations of Jewish artists, and the Yiddish theatre. Strictly political organizations, or organizations with primarily political goals, such as the numerous Zionist youth groups, have been omitted. Admittedly, many of the cultural groups discussed here were explicitly political as well, and it is difficult, if not impossible, to separate their political goals from their cultural aspirations.[2] Separate Jewish organizations existed for almost any kind of professional and personal interest, and many organizations combined both. Many of the separate organizations were formed to meet the needs of specific subgroups of the Jewish community, such as socialist

Zionists, Zionist youth or sports fans. Some of the organizations were quite large, with over a hundred members. Others were much smaller.

In unpublished material from the Museum of the City of Cracow, Zofia Wordliczek lists a total of 305 different Jewish organizations during the inter-war period, from political and religious groups to social clubs and reading rooms, to sports organizations and charitable associations. These groups served the varied interests of a population of 60,000.[3] Each of these was required to register with the police and to report on changes in the status of the organization's officers and policies. Many of them existed only for brief periods, a year or less, but others lasted for nearly the entire inter-war period. Twenty-nine of the 305 organizations, according to Wordliczek's count, were charitable organizations that worked on behalf of Cracow's Jewish children.[4] Nine of the 305 were exclusively women's organizations; four of these were dedicated to charitable goals, two were devoted to the support of working women, and three were specifically nationalist in orientation. The many others were prayer houses and political and cultural organizations. Some organizations sponsored lectures, readings, concerts, plays and libraries. Each provided a specific avenue to participation in a larger Jewish community.

Jewish leaders established these organizations for a variety of reasons. Both anti-Semitism and a desire for a separate Jewish culture played a role. Jews excluded from participation in Polish soccer teams, for example, were able to play on Jewish teams. Those who founded the Jewish theatre societies, however, were motivated more by the desire to improve the Jews' cultural level than by any specific anti-Semitic incident. The impetus for the creation of a Yiddish Theatre Society in Cracow came not from any prohibition against the participation of Jews in the Polish theatre but from the desire to create a Yiddish cultural institution comparable to the best Polish theatres. Some of the organizations described below formed to promote a specific ideology, such as the reading rooms of the socialist Zionists. These ideologies were at least in part a response to the anti-Semitism within Polish society. Still others, like the Association of Jewish Artists, hoped to advance explicitly multicultural goals, such as promoting an inclusive ideology of art while providing opportunities for

Jewish artists to exhibit their work. These various motivations reflect the diversity of the different groups within the Jewish community.

Participation in these different organizations could lead to stronger affiliations with either Jewish or Polish culture. This involvement is difficult to quantify, while the ways in which these organizations affected the identity formation of individual Jews is still harder to assess. In some cases, the contemporary press or memoir literature allows some insight into how the actual activities affected Jewish individuals. We do know, however, the types of activities these organizations sponsored, the kinds of meetings and lectures they held, the games they played, the dramas they performed. The organizations discussed here may have had ties to specific political ideals or cultural orientations, but this certainly does not mean that all who participated in these organizations adhered to them. Those who cheered for the Makkabi sports team may also have gone to the lectures of the more acculturated Social Reading Room; those who attended the Yiddish theatre most likely went regularly to the Polish theatre as well. These organizations did not necessarily create a Jewish or a Polish identity for those who participated in their activities. They did, however, offer opportunities for Jews to encounter specifically Jewish forms of cultural life. Moreover, these opportunities, in settings free of Polish chauvinism, often served as an introduction to Polish cultural life as well.

THE PROMOTION OF JEWISH CULTURE

The goals of many separate Cracow Jewish associations often coincided, though their names reveal a wide range of ideological values and religious beliefs. Some did not promote a specific variant of Jewish culture but rather sought to advance Jewish culture more generally. These groups defined their goals rather vaguely and sponsored a variety of events attracting different audiences. Some of these organizations, such as the Social Club ('Klub Towarzyski'), which sponsored libraries, reading rooms, evening readings, parties, gatherings of an apolitical nature and amateur theatricals, were apparently small and were disbanded because of a lack of members.[5] Some others, such as 'Szir', the Jewish Singing Society, the Union of Hebrew Journalists, or the Radio Social Club, catered to more specific interests.[6] In general, little is known about these organizations' activities, but that does not necessarily mean that they were not important in the lives of some of Cracow's Jews. For example, the influential music critic and lawyer Henryk Apte led 'Szir', an organization named after the Hebrew word for song and that numbered, at one point, fifty-three members. Taken together, these smaller groups, including the general cultural organizations mentioned above, reached out to large numbers of people.

One of the larger organizations was the Jewish Society of People's Education (*Żydowskie Towarszystwo Oświaty Ludowej*).[7] Members of this organization were Bundists and partisans of a united workers' front. The society featured lectures on topics as diverse as the poetry of the Hebrew writer Chaim Bialik, the plays of Poland's Stanisław Wyspiański, biology, politics, trade, medicine, economics and Roman history. This was not an insignificant organization. A police report from March 1935 indicates that 200 people attended a lecture to hear Zofja Dubnow-Erlich speak about Soviet literature. During the same month, eighty people attended the society's Yiddish poetry reading held in the Yiddish theatre building.[8]

The leaders of a similar organization, the Jewish Society for Professional Culture (*Żydowskie Towarszystwo Oświaty Ludowej*),[9] stated in 1937 that its goal was the 'broadening of culture among working Jewish youth, the creation in it of general professional and Jewish knowledge in the spirit of state citizenship, Jewish nationalism, and religious tradition'. These goals were thus both secular and religious and suggest a level of Polish patriotism *and* Jewish national feeling. That Jewish organizations could espouse such apparently conflicting aims shows that Jews, as they had done since the processes of modernization had begun in the nineteenth century, were building their own home, defining their own ethnic and national identity, with reference to both Jewish and non-Jewish culture.

Activities of the 'Toynbe [*sic*] Hala' organization (*Towarszystwo dla szerzenia oświaty wśród Żydów w Małopolsce*, Association for the Development of Culture among the Jews of Małopolska), presumably part of the Toynbee Hall social settlement in

London, included trips, publishing activities, contests, readings and 'the popularization of knowledge in all areas of culture'.[10] This organization was located in the heart of Kazimierz. It appears to have been an active Jewish cultural organization. Large posters in Polish and Yiddish advertised monthly activities. During December 1918 and January 1919, there was a session every Sunday afternoon especially for children.[11] Topics of lectures included Jewish history and culture, the Jewish national fund and Jewish emigration. Scholars often made presentations on the lives and works of both Jewish and non-Jewish writers, including Yitzhok Leyb Peretz and Mendele Mokher Sforim among the former, and Wyspiański, Ibsen and Rostand, among the latter. Influential leaders within the Jewish community participated in these events, including the rabbi and political leader Ozjasz Thon. Henryk Apte, the music critic for *Nowy Dziennik*, gave a piano concert the notice for which was in Polish and Yiddish, and the well-known Jewish educator and Zionist leader Dawid Bulwa also gave a talk. The poster for Bulwa's talk was in Polish and Yiddish, while the stamp of the organization was in Polish and Hebrew, suggesting an awareness that Polish and Yiddish were the daily languages of the community, at the same time recognizing Hebrew as a Jewish language as well. Toynbe Hala tried to be inclusive in its programming and its advertising to the Jewish community. While we can never be certain how many people participated in these types of organizations, the extensive schedule of events and lectures sponsored by Toynbee Hall indicates that the organizers believed there was an audience for such events. Even if one assumes that twenty people or fewer attended each of the lectures sponsored by Toynbee Hall (a low estimate), this is still a significant number of people involved in the monthly events of only one of many organizations.

Another Toynbee Hall group was active in Lwów. The organization in Lwów described its aims as purely educational in nature. The Toynbee Hall group in Lwów appears to have been active and supportive of Jewish culture in its broadest sense. The group sponsored thirty-two lectures in 1928 and twenty-nine in 1929, on history, nature, science, social movements and Palestine. The illiterate could also take courses in Yiddish and Hebrew, which were meant especially for youth aged ten to fifteen years who had not had the benefit of formal education because of the war and conflicts of the immediate post-war period. According to correspondence in Yiddish to the *kehillah* in Lwów, from whom the group received small subsidies, the attendance at Toynbee Hall events averaged roughly 300. The correspondence also stresses that Toynbee Hall sponsored non-partisan events to attract the greatest number of people, those 'who want to acquaint themselves with the problems of life with which they must be concerned as men and citizens'.[12] That the Yiddish letter, meant for the *kehillah*, emphasized the status of Jews as citizens suggests that the conception of Jews as citizens of the Polish state was not simply limited to the linguistically acculturated writers of *Nowy Dziennik* and *Chwila*. Private Jewish organizations promoted Jewish culture in an effort to improve themselves both as private individuals and as citizens of the new political state to which they belonged.

In addressing important social, educational and political problems, these organizations provided answers for the perpetual question of how Jews fitted within the larger society. Cultural organizations with a range of offerings provided opportunities to learn about being Jewish that were not solely from a religious perspective. Polish was often used as an administrative language in the organizations' records, but this should not obscure the extent to which these organizations promoted Jewish, whether Yiddish or Hebrew, culture. Cultural organizations existed especially to promote the development of Jewish culture in Hebrew and Yiddish, demonstrating the support of the Jewish community for cultural development in these languages as well as highlighting the fact that these Jewish languages needed support to attain cultural legitimacy within the Jewish community.

None of these organizations ignored Hebrew or Yiddish literature.[13] Yiddish culture remained an important element in Cracow Jewish life and the place of Hebrew in the city's Jewish cultural life (as well as the strength of Zionism) increased during the inter-war period only with the efforts of the private Jewish schools, as well as many separate Jewish organizations. Though the presence of Yiddish culture in Cracow was minimal compared to other Polish cities, there was still a secular Jewish culture in the city, one that was expressed in the Jews' three languages. The organizations discussed above and below, the Jewish Society for People's Culture, the Jewish Society for Professional Culture, and Toynbee Hall, sponsored meetings and lectures in Yiddish. Indeed, many of them sponsored evenings devoted to specific Hebrew or Yiddish writers, honouring their creative work on their birthdays or their dates of death. Some organizations even specifically promoted Hebrew or Yiddish literature. Some groups sponsored meetings on topics such as the Yiddish theatre, Sholem Aleykhem, Yitzhok Leyb Peretz, H. Leivik, the decline of religion as a way of life, and the family and the national idea. The police often noted the political affiliations of members of those organizations that were specifically organized for workers and regulated any interest in and manifestation of Yiddish. They did not, in the end, ban the general use of Yiddish, though they did occasionally cancel meetings or other activities of Yiddish cultural organizations. Still, police monitored Jewish organizations closely because of the fear that they were simply a front for illegal Communist activity.

Tarbut, an important inter-war Jewish organization in Eastern Europe that took its name from the Hebrew word for culture, encouraged the use of Hebrew in the city. The group sponsored lectures in Hebrew as well as lectures on the need for Jewish youth to learn Hebrew.[14] A 1922 report on a lecture by Mojżesz Gordon noted that Hebrew should be the language of Jewish youth because this was a language that the English, French and Polish Jew could all use to communicate: 'the Hebrew language is presently indispensable for creating Jewish youth and for the raising of a Jewish spirit'.[15] Other lecture topics sponsored by Tarbut included Jewish prophets, Hebrew poetry, Jewish art, Polish literature and its influence on certain Hebrew poets. Thus, while Cracow Jews did not use Hebrew daily, the language did have a presence in the cultural life of the city. The leaders of Tarbut, however, were not able to ignore the fact of the Diaspora; the organization also sponsored talks on Polish literature and published its own reports in Polish.

Jewish participation in general Polish and European culture can be seen in the other specifically Jewish organizations discussed below, including Jewish sports organizations, associations of artists and the Yiddish theatre. Polish culture was present among some Jewish organizations that presented lectures on Polish writers or Polish literary movements as well as on specifically Jewish topics. Linguistically, the community was undergoing a period of transformation, as both Polish schools and Jewish organizations introduced Polish and Polish culture to even greater numbers of Jews, especially youth.

All three cultures of Poland's Jews were represented in Cracow's Jewish cultural life, though to varying extents. Cracow's Jews did not entirely abandon Yiddish or Hebrew in favour of Polish or reject Polish for the exclusive use of Yiddish or Hebrew. They could participate in cultural activities in any and all of the three languages. The Jewish nationalists and Zionists of Cracow privileged the use of Hebrew and the Polish state naturally privileged Polish in its educational and social policies. With the admittedly significant exceptions of the acceptance of Polish citizenship and social pressure to conform to Jewish religious strictures, the Jews of Cracow were not forced to define themselves exclusively in terms of one nationality or culture whether Polish or Jewish. By looking at the different types of organizations that developed to serve their needs, we can better understand how Jews moved between Polish school and Zionist youth organization, synagogue and theatre, Hebrew lessons and soccer games.

SPORT

Cracow's branch of the Jewish nationalist sports organization Makkabi played host to the group's winter 'Olympiad' in the Tatra mountain town of Zakopane in February 1933. This major event drew interest and participation from Jewish youth and leaders throughout all of Poland. The specially organized event included the possibility of taking a chartered train to Zakopane from distant locations and purchasing room and board packages at different levels. Both young students and the wealthiest, most established Jewish professionals were encouraged to come to the event. As elsewhere in Poland, sport played an important role in the development of Jewish life and national identity in inter-war Cracow.

While the largest group dedicated to the promotion of sport

among Jewish youth, Makkabi was not the only option for Jews wishing to participate in and develop recreational activities. Jewish youth, both boys and girls, were often involved in their own sports clubs which competed with Polish ones, and, like young fans everywhere, followed both Polish and Jewish sports enthusiastically. Some of the Jewish sports clubs had a neighbourhood character such as those in Zwierzyniecki and Podgórze, while other clubs were specifically for the working class. Some, like the Jutrzenka and Makkabi sports organizations, were specifically for Cracow's Jews. Jutrzenka was a sports organization founded by socialists and more assimilated Jews, while Makkabi was a part of the international Jewish sports federation and overtly Zionist in orientation.

In his memoir *Wyznanie mojżeszowe* (Mosaic Confessions), Henryk Vogler describes the deep animosity and rivalry between two Jewish soccer teams.[16] Following his family's example, young Vogler was an ardent fan of Jutrzenka. Both sports organizations sponsored other sports as well, including tennis, swimming, athletics and water polo. Jutrzenka declined towards the end of the inter-war period, the result of having been taken over by partisans of the Bund. Jews became involved in socialism, whether as part of the Bund or another, perhaps non-Jewish, socialist party, as a response to the evident class divisions in society; this political activity affected non-political life as well. According to Vogler, the politicization of the Jutrzenka organization resulted in catastrophe as the new leaders occupied themselves with political propaganda and neglected sport. In a short time, the sports complex developed earlier by Jutrzenka had become nothing more than an empty field and some of the group's best athletes joined Makkabi in an effort to continue their activities. It appears that the Bundist version of socialism conflicted with that of the other members of the group, who would have been more inclined to the socialism of the Polish Socialist Party. Such divisions were ultimately disastrous for the group. The dissolution of Jutrzenka left the Zionist Makkabi sports organization the primary alternative for Jewish athletes. What is most significant about the rivalry between these two groups is that it existed at all, and along such ideological lines. In Cracow, the internal politics of Jewish leftists benefited the city's Zionists. Different alternatives existed for

Jewish youth, though these were almost always connected to some larger ideological position that may or may not have interested the youth. Sport was one of the ways community leaders introduced young Jews to different ideologies such as nationalism and socialism.

By contrast, the Cracow branch of Makkabi grew significantly during the inter-war period. Cracow's Jewish elite was active in the organization, with Fryderyk Freund, later one of the leaders of the Yiddish Theatre Society, as its president, and Wilhelm Berkelhammer, the editor of *Nowy Dziennik*, as one of its members.[17] The Makkabi sports field was in Kazimierz, but its offices were found much closer to the city centre. The organization comprised fifteen different sections, including rowing, fencing, riding and chess, among others. From a membership of 400 in 1930, the group more than doubled by 1938.[18]

In comparison, the 1920s were difficult years for the group. Though a Jewish Gymnastics Centre had existed since 1907, its conditions were poor, and Makkabi did not own its own playing field in its early years. Its members were forced to use the field of the Hebrew gymnasium or one of the city's Jewish orphanages. Makkabi did not receive any significant funding from the government (unlike Polish sports groups) and turned to the *kehillah* for support. Without the minimal subsidies from the *kehillah*, the Cracow branch may have been forced to discontinue its activities. The achievements of the group were substantial, if difficult to quantify. As a request to the *kehillah* pointed out, 'Today no Jew will dare to say that we are not able to perform on the field, and no non-Jew would dare to make the charge that Jewish youth are hereditary cowards deserving only of scorn.'[19]

Like the other institutions discussed here, Makkabi clearly set out to redefine how Jews viewed themselves and how they were viewed by others. According to the vice-president of the union of Makkabi groups in Poland, the great merit of Makkabi was its aim to create a 'new Jew, a contemporary individual-citizen'.[20] Because of its importance as an international Jewish group, the Polish State Office of Physical Education recognized Makkabi as the representative of Jewish sport in Poland and at times even provided a small subsidy from state funds. The subsidy was minimal, and Makkabi always needed more funding, but such contact between the state and a private Jewish group suggests the ways in which the Polish and Jewish communities, two peoples so often described as living together yet separately, co-operated. While some Polish officials could not accept the stress Makkabi placed on Jewish national identity on the playing field, others could. The new Jew Makkabi was creating was not only an individual Jew but a citizen of the state.

While Makkabi and Jutrzenka were the two most important Jewish sports clubs in inter-war Cracow, there were several others, with names such as Amatorzy [Polish: Fans], Hagibor [Hebrew: The Hero], Kadima [Hebrew: Forward], and Siła [Polish: Strength].[21] These less popular sports organizations still had approximately fifty to a hundred members each. *Siła* was one of the largest of them, with over a hundred members. The police monitored these sports organizations carefully. They suspected some members and officers of the sports club Gwiazda [Polish Star] of membership in the Poale Zion Left (a socialist Zionist organization) and, according to the police reports, considered all members of Gwiazda as sympathizers of the Communist Party.[22] In 1936, police officials banned Gwiazda because it did not fill a social need; the police claimed there were already enough Jewish sports organizations in the city.[23] The Poale Zion Right (also socialist Zionist) also sponsored its own sports club in the late 1930s, Hapoel.[24] The political and ideological divisions of Jewish Cracow manifested themselves in its sports clubs.

In his memoir, Vogler writes enthusiastically about his early years as a soccer fan in inter-war Poland, weaving together the Polish and Jewish strands of his own life and of Cracow. Vogler was a spectator, not a participant. From an acculturated family living on Floriańska Street in the centre of Cracow, Vogler did not participate in Jewish cultural or sports activities, but he was aware of his Jewish origins and he did follow the Jewish soccer teams. Even such incidental involvement in the Jewish community was important for a young man like Vogler. Vogler recalled a meeting with Leon Sperling, a Jewish soccer player on a non-Jewish soccer team, Cracovia. The Cracovia team was not a specifically Jewish team but, among Jews supporting the left in Cracow, it enjoyed a special sympathy for its courage in fielding players without regard to nationality or religion.[25] Vogler met

Sperling in the Kupa synagogue in Kazimierz, where Vogler's grandfather took him infrequently. During prayer one morning, Sperling was forced to leave the synagogue early as he was late for a match. Vogler, whose uncle had also played soccer, was privileged to go with Sperling to the match and observe how Sperling transformed himself (*Przeistoczenia*) – from a Jew at prayer into a soccer player.[26] It is easy to see how this trans-figuration could affect a young boy so powerfully. Vogler received an early lesson in how an adult Jew could manage a private Jewish life with the more public persona of a soccer player.

As a more acculturated Jew, Vogler was from the outset less interested in this kind of private Jewish life, in which he participated only with his grandfather. Nevertheless, Sperling and the other Jewish soccer players on the Cracovia team served as positive role models for Vogler and other young Jews in Cracow. Still, their presence on Polish teams was an exception and Vogler makes it clear that Jewish fans rewarded Cracovia with their loyalty because it had the courage to accept Jews. Jewish teams were still needed to satisfy the interests of Jews in sport, and Jewish players on non-Jewish teams still won the attention of Jewish fans for breaking a barrier between Polish and Jewish society.

Separate Jewish sports organizations flourished in inter-war Cracow, but groups based on ethnicity did not necessarily separate Jews from Polish culture. Cracow's Jews also tried to participate more directly in the Polish institutions. The best example of this is a conflict over the YMCA building in Cracow. The writers of *Nowy Dziennik* protested against the exclusion of Jews from the newly built local YMCA in 1931 on the grounds that the building had been paid for at least partially with the money of Jews who had responded positively to the YMCA's appeal for funds.[27] This protest arose on the occasion of the building of a new YMCA building in Warsaw. The writer appealed to the Jewish community to withhold support from the Warsaw YMCA because there was no guarantee that Jews would have access to the building's facilities (of most concern was the swimming pool), even if they helped to pay for it. Once the building of the YMCA in Cracow was finished, the YMCA authorities asserted that as representatives of a private organization they could exclude whomever they wanted from their facilities. The YMCA simply betrayed the Jewish community's trust; it allowed Jews to donate money for their building which they then refused them the right to use. One Polish organization, however, did take the side of the Jews. The board of the Polish Swimmers' Union adopted a resolution that stated they would not hold any local, regional, national or international swim meets at the YMCA in Cracow, because of the Cracow YMCA's exclusion of the general public, specifically Jews.[28] This was certainly a success within the community of Jewish sports, but it still did not open the YMCA pool in Cracow to Jews.

That Jews were willing to contribute to the building of the YMCA demonstrates their willingness to participate in institutions that could serve the city as a whole. In addition, the resolution of the Polish Swimmers' Union shows that there was some real, positive co-operation between the two groups. Poles and Jews, throughout the entire inter-war period, were still negotiating ways to live together. This included working out how the minority population could (and would) participate in institutions of the majority. Privileges to use community swimming pools are just one example of specific conflict. The experiences of Jews in Polish public or private schools are others. Not surprisingly, anti-Semitism made the existence of separate Jewish organizations both necessary and desirable. Still, there was the possibility of participating in the institutions of the larger community, of which the Jews considered themselves a part. Sperling's presence on the Cracovia team, Vogler's enthusiasm for integrated non-Jewish teams, and Jewish participation in fundraising campaigns of the YMCA suggest that the Jewish population did not reject the possibility of co-operation and mutual participation.

LIBRARIES AND READING ROOMS

More accessible to the average Jew than the high cultural pursuits of the theatre or visual arts were the libraries and reading rooms sponsored by many different Jewish (and Polish) organizations. A number of reading rooms and community libraries existed in inter-war Cracow specifically for Jews. These were mostly small lending libraries or reading rooms, affiliated with a range of Jewish groups, from the official Jewish community to socialist and socialist Zionist political parties. Reading rooms supplemented the education of many Jews (as non-Jewish reading rooms no doubt did for the non-Jewish populations), serving as a way for individuals to educate themselves independently and informally. Some of the reading rooms played a greater cultural role in the city than a public library might. In the reports of these organizations, one can learn how many people participated in the reading room's activities, how many books were held by the reading room, which languages they were in, and how many books were checked out and by how many people. This does not necessarily indicate the political tendencies of the borrowers, but it does show a popular level of cultural activity that, like the Jewish sports clubs, reflected the political and ideological divisions of the Jewish community.

The *kehillah* sponsored a public reading room for Jews located in its administrative building in Kazimierz. The Public Reading Room and Library 'Ezra' was founded just at the start of the First World War.[29] During the war, the building in which the Ezra reading room was located was used for storage of potatoes or grain, but the *kehillah* reopened it after the war. The president of the *kehillah*, Rafał Landau, was a member of its board. The reading room had a membership of 200. While it was an official organization of the *kehillah*, it did not necessarily serve as the primary reading room for the entire Jewish community.

The People's Reading Room 'Unity' (*Czytelnia Ludowa Jedność/Folkslezehale Aynhayt*) had around 220 members and was located in Kazimierz. The aim of this reading room was similar to that of the more general Jewish cultural organizations mentioned above, to 'raise the cultural level' of its members. The organizers of this reading room reached out to the Jewish working class of Cracow, combining socialist and Zionist ideology. From the police records, we know that all of the members of this reading room also had ties to the Poale Zion Left (100 per cent, according to the report). The reading room was in existence from 1926 to 1938. Though the reasons for its decline in 1938 are unclear, it is significant that this socialist Zionist organization existed as late as the late 1930s.[30] It is likely that it closed as a result of the continual police harassment of those suspected of leftist activity, but there is no record in the police files that this was so or that it was officially suppressed. Its membership was roughly equal to that of 'Ezra', indicating the success of the organization as well as the attraction of its ideology.

The I. L. Peretz Jewish People's Library was in existence from 1928 to 1939.[31] A reading room named after one of the most important Yiddish writers, it had 110 members. Located in Kazimierz, first on Miodowa Street and then Dietl Street, the library maintained a collection of books, held amateur perform-ances and organized readings. The reading room statutes do not suggest any political tendency, but it is likely that the leaders of this organization were closely linked to Yiddish culture and socialist ideology. The Cracow police watched this organization closely. Police labelled at least one of the group's members, the treasurer Stefanja Schenker, 'politically suspect'. The police noted previous arrests of the organization's officers as well as their membership in the Anarchist Federation of Poland. Further notes on the members show that all of them were members of Poale Zion Left and members of Antifa, an organization described as an 'enemy of the Polish state'. An additional note in the police files terms the locale of the organization a 'rendezvous and meeting place for persons suspected of Communist activity'.[32] The organization was still relatively active in 1937, when a general meeting drew sixty-two members and the number of readers using the library was 440. The library at that time held 3,370 books. An inventory of its library indicated that it contained 1,805 books in Yiddish, 1,046 in Polish and 300 in German, demonstrating the organization's commitment to Yiddish as well as secular culture. Most interestingly, this is the only organization (besides the Yiddish Theatre Society) that seems to have placed more emphasis on Yiddish culture than Polish or Hebrew.

Not all of the reading rooms for Jews were located in Kazimierz. One of the most important in inter-war Cracow was an organization of the Jewish intelligentsia, called the Social Reading Room (*Czytelnia Towarzyska*), located on Rynek Główny, the main market square.[33] This reading room is noted as a Jewish organization, but there was nothing specifically Jewish about its activities. Non-Jewish memoirists often note the programme the Social Reading Room sponsored. The Social Reading Room was one of the most important intellectual associations in the city, whether Polish or Jewish. Non-Jewish memoirs make no mention of this organization's Jewish origins, however, and the only reference found to the Jewish origins of this reading room is in Henryk Vogler's memoir. Vogler writes that the Collegium of Scientific Lectures (*Kolegium Wykładów Naukowych*), part of the reading room's official activities, was very much like other Cracow organizations of this type but that it was an organization of the Jewish intelligentsia. Vogler writes,

> On Rynek Główny from Floriańska to Sławkowska and Szczepańska ... on the first floor of apartment building number 39 was found the home of a cultural and educational institution, similar to many Cracow organizations of this type, only that this one was an organization of the Jewish intelligentsia. But this institution did not dedicate its attention to Jewish problems; rather, it avoided them. This society was always in general culturally and educationally ambitious, and it constantly tried to place itself in the avant-garde. Antoni Słonimski stressed this in his malicious travesty of Słowacki, writing: 'Let the Jews not lose hope, let them carry education, not a lamp, before the nation ...'[34]
>
> The reading room owned a rich library as well as a large collection of the current press from around the country and from abroad. Here met, for bridge and for chess, young sons of lawyers, doctors, bankers, rich merchants, the second generation of the new intelligentsia born in the Cracow atmosphere of Young Poland ... newcomers from the depths of the ghettos of Eastern Galicia ... all became the bards of the city's literature, celebrating it with enthusiasm and the fervent love of the neophyte.[35]

Membership in the Social Reading Room was already over 300 in 1913, including such important Jewish political and cultural figures in Cracow as Adolf Gross, Rafał Taubenschlag, the Landau families, the Tilles family, and Henryka Fromowicz-Stillerowa.[36] By 1919, the Social Reading Room had already become one of the most important cultural organizations in inter-war Cracow, sponsoring literary and other evenings featuring the very best of Polish writers and intellectuals. The Social Reading Room held weekly classes in English, Esperanto, French and Italian, and sponsored chess, sports, music and other activities. The organization subscribed to many newspapers, including the Cracow newspapers *Czas* [*Time*], *Głos Narodu* [*Voice of the Nation*], *Ilustrowany Kurier Codzienny* [*Illustrated Daily Courier*], *Nowy Dziennik* and *Robotnik* [*The Worker*] as well as the English *New Era* and *Times Literary Supplement*, the Esperanto periodical *Verda Stelo*, the French *L'Illustration*, and the German *Berliner Tageblatt*, and the Viennese *Neue Freie Presse*.

The activities of this reading room went well beyond lending books and often reflected a strong attachment to Polish culture. Members organized lectures and literary and theatrical evenings that were often well attended and the topics of which included the future of Polish poetry, the philosophy of Kant, or the works of such seminal Polish literary figures as Jan Kochanowski, Juliusz Słowacki, Ignacy Krasiński, Adam Mickiewicz and Lucjan Rydel. Additional activities throughout the years included a lecture by the poet Julian Tuwim, an evening dedicated to the Polish military, and a vaudeville production by Stanisław Mandelbaum with the music of Józef Frist and the work of the club's own drama group. Further indicating the organization's attachment to Polish culture, the Reading Room purchased a commemorative brick to be placed at Wawel, Cracow's royal castle, in honour of the organization's first ten years. The year after its tenth anniversary, the organization had grown to 864 members. In over ten years of existence (including the years of the First World War and the difficult post-war period), there were a total of over 1,700 lectures and readings.[37] The Polish community took note of the Reading Room's extraordinary growth, as a subvention of the Ministry of Art and Culture attests.[38] In 1924–25, the organization received a subsidy from the Cracow city council, and in the next year it bought the latest technological innovation, a film projector, in order to show pictures for art and natural sciences lectures.

The Collegium did not limit itself to the presentation of academic lectures, however. It also sponsored the cabaret *Bury Melonik*, which became known thanks to the efforts of Bruno Hoffmann and Adam Polewka as well as the actor Jasiu

Ulreich.[39] The work presented in this cabaret was primarily *szmonces*, or linguistic jokes based on the Polish-language skills of Jews. This type of humour, satirizing the Jewish use of Polish, was especially popular in the cabarets of Warsaw, Lwów and Cracow.[40] Tuwim himself wrote *szmonces*. These played well to inter-war cabaret audiences, which, according to Vogler and many other memoirists, were predominantly Jewish.[41] Vogler described *Bury Melonik* as a worthy successor to the pre-war *Zielony Balonik* [*Little Green Balloon*] cabaret held in the *Jama Michalika* cafe on Floriańska.

The Social Reading Room on Rynek Główny may have been one of the most influential reading rooms in the city but, in catering to the acculturated Jewish intelligentsia, it did not serve the needs of the larger Jewish community. The precise size of this intelligentsia is difficult to determine; the 864 members of the Social Reading Room provide some clue, but it is possible that at least some of this number were Poles. The Social Reading Room did, however, succeed in providing a space for the Jewish intelligentsia to pursue cultural endeavours they may have not been able to pursue in non-Jewish settings. At the same time, they served as an organization that might bring acculturated/ assimilated Jews closer to Polish culture and to Poles who were interested in similar intellectual pursuits. From press reviews and memoir literature, we know that the Polish intelligentsia knew of and participated in the activities of the Collegium, but it is difficult to assess the effect the Collegium might have had on Polish–Jewish relations in the city.[42] The Collegium did not speak specifically of increasing mutual understanding between the two peoples or working in specific ways towards improving Polish–Jewish relations. Rather, it simply pursued cultural goals that assumed familiarity with the highest level of Polish culture. Groups like the Association of Jewish Artists (discussed further below) worked towards improving the Jewish community while attempting to gain some understanding of Polish society. In contrast, the founders of the Collegium took their legacy of Polish culture for granted. This in itself indicates the level of acculturation that had already taken place. The Collegium founders did not identify themselves as Jews in any of their published materials or press announcements and their Jewish identity was not relevant for their goal of 'spreading' culture. This alone makes them unique among Jewish organizations in Cracow.

The Social Reading Room clearly neglected Jewish culture in favour of Polish. One might argue that the Polish Jews who founded the Social Reading Room had already achieved a level of mutual understanding by adopting the content and forms of Polish culture as their own. The price for this, however, was neglect of Jewish culture and identity. While this may not have been an outright denial of Jewish identity on the part of the Collegium founders, it was a privileging of one culture over the other. Some members of the Social Reading Room, however, were also actively involved in Jewish community life. Adolf Gross and Samuel Tilles were leaders in the *kehillah* and Fromowicz-Stillerowa wrote for *Nowy Dziennik* and *Nasza Opinja* and established a children's magazine for Jewish children, *Okienko na Świat*. Still, important questions remain unanswered. Why were these Jewish community leaders, so actively involved in Jewish causes, members of an organization that has been described by a reliable source (Henryk Vogler) as having avoided Jewish culture? Leaders such as Gross, Tilles and Fromowicz-Stillerowa apparently did not wish to remain separate from either Polish or Jewish culture. Still, Vogler's assertion that the Reading Room was an organization of the Jewish intelligentsia suggests the limits of acculturation short of conversion. This segment of Cracow Jewry deserves more study, not least because the cosmopolitan nature of the Reading Room suggests similarities to the Jewish intellectual tradition of Vienna.

Both Polish and Yiddish culture were highlighted in the activities of the different reading rooms for Jews. The reading rooms formed to serve different sub-populations within the Jewish community, assimilated Jews, women, or those of the Yiddish-speaking left. The division of the Jewish community into these different groups is not as important as the idea that these reading rooms, in spite of their individual characteristics, represented the collective efforts of the Jewish community to raise its own cultural level. Such informal educational efforts take on even greater importance when one remembers that most Jewish children received their education in Polish and only the most rudimentary Jewish religious instruction in public schools. With the notable exception of the Social Reading

Room, these separate cultural activities ensured a commitment to Jewish ethnicity and promoted an attachment to Jewish nationalism without compromising the development of Polish patriotism. At the same time, the Social Reading Room is one marker of the entrance of Jews to the Polish nation's elite literary culture.

JEWISH ARTISTS

Just as Jewish sports organizations and reading rooms furthered the development of a secular Jewish culture in Cracow, Jewish visual artists began to organize themselves into associations that furthered their art in secular contexts. The goal of the Jewish Society for the Spreading of the Fine Arts was, simply, the development of the fine arts among Jews.[43] Artists in the Association of Artists 'Union', including Leon Lewkowicz, Szymon Muller and Jakób Pfefferberg, defined their goal as the 'spreading of a love for art through lectures and the exhibitions of paintings and sculptures of our members'.[44] During the inter-war period, Jewish leaders organized cultural life along specifically Jewish lines, taking advantage of an opportunity that had not presented itself during the final years of the Habsburg Empire.[45]

That such organizations focused almost solely on the 'spreading' (the Polish words most often used include *krzewienie, rozpowszechnienie, rozszerzenie* and *szerzenie*) of 'culture' or, sometimes more specifically, 'Jewish culture,' indicates a growing recognition on the part of the Jewish cultural leaders that significant segments of the Jewish community were excluded from participation in any kind of formal cultural life. Unlike the acculturated Jewish elite who founded the Social Reading Room, the Union of Jewish Artists confirmed its own Jewish identity and expressed a willingness to 'spread culture' among Jews. Their organizing into an association of artists demonstrates the need for Jewish leadership and the development of a specifically Jewish secular culture, especially given the more acculturated Jewish elite's abandonment of specifically Jewish cultural goals. In an effort to reach out to a larger segment of the Jewish community, the artists' efforts aimed to improve the number and kinds of opportunities afforded Jewish artists as well as those offered to Jewish audiences. The two goals were intertwined in the statements of the organizations themselves, suggesting that Jewish cultural leaders understood the need to cultivate Jewish audiences to support their work. Further, Jewish artists expressed hope that the relationship between artist and audience could lead to greater mutual understanding within Poland. In the journal *Sztuka i Życie Współczesne* [*Art and Contemporary Life*], published in February 1934 in Cracow, a group of Jewish artists proclaimed their hope that art could overcome the hatred unleashed in Europe in recent years.[46] This periodical was the work of the Association of Jewish Artists, Painters and Sculptors. Founded in 1933, the association grew to a not insignificant membership of 171. The association included the participation of Wilhelm Berkelhammer, the editor of *Nowy Dziennik*, Henryk Apte, the music critic for *Nowy Dziennik*, as well as the artists Leo Schoenker, Norbert Nadel, Ignacy Muller and Leon Lewkowicz.[47] In *Sztuka i Życie Współczesne*, these artists called for greater co-operation between the artist and the audience, a co-operation that should not be limited to one national group but that should serve the greatest number of people possible. Moreover, they expressed hope that this would lead to a greater level of understanding between Poles and Jews. As the articles of the journal show, the artists were interested in local Jewish art, working to establish a Jewish Museum in Cracow and in areas as diverse as French impressionism and Soviet film.

The writers in *Sztuka i Życie Współczesne* exemplify how the educated Jews of Cracow also worked on behalf of the Jewish community. Engaged in current debates regarding contemporary art, cosmopolitan in orientation, and significantly less traditional than the typical Jew of Kazimierz, the artists of the Association for Jewish Artists were none the less involved in local affairs, as their concern for a museum proposed by the *kehillah* attests. Jewish artists, like other Jewish intellectuals, turned to separate Jewish organizations to maintain their ethnic identity without abandoning the majority culture. They promoted what we would call today greater multicultural understanding amid the realities of cultural diversity. They promoted different kinds of art equally, and they worked to advance local causes such as the *kehillah* museum.

One of the most important and more ideologically oriented articles in *Sztuka i Życie Współczesne* came from Leon Chwistek, a non-Jewish Polish artist and intellectual from Lwów. His article, 'Questions of the Artistic Environment', pointed out that the idea of 'national art' had still not been overcome. Chwistek saw his era as one of great prejudices. He was clearly against 'national art', that is, art that would somehow privilege one nation, one community, over another.[48] Taking his ideas even further, Chwistek asserted that chauvinism was connected with crime and would always act as a brake on the development of spiritual culture. Tolerance, in contrast, always leads to the blossoming of culture and a higher cultural level. As proof, Chwistek compared the Poland of Casimir the Great and the Jagiellonians to fifteenth-century Spain and the Inquisition. Chwistek noted that it was the artists from foreign countries that made Paris the centre of the art world in the inter-war period. In fact, the further the origins of these artists from Paris, the stronger the proof that Paris was the centre of the art world.

There was a spark for great art in Poland, according to Chwistek, but it disappeared quickly. Great art could exist even in the Carpathian mountains, Chwistek felt, but without the support of a great centre it would drown. Advocates of 'averageness' (*przeciętność*) asserted that artistic innovations were, by definition, foreign, specifically Jewish, and therefore should be liquidated. According to Chwistek, Poles had never understood that they were destined for the great task of the working people. He thought Poles could solve their problems by promoting the cause of social justice for all nations. This task plainly involved tolerance for other nations and other types of art. Then and only then would Poles not have to go abroad to look for examples of great art because all races/nations would feel drawn to Poland as an artistic centre.[49]

In a review of an exhibition sponsored by the Association of Jewish Artists, Painters and Sculptors in Cracow,[50] the Jewish artist Henryk Weber asked the recurring question about Jews and art – were they Jewish artists or artists who happened to be Jewish? Weber did not give a definitive answer to this question, but he did state that national categories did not help artists.

Taking Chagall as an example, Weber suggested that what was important for an artist was to be rooted in his environment, concluding that many different characteristics could define an artist, none of them necessarily dependent on nationality.

Both Chwistek and Weber espoused an inclusive philosophy of art that transcended national distinctions. This philosophy allowed for Jews to be included in the art world, to be exhibited alongside other artists, to be viewed objectively, not to be discriminated against as Jews, and to appeal openly to non-Jewish audiences. According to Chwistek and Weber, art could not be limited by national boundaries and national character-istics could not and should not determine the nature of an individual's art. These artistic values were of great importance to a minority community that could simply not take any other position. The call for greater multicultural understanding among artists was the most effective way for Jews to ensure that they would be taken seriously as artists. Not surprisingly, they advocated the work of artists of other nationalities as well, writing about Soviet film or French impressionism. Advocating the organization of artists' groups along ethnic lines, this association of Jewish artists also reached out to artists from other ethnic groups, declaring their solidarity while separating themselves from them at the same time.

THE YIDDISH THEATRE IN INTER-WAR CRACOW

In terms of innovation, the most significant Jewish cultural institution during the inter-war period was the Cracow Yiddish Theatre Society, established as a formal organization in 1926. This group was formed largely thanks to the efforts of Mojżesz Kanfer, who was appointed literary editor and theatre critic of *Nowy Dziennik* in 1923. The Yiddish Theatre Society went through difficult periods during the 1920s and 1930s, even ceasing to exist for several years. Kanfer's effort to establish a standing professional Yiddish theatre troupe in Cracow is notable for several reasons, not least of which is the fact that it was led by a journalist writing in Polish. It is also notable for the determination of its leadership and for its ultimate lack of success. Kanfer and his society thought the current level of

Yiddish theatre in Cracow to be shamefully low and they continually tried to improve its artistic quality. Kanfer faced a difficult battle, though, as he did not have the support of the city's Jewish intelligentsia who, according to Kanfer and the memoir literature, attended the Polish theatre with much more regularity. Nor did the society enjoy the unquestioned support of other Yiddish cultural institutions in the city. The society was thus charged with the task of developing and maintaining a Yiddish-speaking audience as well as winning the support of the predominantly Polish-speaking Jewish intelligentsia, who had already abandoned Yiddish as a daily language.

Yiddish productions had taken place in Cracow as early as the 1880s. Tracing the history of Yiddish theatre in Cracow, Rachel Holcer noted the formation of the Jewish 'Szopka' Satirical Puppet Theatre in 1919.[51] The director of the puppet theatre was Mojżesz Jacob, a former censor under Habsburg rule who after the end of the First World War received a government concession to present Yiddish plays. The Puppet Theatre was held on the Planty in the 'Royal' *kawiarnia* [coffee shop] and attracted the attention of Kanfer, Wilhelm Fallek and other Jewish intellectuals who described it as political satire of the highest order.

According to Fryderyk Freund, one of the early leaders of the group, the efforts to form the Yiddish Theatre Society had begun as early as 1924, but the organization formed then, the Society of Friends of Jewish Art, did not receive the necessary concession from the government. This organization, with Freund as president and Kanfer and Mordecai Gebirtig on the board, sponsored a series of lectures in 1925 by such prominent Jewish cultural figures as the writers Meylekh Ravitch, Sholem Asch, H. Leyvik, and Joseph Opatoshu. The efforts of those involved in the Yiddish Theatre Society in Cracow were tireless, and, judging from the well-known list of authors invited to lecture in 1925, not entirely unsuccessful.[52] The Polish director Antoni Piekarski attributed the early achievements of the Yiddish theatre in Cracow to the strength of Jewish solidarity. But Kanfer, more than anyone, recognized that when it came to organizing a Yiddish theatre, there was no Jewish unity that could be relied on for support. In fact, Kanfer was a pioneer in the development of the Yiddish theatre, and he faced many difficulties, even from within the Jewish community. Thus, the society initially focused on sponsoring lectures and bringing in visiting Yiddish theatre troupes.

Recalling the first years of the Cracow Yiddish Theatre Society, Freund reported that the society received its concession from the government because it promised not to interfere with the *Teatr Miejski* [City Theatre]. Most importantly, Freund argued that the Yiddish Theatre Society benefited Polish culture as well.[53] It seems an unlikely concern, but it appears the city was worried about possible competition the City Theatre might face from another theatre in the city. In 1939, the city's Yiddish theatre was a topic for debate in the Cracow city council. Kalman Shtayn, a Jewish delegate to the city council, asserted in 1939 that the Yiddish Theatre Society was a valuable cultural institution for the city of Cracow as well as for the Jewish population.[54] Shtayn argued forcefully against the well-known Polish academic and city leader, Stanisław Pigoń, who had suggested dropping the subvention for the Cracow Yiddish Theatre Society from the city's cultural budget. Shtayn asserted that Cracow was the cultural centre of Poland and argued further that Jewish culture in Cracow, like Polish culture, should be on the highest level possible. Shtayn even quoted Pope Pius XII's affirmation of the dignity of the individual, which, according to Stein, could be respected only if the individual had equal rights in culture and education. The budget for culture was approved to the displeasure of the representatives of the Polish right, who walked out of the council meeting. Like Freund, Shtayn asserted that the development of Jewish culture would somehow improve Polish culture. Neither defined precisely how this benefit for Polish culture would be realized; they simply asserted that any improvement in Jewish life would at least bring some recognition to the city.

The city's subvention never helped to solve Kanfer's problems within the Jewish community, however. His daughter, Irene Kanfer, helps to explain the difficulties her father faced. Kanfer, in his columns in *Nowy Dziennik*, repeatedly encouraged the more assimilated Jewish intelligentsia of Cracow to attend the Yiddish theatre, usually to no avail, perhaps because of his critical tone. Recalling his description of the Jewish theatre-going audience, Irene Kanfer writes, 'my father spoke about the

Jewish theatre public of Cracow with sarcasm: assimilated snobs for whom the Jewish language was a type of jargon and for whom real theatre is – Polish theatre'.[55]

Kanfer's writings suggest that part of his goal was the preservation of a Yiddish and Jewish culture that many assimilated Jews were in danger of leaving behind completely. He wrote in 1931,

> Even the assimilated Jewish intellectual, who preserved in his soul the cult of the traditional tsholent, delighting in Jewish fish and growing mystical at the sound of the shofar, even this assimilated Jewish intellectual senses a nostalgic recognition that Jewish culture is not dead, that Sholem Aleykhem, Peretz, Asch, Leyvik, and Anski speak to him from the stage.[56]

Kanfer's activities were an institutional affirmation of the city's Yiddish culture, a culture the city's Jewish elite did not acknowledge in any other official way.

Kanfer not only had to win over the more assimilated, but he also had to court the Orthodox if he wished his theatre society to succeed. He wrote, ' … we find ourselves in the tragic situation that an important segment of Jewish society takes a decidedly hostile position to Jewish theatre.'[57] His daughter recalled of her father, 'He also frankly characterized the fanaticism of the Orthodox Jews, for whom, as for all Puritans, *any* theatre was sinful – they did not allow their own children to participate in theatrical productions.'[58]

The differences within the Jewish community were real. While some Jews embraced both the Jewish and non-Jewish theatre as one of the highest expressions of art, others were vocal in the implications of the development of an active theatre scene. According to the Cracow correspondent of the Lwów Yiddish daily, *Najer Morgen*, Yiddish theatrical performances in Cracow had never occurred on Shabes or Jewish holidays.[59] But in May 1934, the visiting theatre director B. Yakubovitsh announced that the première of *Yankel muzikant* would take place on a Friday night. This announcement caused the Hasidim of Cracow to join together in calling an informal court made up of representatives of the city's Shomer Shabes group, an organization devoted to maintaining the observance of the Sabbath and deterring any desecration of the holy day. According to *Najer Morgen*'s correspondent, several of the artists involved with the production appeared at the informal hearing, explaining that they performed on Shabes in even the smallest shtetls. Collectively, they wondered why sixteen artists should be put out of work when leaders of the political parties, cultural activists, and Jewish city council members could attend cabaret performances in luxurious coffee houses on Shabes. A delegation of artists also went to Rafał Landau, the head of the *kehillah*, and asked him to intervene. In response, Landau questioned why the artists even felt the need to ask for the permission to perform. The Shomer Shabes group, Landau pointed out, did have some authority within the community, but it was not the *kehillah* nor even necessarily representative of Cracow Jewry.

Kanfer was presented with a gap between two different segments of Jewish society, the Orthodox more likely to use Yiddish but opposed to the theatre, and the more assimilated Jewry who were open to the theatre but found Yiddish to be marginal to their cultural identity. In establishing a modern Yiddish theatre, Kanfer self-consciously developed a middle ground between these different groups. In Kanfer's mind, his efforts to build a theatre society occupied a place in Cracow Jewish society between the assimilated and the Orthodox, providing a Jewish institution in which other Jews, who may have moved outside of the strictly Orthodox world but who were not completely assimilated, could take part, learning something about Jewish culture. Not insignificantly, Kanfer wrote for *Nowy Dziennik*, itself a Jewish institution that, as a Polish-language Zionist newspaper, bridged two different cultures. Rachel Holcer confirms this balancing act of Kanfer in her memoirs, writing that the Yiddish theatre in Cracow 'became the basis of a constant cultural centre in a stronghold of assimilation and Orthodoxy'.[60]

Sometimes Orthodox Jews crossed the boundaries dividing traditional Jewish life from Kanfer's society. In spite of the many public failures of the society, this was perhaps its most important success. Irene Kanfer noted how some children of Orthodox Jews attended performances in violation of their parents' religious beliefs, and one, her friend, attended the actors' studio without telling her parents. Kanfer introduced at least some traditional Jews to secular culture. Though in Yiddish and part of Yiddish culture, the Cracow Yiddish Theatre Society was not an example of a traditional Jewish institution. Rather, it was clearly part of modern artistic movements, expressing in Yiddish the works of different literary movements in different European languages and developing its own artistic preferences and forms. Moreover, it was part of a cultural and national movement of the Jews, led by the literary critic of a Polish-language Zionist newspaper. The theatre society did not reflect the hopes and dreams of the Yiddish-speaking Orthodox majority but rather the goals and education of a Jewish intelligentsia that was in the process of transforming traditional Jewish life. In disobeying her parents, Irene Kanfer's friend introduced herself to a larger world that, while still linguistically distinct from the culture of the majority, was not a part of her parents' experience.

Attracting large audiences was a problem that plagued Kanfer throughout the inter-war period. Kanfer's tendency to blame this on the fact that Cracow's more acculturated Jews attended the Polish theatre was to some extent justified. Writing on the Yiddish theatre, the critic N. Wejnig argued that the problem of reforming the Yiddish theatre was not dependent on the audience's supposed dislike of classical theatre – proof of this lay in the fact that Jews attended the 'theatre of other nations to satisfy their aesthetic hunger'.[61] The Jews of Cracow did not see the Yiddish theatre as their only cultural option. Some of the most important memoirs of inter-war Cracow Jews mention the Yiddish theatre, but only fleetingly. Henryk Vogler and Henryk Ritterman-Abir attended the Polish theatre, not the Yiddish. Vogler writes that he never knew the Yiddish theatre when he was growing up in inter-war Cracow. According to Vogler, attendance at the theatre (at least the Polish theatre) was not for the proletariat and surrounding peasantry for many reasons, not least of which was financial.[62] Rather, the theatre depended on students and the richer urban bourgeoisie for its audiences. In the early 1920s, Vogler's parents subscribed to loge seats in the Słowacki theatre, and, like Ritterman-Abir, he grew up knowing the pleasures of the theatre, but in Polish. Ritterman-Abir notes that he did have some contact with the Yiddish theatre, seeing Ida Kaminska's troupe perform in the theatre on Bocheńska Street and getting to know some of the Yiddish actors. Still, Ritterman-Abir's experiences in the theatre grew out of his time as a student at the Sobieski gymnasium. In addition, the *Teatr Szkolny* programme of Juliusz Osterwa introduced Jewish children all over Cracow to Polish theatre. Polish educational and cultural authorities could use the Polish schools and administrative system for their own goals, which included introducing young Polish citizens to the high culture of Polish theatre. Yiddish cultural leaders did not enjoy the advantages of a centralized school administration. Thus, the efforts of the theatre societies in inter-war Cracow were all the more necessary to develop and sustain a vibrant theatrical life among Cracow's Jews.

Though Vogler and Ritterman-Abir did not attend the Yiddish theatre, other Jews inclined towards the use of Polish did. Irena Bronner cites her knowledge of the poetry of Tadeusz Żeleński (Boy) alongside her brief reminiscence of her parents' attending the Yiddish theatre as a young girl.[63] Interestingly, she recalled how they used to return home repeating or singing the contents of the performance. The specific incident she chose to relate regarding the Yiddish theatre is telling. She remembered how one night her parents returned home retelling the scene from Sholem Aleichem's *Tevye der milkhiger* in which Tevye's daughter Hodel runs off with a non-Jew. They then later jokingly cited this line to their daughter more than once.

The Yiddish Theatre Society did not limit itself to presentations of Yiddish plays. Presenting non-Yiddish plays in Yiddish was a sign of the maturity of Yiddish theatre, an indication that it was interested in introducing its audience to other playwrights and other cultures using one Jewish vernacular. The Yiddish Theatre Society performed two plays of Stanisław Wyspiański in 1927 and later in 1932. One of these, *Daniel*, an opera libretto written by Wyspiański in 1893 on the Biblical themes in the Book of Daniel, was performed in Yiddish for the first time in 1927. *Sędziowie* [*The Judges*], a story based on a contemporary trial in Poland and written in 1907, received its first production, in any language, in Yiddish, in 1927. *Daniel* is an allegory concerning a nation divided by foreign powers and subject to slavery, important for both Polish and Jewish national thought. One Polish reviewer wrote about the staging of *Daniel*, 'What was for us an allegory, the Zionists take today as their own national reality.'[64] Both plays presented significant challenges for the theatre society. The director of *Daniel*, Antoni Piekarski, barely understood Yiddish. *Daniel* required an elaborate staging that necessitated the use of the gallery space by the actors, and *Sędziowie* contained Jewish characters that had been labelled anti-Semitic by another Yiddish theatre director, Michał Weichert.[65]

While Kanfer and the Yiddish Theatre Society were still interested in the majority culture around them, Polish theatre critics were unaware of the Jewish cultural efforts going on in Kazimierz until they attended these first Yiddish productions of Polish plays. Upon attending the Yiddish Theatre on Bocheńska Street in Kazimierz, two Polish theatre critics described their trip to the theatre as entering another world. Both claimed they had never heard of this street name before, in spite of being longtime residents of Cracow.[66] The Polish reviews of the two plays were generally favourable, in spite of the Polish reviewers' startling ignorance of the Jewish community in their city. The translations of the Zionist activist D. Leibl were uniformly praised.

Thus, the theatre society acted as an organization that introduced Polish culture to its Yiddish-speaking audience (also part Polish-speaking, of course), even including Polish national art in its own repertory. While certainly a Jewish organization, the Yiddish Theatre did not serve to isolate its audience. It produced plays originally written in German and English as well, acting as an intermediary between the Yiddish-speaking public and the larger society. A reviewer for *Ilustrowany Kurier Codzienny* commented on the importance of the stagings of the Wyspiański plays for the Jewish audience: 'These presentations are a most effective attempt to popularize Polish national poetry among the Jewish masses for which the theatre under the direction of J. Turkow deserves sincere recognition.'[67] It is quite possible that the Wyspiański plays reached a different audience from that reached by some of the more traditional plays performed by the Cracow troupe. Interestingly, in his writings on the Yiddish theatre, Sholem Freund noted that the performances of Wyspiański's plays 'in truth were more successful among the Polish and Jewish-Polish audiences than among the Jewish'.[68] To be fair, this was in part Kanfer's goal: to expand the range of Yiddish theatre, both in repertory and audience. By presenting a Polish play in Yiddish, Kanfer reached out to both audiences, the Polish and the Jewish, introducing each to the other.

Kanfer's efforts never ceased during the inter-war period. He continually looked for ways to keep the society active even during difficult times. In 1930, after the relative failures of the 1927–28 season, Kanfer called for a national conference on Yiddish theatre, recognizing that Cracow alone could not support a permanent residential troupe in Yiddish. In addition to the theatre on Bocheńska, the Yiddish Theatre Society also sponsored evenings of theatre and cabaret in a smaller space on Szpitalna Street in the centre of the city (in the building that is today the US Consulate). These evenings were intended to be smaller events, attracting a higher class of audience than the performances on Bocheńska. Mordecai Gebirtig, the Yiddish composer, participated in these evenings, evidence that the presentation of Yiddish culture was not limited to Kazimierz. In his 1937 report on the theatrical activities on Bocheńska and Szpitalna, Kanfer admitted difficulties, but claimed that he had developed a permanent residential Yiddish theatre in Cracow. The theatre still had not grown to its full potential and still needed the support of the broadest part of the Jewish intelligentsia.[69] The theatre had been inactive for much of the 1930s because of the economic crisis, and Kanfer expressed hope that it would become active again and even hoped to build a new theatre building. Until then, guest performances by visiting theatre troupes would be held at the theatre on Bocheńska. Kanfer encouraged everyone to support Yiddish theatre even during hard economic times.[70]

Kanfer himself was the first to admit the difficulties in organizing the society and in presenting Yiddish plays to Jewish audiences. He wrote in 1931, the period late-twentieth-century scholars of Yiddish culture might regard as the heyday of Yiddish drama, that 'Yiddish theatre in Poland is dying away and declining from day to day.'[71] Kanfer was one of very few Jewish intellectuals in Cracow who worked diligently on behalf of Yiddish culture. That he was not entirely successful should not diminish the importance of his efforts. While theatre troupes in Vilnius, Warsaw and even Łódź may have been more active during the inter-war period, Kanfer's efforts to establish a permanent residential theatre troupe made the Cracow society unique. Yiddish culture in Cracow did not happen without effort. The formation of the society itself implied that Yiddish culture needed such organization. The society's failures demonstrate that the necessary effort to make Yiddish theatre a successful venture was indeed quite significant.

That the Yiddish press did not uncritically support the Yiddish theatre also did not help Kanfer attract Jewish theatre-goers.[72] Moyshe Blekher, the editor of the Yiddish periodicals *Der reflektor* and *Di post*, often criticized Kanfer's use of Polish in organizing the Yiddish Theatre Society, deriding it as the product of assimilationists. Blekher did not acknowledge the difficulties Kanfer encountered in establishing an important Yiddish cultural institution, nor did he offer real support. In a sharply critical article about Kanfer's theatre society in the Yiddish press, one writer (in an unsigned article, most likely Blekher) noted that 'the theatre society has already fallen apart seven times and been reorganized ten times'.[73] In all their years of its existence, the unnamed author wrote, the theatre society had failed to do anything substantial, either for the audience or for the actors. Many members of the theatre society had left the group as a protest against its leaders, leaving the society in a poor position. And, according to the article, neither Freund nor Kanfer protested when the theatre society brought in 'hungry actors to play in *shund* and pornographic musical theatre pieces for a bite of bread'.[74] This was precisely what Kanfer wanted to change about the Yiddish theatre. He wanted to provide actors and audiences with the opportunity to create and enjoy theatre of the highest order, a goal which, in spite of the criticism, he achieved, if only partially. The article further criticized Kanfer and his theatre society for being 'dilettantish', a quality apparent in the then current production of H. Leyvik's *Shop*. According to the article, this was not the level of the plays of Michał Weichert or Mark Arnshtayn in Warsaw.[75]

The writer disparaged Kanfer's effort to develop an actors' studio as well. According to the author, a studio implied a school for experimentation and training for actors, not acting students. The writer granted that those in the studio were good candidates for training but argued that they were being exploited in order for the theatre to receive the concession to present Yiddish plays.[76] The formation of studios, even if they were short-lived, implies that artistic innovation and improvement were the goals of those involved in Cracow's Yiddish theatre. Yiddish actors and cultural activists pursued and supported their craft professionally. The writer in *Der reflektor*, however, claimed that the problems of the theatre society could not be solved by the formation of a studio, but that better directors were needed for the actors. Only then would the Yiddish Theatre Society assume an 'important cultural position in our assimilated city'.[77]

Polish-language posters of the theatre society advertising productions in Yiddish were also subject to criticism. The writer of an article in *Der reflektor*, most likely Blekher again, claimed that such posters were 'foreign' to the goals of the society because they were in Polish. The Yiddish Theatre Society was, in theory, the *kultur-treger* [bearer of culture] of Yiddish language and drama in the city, so such a poster did seem odd to the Yiddish writers of *Der reflektor*. But the Polish poster also reflected an acknowledgement of reality on the part of the theatre society. While there is no doubt that the theatre society could have advertised in Yiddish (as many other Jewish organizations did), advertising in Polish reached a Jewish audience that may have been interested in Yiddish culture even if they had given up Yiddish as a daily language.

Blekher did not hide his disdain for Kanfer and the other leaders of the theatre society in *Di post*, the Yiddish periodical he founded two years after the demise of *Der reflektor*. Here too Blekher criticized these cultural leaders severely for such things as not using Yiddish in their private lives and, like *Der reflektor*, advertising for the Yiddish theatre in Polish. Admitting that a Yiddish theatre in town did highlight Yiddish culture in an assimilated city like Cracow, Blekher none the less reproached Yiddish actors and actresses who behaved like 'stars' by appearing in Polish posters. Reporting on a meeting of the theatre society, Blekher termed Kanfer, Freund and the other leaders of the theatre society, 'cultural martyrs', a term they may have taken positively. Blekher, however, used it ironically, implying that their commitment to Polish-language culture outweighed their involvement with Yiddish. Blekher did not believe that Kanfer and the others were sincerely interested in Yiddish culture. For Blekher, the Yiddish culture of Kanfer's society was not representative of the Yiddish culture of Cracow because the Jewish intelligentsia presenting that culture in Yiddish, in his view, had only a tangential relationship to Jewish life.

Clearly, those in the city involved and interested in Yiddish culture did not always work together, and Kanfer found greater co-operation among those Jews who promoted a Polish-language Jewish culture, such as the writers of *Nowy Dziennik*. Further, the conflict between *Der reflektor* and *Di post* and the theatre society indicates that, for many, a Yiddish *kultur-treger* in the city was both a desired and a necessary goal. There was no obvious candidate among the Jewish institutions of the city for such a title, a sign of the weakness of Yiddish culture. The theatre society was often inactive and *Der reflektor* only lasted for a couple of issues. To be fair, *Di post* began publishing in 1937 and was still publishing full issues in August 1939. Blekher's was the only voice in the city that called for a more assertive Yiddish culture in Yiddish for a Yiddish-speaking population. *Der reflektor* failed; *Di post* did achieve some success and remained in print until the outbreak of the war. Kanfer and Blekher both promoted Yiddish culture, each in his own way. Unlike Blekher, Kanfer aimed to link the different Polish and Yiddish cultures. The absence of a true Yiddish *kultur-treger* in Cracow highlights how the city's Jews were creating Jewish cultures with different agendas. Blekher's strong Yiddishist views contrast with Kanfer's attempt to create a Jewish culture that was neither entirely Polish nor entirely Jewish, focused on neither Hebrew nor Yiddish, neither assimilationist nor separatist.

At least two other organizations in inter-war Cracow were concerned with the theatre, proof that even within the relatively small community of 60,000, there was room for more than one theatrical society. The Jewish Stage (*Scena Żydowska* or *Idysze Bine*), like the Yiddish Theatre Society, was formed in 1926. There is no indication that this organization was involved with the Yiddish Theatre Society, however. The leaders of the organization included Juljusz Witkower, a university student, and Róża Holzer-Rymplowa.[78] The goals of the organization did not specify Jewish art or a Jewish audience, but were stated simply as 'the spreading and deepening among its members of art and culture in the general sense, but especially the theatrical'.[79] Clearly,

Kanfer's Yiddish Theatre Society did not serve all of the Jews of Cracow.

The Jewish Amateur Scene Club, established in 1922, also stated its goals in a particularly unusual way.[80] The founder of this organization was the owner of a box factory and, given the addresses of its officers, was based in Podgórze rather than Kazimierz. Its goal was to 'bring the Jewish masses not yet having a good command of proper Polish closer to culture, to instruct the masses intellectually, to develop and spread the idea of the beauty of the fine arts by organizing in Yiddish and Polish amateur presentations, readings and lectures and maintaining a periodical and library in Polish and Yiddish'.[81] This statement suggests the level of linguistic assimilation much more reliably than census statistics. For the Jewish founders of this organization, the general Jewish population did not speak Polish as well as the founders thought they should. Therefore, an organization was established to help them master the Polish language and introduce them to Polish culture. While others, most notably Sore Shenirer, were concerned that Jews were turning to Polish in ever greater numbers, this Jewish organization specifically included an improvement of Polish in its goals. The founders' statement also indicates the Yiddish-speaking nature of Cracow's Jewish population. Cracow's Jews had begun a process of changing linguistically but had not yet completely switched languages.

The various dramatic societies had somewhat different goals. The two smaller organizations that did not share the high profile of Kanfer's Yiddish Theatre Society had somewhat lesser (yet perhaps more realistic) objectives in mind. They were concerned with 'spreading culture' among the general population and aimed to be more instructional in their activities than artistic. Kanfer, the literary critic, on the other hand, would settle for nothing less than a permanent residential Yiddish theatre troupe in Cracow, one that would perform on a consistently high artistic level. As the literary critic of *Nowy Dziennik*, Kanfer had the high profile within the Jewish community necessary to undertake the ambitious goal of starting a Yiddish theatre.

None of these drama societies, with their emphasis on Yiddish culture, served to separate the Jewish community from the Polish majority. For all his advocacy of the Yiddish theatre,

Kanfer wrote in Polish and, as a theatre critic, was involved in Polish theatrical life as well, consistently reviewing the plays performed in the Słowacki Theatre and other venues in Cracow. The goal of establishing a separate Yiddish theatre was meant to promote Yiddish culture, and to establish a Jewish cultural organization that would have been on an equal artistic level with the Polish theatre. Kanfer was not abandoning the Polish theatre in favour of Yiddish; he clearly wanted to be a part of both. He simply recognized that more work was necessary before Yiddish theatre in Cracow could meet his exacting artistic standards, and he was willing and generous enough to take this work on himself. On another level, the two smaller organizations did not exclude Polish culture from their consideration at all. In fact, these groups were less exclusively Yiddish oriented than Kanfer's theatre society. One of the two specifically included Polish culture, recognizing that a mastery of the Polish language and culture was a priority for Cracow's Jews and the other did not specify Yiddish culture in its goals. None of the organizations would have completely isolated its members or audiences from the majority culture. Rather, it is likely their members and those involved in the organizations' activities participated in both Polish and Jewish culture to a greater extent precisely because of their involvement in specifically Jewish cultural organizations.

The efforts of Kanfer and the leaders of the other smaller societies should be viewed in the larger context of Jewish life in Cracow. These leaders faced tremendous obstacles in their attempts to develop a Jewish theatrical culture in the city, including increasing linguistic assimilation and a more influential Polish theatre that attracted a Jewish audience. Nevertheless, their efforts ensured that the trilingual culture of Polish Jewry in Cracow continued to thrive. Thanks to Kanfer and the other Yiddish cultural leaders, Cracow's Jews could participate in a secular Jewish culture without abandoning their Jewish identity.

Taking a *kawiarnia*, or coffee house, as his vantage point from which to survey Jewish culture in Cracow, the young writer M. Bornstein expressed his hope that Jewish culture in the city would continue to grow. Bornstein praised the performances of the Yiddish theatre and the lectures and art exhibitions so many groups sponsored. But such expressions of Jewish participation in Jewish culture were not enough for Bornstein, who made known his dismay that there was no established Jewish literary magazine in the city. At the time Bornstein was writing, *Di post* had been publishing for a couple of weeks, but, according to Bornstein, had failed to attract older or younger readers. Bornstein's assessment of Jewish cultural life in Cracow reflects many of the difficulties Cracow's Jewish cultural leaders faced. Bornstein concluded his survey of Jewish culture in Cracow by writing, 'at least there's a nice bar', referring to the well-known *Szmatka kawiarnia*. For Bornstein, this informal gathering of Jewish artists and intellectuals was just as important as any formal cultural organization. More significantly, though, it was an important feature of Jewish cultural life in a city the Jewish population of which was still learning to appreciate different forms of Jewish cultural expression.

That the cultural organizations discussed above did not yet satisfy writers like Bornstein should not diminish their importance and influence within the Jewish community. This review of Jewish cultural organizations in inter-war Cracow considered only a few of the 305 organizations on Wordliczek's list. Those organizations examined here contributed to the cultural diversity of the city and the Jewish community, working towards the development of a secular Jewish culture that was one of the goals of writers like Bornstein.

Taking part in the activities of the organizations mentioned in this chapter indicates, at least to some extent, a self-identification with Jewish life. This is especially important for more acculturated Jews who did not participate in religious observances. Ethnic identity can be expressed by participation in a separate ethnic organization, whether that means simply attending lectures infrequently or taking a leadership role. Simple participation in an ethnic organization does not, of course, always signify lasting ethnic allegiance. But as this survey of the various associations Jewish community leaders established demonstrates, Jews in Cracow had the opportunity to participate in all kinds of separate Jewish activities, from soccer teams to theatrical productions. Jewish children attending private Polish schools could go to soccer matches where exclusively Jewish teams such as Makkabi and Jutrzenka would play. The establishment of the private Jewish organizations discussed in this chapter ensured that the Jews of Cracow would have the opportunity to play, to read, to paint, to act as Jews.

At least two different important Jewish cultural organizations had substantial connections to Polish culture, the Association of Jewish Artists and the Cracow Yiddish Theatre Society. Other organizations, such as the private Jewish sports clubs, did not preclude participation in and co-operation with Polish sports organizations. Just as private Jewish schools served as a bridge to Polish culture (as well as an introduction to Jewish culture) for many Jews, so cultural organizations meant exclusively for Jews were not entirely separated from Polish culture. All of the organizations discussed in this chapter aimed to improve the cultural level of Jews, culturally, intellectually or physically. Their achievements can be measured in different ways, according to the number of events they sponsored, the number of individuals who participated, or the profile of the organization within the Jewish and non-Jewish communities. Paul Brass has argued that an ethnic group 'establishes' itself as a nationality if it achieves 'recognized group rights in the political system'.[82] The Jews of Cracow used their limited political rights to develop their own, often separate, community structures. By establishing such a broad network of social and cultural organizations, the Jews of Cracow were defining themselves as something other than merely 'Poles of the Mosaic faith'. Though they were not able to define themselves as a political nation, the Jews of Cracow, especially those active in the organizations discussed in this chapter, did aspire to a separate cultural identity as Polish Jews.

NOTES

1. Sholem (Fryderyk) Freund, 'Pierwszy społeczny teatr żydowski w Polsce (Krakowski Teatr Żydowski)', in *Teatr Żydowski w Krakowie*, ed. Jan Michalik and Eugenia Prokop-Janiec (Cracow: Międzywydziałowy Zakład Historii i Kultury Żydowskiej w Polsce), 162. Freund's article originally appeared in *Yidish teatr*, 1927, Nr 1–2 and was translated by Anna Ciałowicz for publication in *Teatr Żydowski w Krakowie*.
2. In addition, I have omitted an analysis of Jewish religious and charitable organizations, primarily because they deserve separate treatment. A study of Jewish

social work in inter-war Poland would be especially useful as it is likely to yield important insights into the activities of Jewish women, who were more active in social work than in political or cultural activities. It would also help us to understand better the consequences of the dire economic circumstances faced by both Jews and Poles.

3. Zofia Wordliczek, 'Wystawa'. Collection of unpublished materials in the library of the Museum of the City of Cracow, Old Synagogue (Muzeum Miasta Krakowa, Stara Synagoga).

4. Ibid.

5. Wojewódzkie Archiwum Państwowe w Krakowie, Starostwo Grodzkie Krakowskie (WAPKr, StGKr) 241 Klub Towarzyski w Krakowie 1932–39.

6. StGKr 249 Żyd. Tow. Śpiewane 'Szir' 1920 1923–28; StGKr 139 Zrzeszenie literatów i dziennikarzy hebrajskich w Polsce Oddział w Krakowie; StGKr 241 Radio Klub Towarzyski w Krakowie 1924–38.

7. StGKr 249 Żydowskie Tow. Oświaty Ludowej (1913–18), 1920–39.

8. StGKr 139, March 1935.

9. StGKr 249 Żyd. Tow. Oświaty Zawodowej 1937.

10. StGKr 246 'Toynbe Hala' Towarzystwo dla szerzenia oświaty wśród Żydów w Małopolsce 1904–17, 1920–35.

11. The police file indicates that the organization lasted until 1935, but this is the only record of its activity located in the file.

12. Central State Historical Archives, L'viv, Fond 701, Opis 3, Sprava 1050, 15–17.

13. The notable exception is the *Czytelnia Towarzyska* [Social Reading Room], discussed further below.

14. StGKr 249 Żyd. Stow. Kulturalno-oświatowe 'Tarbut' w Krakowie 1922–38.

15. Ibid.

16. Henryk Vogler, *Wyznanie mojżeszowe* (Warsaw: Państwowy Instytut Wydawniczy, 1994), 12.

17. StGKr 249 Żyd. Klub Sportowy 'Makkabi' 1911, 1923–38.

18. StGKr 249 Żyd. Tow. Gimnastyczne w Krakowie (1901–14) 1919–38.

19. ZIH GWZKr 905.

20. M. Dickes, 'Makkabi a władze sportowe', *Chwila*, 7 August 1934, 10.

21. For more information, limited as it is, on these and other sports organizations, see the following StGKr 248 Żydowski Klub Sportowy 'Adria' 1922–25; StGKr 248 Żydowski Klub Sportowy 'Amatorzy' w Krakowie 1921–30; StGKr 248 Żydowski Klub Sportowy 'Bar-Kochba' w Krakowie 1924; StGKr 248 Żydowski Klub Sportowy 'Dror' 1922–28; StGKr 248 Żydowski Klub Sportowy 'Gewira' 1922–30 Podgórze; StGKr 249 Żydowski Klub Sportowy 'Hagibor' 1928–38; StGKr 249 Żydowski Klub Sportowy 'Hakudur'; StGKr 249 Żydowski Klub Sportowy 'Hakoah' 1922–28; StGKr 249 Żydowski Klub Sportowy 'Hasmonea' w Krakowie 1922–29 Podgórze; StGKr 249 Żydowski Klub Sportowy 'Jehuda' 1923–30; StGKr 249 Żydowski Klub Sportowy 'Kadimah' 1922–25; StGKr 249 Żydowski Robotniczy Klub Sportowy 'Siła' 1922–39.

22. StGKr 249 Żyd. Robotniczy Klub Sportowy 'Gwiazda' 1927–38.

23. StGKr 248 Żydowski Klub Sportowy 'Gideon' w Krakowie 1926–27–28. 'Gideon' merged with 'Gwiazda'.

24. StGKr 249 Żyd. Rob. Klub Sportowy 'Hapoel' w Polsce Oddział w Krakowie 1936–37.

25. Vogler, *Wyznanie mojżeszowe*, 11. Cracovia's rival, Wisła, did not enjoy such a reputation, at least partly due to an anti-Semitic remark made by one of Wisła's players about a Jewish referee. Jewish soccer fans of inter-war Cracow rewarded the more tolerant Polish soccer team, Cracovia, with their enthusiasm and loyalty.

26. Vogler, *Wyznanie mojżeszowe*, 9–10.
27. Dr J. H., 'Antysemityzm krakowskiej YMCA, a żydowskie pieniądze', 24 March 1931, 6.
28. Ibid. No date is given for the resolution.
29. StGKr 239 Biblioteka i Czytelnia Publiczna 'Ezra' w Krakowie 1930, 1938.
30. StGKr 239 Czytelnia Ludowa 'Jedność' w Krakowie 1926–38; Folkslezehale 'Aynhayt' in Kroke.
31. StGKr 248 Żydowska Biblioteka Ludowa im. J. L. Peretza 1928–39.
32. Ibid. Note of Wiktor Olearczyk, February 1938.
33. StGKr 239 Czytelnia Towarzyska w Krakowie /1917/ 1918–25–39. This file includes the *Sprawozdania za rok zawiadawczy 1932*. See also WAPKr, Syg. 2475 *Sprawozdanie Wydziału Czytelni Towarzyskiej w Krakowie z czynności za (I) rok zawiadawczy 1912/13* (Cracow: Drukarnia Ludowa, 1913) and *20 lat Czytelni Towarzyskiej w Krakowie Sprawozdania roczne 1932* (Cracow: Nakładem Czytelni, 1932).
34. Słonimski was very cleverly playing with Słowacki's words. The original quote from Słowacki comes from his poem, 'Testament moj':

> Lecz zaklinam – niech żywi nie tracą nadziei
> I przed narodem niosą oświaty kaganiec;
> A kiedy trzeba – na śmierć idą po kolei,
> Jak kamienie przez Boga rzucane na szaniec! ...

'Kaganiec' is a word no longer used in contemporary Polish. 'Kaganek' is a small source of light, like a candle (a kind of oil lamp). The word 'oświata' (education) derives from święcić, oświęcać (to shine, turn on the light).
35. Vogler, *Wyznanie mojżeszowe*, 91–2.
36. WAPKr, Syg. 2475 *Sprawozdanie Wydziału Czytelni Towarzyskiej w Krakowie z czynności za (I) rok zawiadawczy 1912/13* (Cracow: Drukarnia Ludowa, 1913).
37. For a complete listing of the events sponsored, see *20 lat Czytelni Towarzyskiej w Krakowie Sprawozdania roczne 1932*.
38. The subvention is confirmed for at least the year 1921 to 1922. See the entry for that year in *20 lat Czytelni Towarzyskiej w Krakowie* (Cracow: Nakładem Czytelni, 1932).
39. Vogler, *Wyznanie mojżeszowe*, 93.
40. The most well-known writer of *szmonces* in Cracow was Dr Alfred Winterstein, or Alwin. Alwin's work appeared in inter-war Polish Jewish newspapers as well, especially *Chwila*. Alwin even had his own small theatre in Cracow in the Sala Bolońska in the Pałac Spiski on Rynek Główny.
41. Vogler, *Wyznanie mojżeszowe*, 40, 94.
42. For a description of a lecture by the important Polish artist and philosopher Leon Chwistek, see Józef Dużyk, 'Życie literackie', in *Dzieje krakowa, Kraków w latach 1918–1939*, v. 4, eds Janina Bieniarzówna and Jan Małecki (Cracow: Wydawnictwo Literackie, 1997), 343–4.
43. StGKr 249 Żyd. Tow. Krzewienie Sztuk Pięknych 1929–30.
44. StGKr 241 Stow. Artystów Plastyków 'Zjednoczenie' 1933–37.
45. The Jewish artists discussed here were those active within the Jewish community. Other artists of Jewish origin from Cracow were more active in the Polish art world; their careers await further study. The most important of these artists, Jonasz Sztern, survived the Holocaust and included Jewish themes in his later work. Sztern was a part of *Grupa Krakowska* [Cracow Group], which attracted other artists of Jewish origin as well. Art historians have focused attention on the group's art but have not examined it as an inter-ethnic artistic circle. This remains an important topic of study for those interested in relations between Jews and Poles. See Helena Blum, *Jonasz Stern* (Cracow: Wydawnictwo Literackie, 1978); *Leopold Lewicki i Grupa*

Krakowska w latach 1932–1937 (Cracow: Stowarzyszenie Artystyczne, Grupa Krakowska, 1991); *Erna Rosenstein* (Cracow: Stowarzyszenie Artystyczne Grupa Krakowska, 1992).

46. 'Od redakcji', *Sztuka i Życie Współczesne* (Czasopismo Zrzeszenia Żyd. Art. Malarzy i Rzeźbiarzy w Krakowie) 1 (February 1934): 2 (*Art and Contemporary Life*. Journal of the Association of Jewish Artists, Painters and Sculptors in Cracow). This was the first issue and the only issue I have been able to locate.

47. WAPKr, StGKr 247 Zrzeszenie Żyd. Artystów Malarzy i Rzeźbiarzy 1933, 1938. Also involved were Emil Schinagel, Leon Fiszlowitz, Abraham Neuman, Erna Zollmanowa and Helena Grabschriftówna.

48. Leon Chwistek, 'Zagadnienie środowiska artystycznego', *Sztuka i Życie Współczesne*, 1 (February 1934): 3–4.

49. For a fuller discussion of different types of Polish nationalism, see Jerzy Jedlicki, 'Polish Concepts of Native Culture', in Ivo Banac and Katharine Verdery, eds, *National Character and National Ideology in Inter-war Eastern Europe*, (New Haven, CT: Yale Center for International and Area Studies, 1995), 1–22. Jedlicki discusses the romanticized, more inclusive nationalism harking back to the Polish-Lithuanian commonwealth as well as a 'folk-oriented' nationalism that writers and artists developed in their work. Also see Brian Porter's *When Nationalism Began to Hate*, where Porter discusses the intellectual changes of the nineteenth century that made possible an exclusive and intolerant Polish nationalism.

50. *Nowy Dziennik*, 28 November 1931, 5–6.

51. Rachel Holcer, 'Teatr Żydowski w Krakowie', in *Teatr Żydowski w Krakowie*, 199. Originally published in *Jidiszer teater in Ejrope cwiszn bejde welt-milchomes* (New York, 1968), 276–85. *Teatr Żydowski w Krakowie* is a collection of essays and important primary sources translated from Yiddish into Polish. See especially Mirosława Bułat, 'Kraków – żydowska mozaika teatralna', 29–62. For a collection of articles on the Yiddish theatre elsewhere in Poland, see the special issue of *Pamiętnik Teatralny*, XLI (161–4) (Warsaw, 1992). See especially the following articles: Michael C. Steinlauf, 'Teatr żydowski w Polsce. Stan badań', 7–21 and Kazimierz Nowacki, 'Teatr żydowski w Krakowie', 353–77.

52. Freund, 'Pierwszy Społeczny teatr Żydowski w Polsce (Krakowski Teatr Żydowski),' in *Teatr Żydowski w Krakowie*, 163.

53. Ibid., 167.

54. Kalman Shtayn, 'Di yidn in krokover shtotrat tsvishn di tsvey velt-milkhomes', *Yorbukh* (Buenos Aires: World Federation of Polish Jews, 1969), 320.

55. Irene Kanfer, 'Słów kilka o teatrze żydowskim w Krakowie', *Teatr Żydowski w Krakowie* 207.

56. Mojżesz Kanfer, 'O sanację teatru żydowskiego w Polsce', *Nowy Dziennik*, Nr 139, 1931, 10–11.

57. Ibid.

58. Irene Kanfer, 'Słów kilka o teatrze żydowskim w Krakowie', 207.

59. 'Din Toyre tsvishn di krokever "Shomrey Shabes" un di yidishe artisten', *Najer Morgen*, 25 May 1934, 3.

60. Rachel Holcer, 'Teatr Żydowski w Krakowie', in *Teatr Żydowski w Krakowie*, 200.

61. N. Wejnig, 'Medytacje o teatrze żydowskim', *Nowy Dziennik*, 6 September 1918, 3–4.

62. Vogler, *Wyznanie mojżeszowe*, 40.

63. Bronner, *Cykady nad Wisłą i Jordanem*, 46–8.

64. Tadeusz Sinko, 'Wyspiański w żargonie', *Czas*, Nr 1918, 1927, 2. Reprinted in *Teatr Żydowski w Krakowie*, 177.

65. Mojżesz Kanfer, 'Sędziowie i Daniel Wyspiańskiego, Tłum. D. Leibla Reżyseria Antoniego Piekarskiego', *Nowy Dziennik*, Nr 14, 1927, 4.

66. Marian Szyjkowski, 'Misterium Żydowskie', *Ilustrowany Kuryer Codzienny*, Nr 146, 1921, 2 (reprinted in *Teatr Żydowski w Krakowie*, 156); Ludwik Szczepański, 'Szojlik syn Todresa, Krótka wyprawa w nieznany świat', *Ilustrowany Kurier Codzienny*, Nr 80, 1922, 3 (reprinted in *Teatr Żydowski w Krakowie*, 158).
67. (j.f.), 'Daniel i Sędziowie St. Wyspiańskiego na scenie teatru Żydowskiego w Krakowie', *Ilustrowany Kurier Codzienny*, Nr 21, 1927, 9. Reprinted in *Teatr Żydowski w Krakowie*, 176.
68. Sholem Freund, 'Pierwszy Społeczny teatr żydowski w Polsce (Krakowski Teatr Żydowski)', in *Teatr Żydowski w Krakowie*, 163.
69. 'Walne Zebranie Żydowskiego Towarzystwa Teatralnego', *Gazeta Gminna*, 18 October 1937, 14.
70. 'Z działalności Tow. Krakowski Teatr Żydowski', *Gazeta Gminna*, 10 February 1938, 10.
71. M. Kanfer, 'O sanację teatru żydowskiego w Polsce', *Nowy Dziennik*, Nr 139, 1931, 10–11.
72. The Polish-language Jewish press was, of course, favourable to the cause of the Yiddish theatre, as Kanfer was the literary editor of *Nowy Dziennik*.
73. 'Notitsn fun a teater-retsenzent', *Der reflektor*, July–August 1935, 26–8.
74. Ibid. In the *Modern English-Yiddish/Yiddish-English Dictionary*, Max Weinreich defines *shund* as 'literary trash'.
75. For more on Mark Arnshteyn and the connections of these other artists to Polish culture, see Michael Steinlauf, *Polish-Jewish Theater: The Case of Mark Arnshteyn: A Study of the Interplay among Yiddish, Polish and Polish-language Jewish Culture in the Modern Period* (Ann Arbor, MI: UMI Dissertation Service, 1988).
76. 'Notitsn fun a teater-retsenzent', *Der reflektor*, July–August 1935, 26–8. Irene Kanfer recalls that the Yiddish actress Runa Wellner at one time led an actors' studio in Hebrew. Irene Kanfer, 'Słów kilka o teatrze żydowskim w Krakowie', in *Teatr Żydowski w Krakowie*, 206.
77. 'Notitsn fun a teater-retsenzent', *Der Reflektor*, July–August 1935, 26–8.
78. WAPKr, StGKr 241 Scena Żydowska (Idysze Bine) 1926.
79. Ibid.
80. WAPKr, StGKr 248 Żydowski Amatorski Klub Sceniczny w Krakowie 1922–29.
81. Ibid.
82. Paul R. Brass, 'Ethnic Groups and Nationalities', in *Ethnic Diversity and Conflict in Eastern Europe*, ed. Peter F. Sugar (Santa Barbara, CA: ABC-Clio, 1980), 4.

Conclusion

Stay well, my Kroke
Blessed is your earth
My parents rest in you
Near them I was not destined to lie
Somewhere far away a grave waits for me.
　　　　Mordecai Gebirtig, 'Blayb gezunt, Kroke', *Mayne lider*

Although the Jews of Cracow established separate cultural institutions during the inter-war period, they also began a process of integration that the outbreak of the Second World War interrupted. The processes discussed throughout this study – the development of a Zionist press in Polish, the education of Jews in a non-Jewish culture, and the participation of new generations of Jews in separate cultural organizations – combined to change the way Jews thought of themselves as Jews and as Poles. The emergence of Polish Jewish subcultures in Cracow allowed Jews to attend a public school but play soccer with other Jews; or to attend one of the most exclusive private schools in the city but go to the Yiddish theatre; or to edit a Polish-language Jewish newspaper but work for the establishment of a Jewish state in Palestine.

The combination of a newly modernizing state and a trilingual Jewish culture meant that Jews would identify as Jews in different ways, at different times and in different languages. Writing and speaking and teaching in Polish, the Jewish nationalists themselves did not deny their experience of the majority culture. In showing how the Jewish nationalists of *Nowy Dziennik* and the Hebrew gymnasium developed a rhetoric that allowed both for the growth of Jewish nationalism and for an identification with Polish culture, I have demonstrated how Cracow's Jews hoped to remain both Jewish and Polish. The Jews of Cracow were taking the first step towards developing a multicultural society in which all groups were respected. Jewish community leaders recognized the necessity to integrate into Polish culture and to remain Jews at the same time. Acknowledging their difference from the Poles, the Jews of Cracow defined and asserted their own versions of ethnic identity.

The establishment of private Jewish institutions such as newspapers, schools or theatre societies is the best example of how Jews hoped to achieve this goal. These institutions are evidence of a burgeoning civil society. The twenty years of Poland's Second Republic is the one period in twentieth-century Polish history when Poles, Jews and the nation's other minorities had the opportunity to found institutions of civil society that would serve the peoples of a liberal democratic state. After the founding of an independent Polish state, Jewish community leaders identified a real need for a separate press, educational system and network of cultural organizations. Whether their goals were to maintain tradition or to teach Jews Polish, these institutions provided the private space for the expression of various forms of Jewish identity. These expressions of separate identities, however, did not negate the affiliation with the majority Polish community. As this work shows, it often strengthened that affiliation.

The need for private Jewish institutions arose partly from the exclusive aspects of Polish nationalism and from Polish anti-Semitism. Anti-Semitism was one of the major factors in the establishment of most of the private Jewish organizations discussed. It spurred the establishment of *Nowy Dziennik*, the founding of private Jewish schools, and the development of private Jewish sports clubs. Private Jewish institutions were a way in which Jews could express their own specific goals and protect themselves from an often hostile majority, even as the activities in those institutions prepared them to function in that majority culture. The number and range of Jewish institutions founded in inter-war Cracow testifies to the vibrancy and hopes of the community as well as to the need for a separate, protected public space where Jews could feel safe. As late as 1937, Jewish leaders established private Jewish schools with Polish as the language of instruction precisely because they envisioned a Polish future in which the Jews would play an active role.

The Zionists of *Nowy Dziennik* founded a newspaper the goal of which was at least in part to bridge the gulf between Jews and Poles. With their own forum to raise important Jewish issues, the Zionists could fight against anti-Semitism in a language both minority and majority could understand. The editors of *Nowy Dziennik* set themselves apart from earlier assimilationist leaders by championing a Jewish national identity. In fashioning this identity, they were careful to include an aspect as loyal citizens of Poland. Making the distinction between loyalty to the Jewish nation and allegiance to the Polish state, the Zionists integrated the two different cultures in which they participated. The views of the intellectuals gathered around *Nowy Dziennik* on national identification and assimilation were positions of integrity, of, literally, wholeness. However one may evaluate their Zionist ideology or assimilationist stance, they compensated for their minority status by participating in the majority culture and for their linguistic assimilation by asserting a unique ethnic and national identity. Unwilling to compromise their Jewish or Polish identities, they created a Polish Jewish subculture.

The Zionists of *Nowy Dziennik* are not representative of the entire Jewish press in Cracow. Yiddish-language publications stood apart from the majority and expressed different priorities for different audiences. *Dos yidishe vort* and *Di yidishe shtime* aimed to reach the city's Orthodox. They stood for the maintenance of Jewish tradition in Cracow; they qualify the Polish nature of the Cracow Jewish community. Still, it is possible to see evidence of change among Cracow's Orthodox in these newspapers as well. *Dos yidishe vort* advocated Jewish education of any sort, in any language; *Dos likht* took note of Orthodox Jews moving outside of Kazimierz. *Der reflektor* and *Di post* represent yet another variant of Jewish culture in Cracow, one that advocated Yiddish as the representative language of the Jewish community. The Yiddish cultural politics expressed in these newspapers fought the linguistic and cultural assimilation *Nowy Dziennik* represents.

While the editors and writers of *Nowy Dziennik* and *Di post* made considered decisions about their use of language, Jewish children in public schools had no such choice. The required weekly religious instruction was the only institutional allowance for the expression of a Jewish identity. The overwhelming majority of Jewish children attended public schools, but this did not necessarily threaten the future development of private Jewish institutions. Attendance at a public, private Polish, or private Jewish school was not a certain indicator of a Jewish child's future allegiances. Jewish children in public schools were not unaware of their Jewish identity and, during the inter-war period, had the opportunity to participate in a wide range of separate Jewish cultural initiatives. Such extensive minority participation in public education does indicate that the Jewish community in Cracow was likely to complete the process of linguistic assimilation begun in the nineteenth century, unless steps were taken to stop this through political action or the development of cultural institutions. Private Jewish schools provided a check on the process, ensuring that the Jewish community would in some way remain apart from the majority even as they integrated into the majority society.

The establishment of private Jewish schools tells us that many Jewish parents wanted more than weekly religious instruction for their children, even as they realized that an education in Polish was essential for their children's economic success. The founding of the Hebrew gymnasium, the *Cheder Iwri* schools and the Jewish trade schools demonstrates the variety of ways Jewish parents provided for their children. The private schools Jews founded served to train Jews in Zionist ideals, maintain religious tradition, or to provide Jews with practical skills for employment in Poland or future emigration to Palestine. The growth of the different types of schools suggests that the need for private Jewish education was felt throughout the community. The schools provided a safe atmosphere where Jewish students could be free from anti-Semitic taunts as well as the pressure to perform academically in an effort to compensate for their minority status.

Along with the Jewish press and schools, the many smaller Jewish cultural organizations also helped to check further assimilation. The sports clubs, reading rooms and theatre societies discussed here were only the beginnings of a civil society that promised many opportunities for Jews of all ages to affiliate with other Jews and Jewish issues. The goals of many of these organizations, such as *Nowy Dziennik*, hoped to integrate Jews into the majority culture as well. These were not organizations that promoted resistance against the government or threatened political destabilization, even though the continued police surveillance speaks eloquently of the government's suspicions. They were groups that sought to offer Jews the chance to swim in a new swimming pool, learn a language or attend a lecture on Jewish politics. Remaining in some way apart from the majority community, these cultural organizations ensured the separateness of the Jewish community even as Jewish schoolchildren entered the larger society on a daily basis. For a community whose children and adults could not avoid the influence of Polish culture, the Jewish organizations were the private space for the development of a Jewish identity uniquely Polish in nature.

This work has concerned the institutions the Jews themselves founded to address, in part, the needs of the community. The founding of separate Jewish newspapers, schools, sports clubs and reading rooms still brought Jews into contact with Poles. This contact was in part voluntary, such as at a soccer match, and in part required, as Polish inspectors entered Jewish schools. In either case, the development of a Jewish civil society in inter-war Cracow did not signify an escape from the majority culture. The emerging Polish Jewish subcultures of inter-war Cracow suggest that contact between Jews and Poles was at times neutral and not entirely negative. While the state required Jewish educational leaders to include Polish subjects in their curriculum, they were not forced to publish Jewish children's literature in Polish. Polish school inspectors monitored Jewish schools to ensure that teachers were following the state curriculum but also to encourage the repair of inadequate facilities. In addition, the Jewish intellectuals and middle class of Cracow were not forced to attend the Polish theatre or to sponsor literary readings with Poland's most well-known authors.

At least one scholar has already noted that the linguistic assimilation occurring in Poland resembles the linguistic assimilation among Jews in the United States.[1] This important similarity to the American Jewish community also made Cracow stand somewhat apart from other Jewish communities in Poland. More acculturated and linguistically assimilated than the Jews of Warsaw, Vilnius, or Łódź, the Jews of Cracow built an ethnic and national community that recognized the importance of the majority culture. The Jews of Cracow represent an alternative solution to the 'Jewish question': integration into the majority community without any loss of ethnic or national integrity.

This attempt to reconcile Jewish identity with Polish citizenship was a valiant effort of a national minority community to maintain, and even develop, itself in the face of changing political structures and the growth of a Polish anti-Semitic nationalist movement. The effort shows both the success that can be achieved and the limits a minority community confronts. Able to found the institutions that would teach their children Hebrew or Polish, the Jews none the less could not control the attitudes of the majority community. As Polish nationalists of the right challenged Jewish citizenship and sought to forbid traditional Jewish practices in the late 1930s, it became clear that internal efforts of the Jewish community were even more necessary to support and defend Jewish culture.

So did these efforts to integrate fail? The anti-Semitism of the late 1930s suggests that the answer may be yes, but this would contradict the testimonies of the Jews from Cracow who attest to their connection to Poland and Polish culture even after experiencing the horrors of the Second World War and the Holocaust. Cracow's Jewish press educated its readers in the ways of Polish citizenship and Jewish national identity; the private Jewish schools succeeded in teaching students to be both Jews and Poles; and the cultural organizations provided a space for Jews to be Jewish even as they assimilated linguistically. The cultural initiatives discussed here enabled Cracow's Jews to live as Jews and as Poles. Changing the prevailing attitudes of anti-Semitism both inside and outside of Poland was only a part of their goal; that they failed to do this should not diminish our estimation of the success of institutions such as *Nowy Dziennik* or the Hebrew gymnasium.

With the press, schools and cultural organizations that acted as their institutional homes, Cracow's Jews built a national community that could exist in a multicultural state. Ethnic minority groups in Eastern Europe and elsewhere still confront the same predicament as the Jews of inter-war Cracow: how to build a national community amid hostility because of marked religious, linguistic and cultural difference. This study shows that the minority can be successful in organizing the community to remain cohesive in spite of its own diversity, the tendency to assimilate towards the majority culture, and the hostile attitudes among the majority. Such efforts as the cultural initiatives of the Jews of inter-war Cracow could not, however, protect the Jews from the hostility of outsiders. The cultural history of the Jews of inter-war Cracow provides a lesson to other minority communities struggling to adapt to a majority culture in a multi-cultural state. The home one builds in a multi-ethnic society can stand, but support from the majority community is vital to strengthen the foundation and protect it from outside violence.

Though this study has been limited to Cracow, I hope to have made clear that the trends present in Cracow were far from absent in Poland's other large Jewish communities. These trends, including linguistic assimilation and the education of Jewish children in a Polish cultural environment, were perhaps most evident in Lwów, Cracow's sister city in Galicia. The Yiddish cultural activist Moyshe Blekher often gave Vilnius, a city with a Jewish population comparable in size, as an example of a Jewish community with a real *yerushe*, or heritage, in contrast to Cracow, which, in Blekher's opinion, had long been under the influence of assimilationists. While Vilnius was certainly a city with more Yiddish cultural activity, Blekher's dismissal of Cracow's Jewish culture solely because that culture was usually expressed in Polish seems unnecessarily harsh. The diversity of Jewish cultural life, while often regarded as a weakness, was also the strength of Jewish life. That Jews could change aspects of their identity yet remain Jews contributed to the strength of the community just as the Jewish nation was to undergo its most difficult test.

The Holocaust would change Jewish identity in Poland in ways that could not have been anticipated. The trauma of the Holocaust challenged both traditional religious belief and a secular identification with a persecuted minority community. The history of the Nazi persecution of the Jews in Cracow has received its share of attention. Most familiar is the story of Oskar Schindler, thanks largely to Thomas Keneally and Steven Spielberg.[2] Schindler's rescue efforts should not overshadow the stories of the Jews themselves, though; these deserve their telling as well. Many survivors from Cracow have written of their experiences during the war in the Cracow ghetto, established by the Nazis in 1941. They have also detailed their time in Płaszów, the labor camp on the city's outskirts, and in subsequent concentration camps.[3] Though the war and its effects on Cracow's Jews are not the focus of this study, these memoirs deserve mention, in part because they often address Jewish life and culture in pre-war Poland but also because they commemorate those Jews who made possible the creation of vibrant Polish Jewish subcultures.

Though the Holocaust often overshadows our understanding of Jewish life in Poland and the relationship between Jews and Poles and Polish culture, my intent has been to focus on the ways in which Jews defined their community and developed a society capable of change and development before the war. Though the increase of anti-Semitism in Poland in the late 1930s indicated to some the danger that lay ahead, the establishment of new cultural institutions during the same period suggests that many Jews committed to the development of the community at the time when it was most vulnerable.

This work has been an attempt to describe the community as it was before its destruction. Though one of the smaller of Poland's larger Jewish communities, Cracow was home to a number of Jewish groups, each with its own mission and history. To limit the focus of the study, I chose to omit discussion of specifically religious, political and charitable groups, in favour of those organizations with specifically cultural goals. Though this means that this study must remain in some way incomplete, this decision allowed me to concentrate on the new development within Cracow Jewry, that is, the proliferation of organizations and institutions that came to represent the Jewish community to itself and to Polish society. In doing so, I have been able to highlight how Jewish community leaders accommodated their institutions to Polish governmental rule, Polish culture and changing Jewish nationalist ideas. My goal has been to learn more about the community when it was alive, vibrant and still hopeful.

The unprecedented nature of the Holocaust for ever changed the community unexpectedly. War came to the Jews of Cracow immediately upon its outbreak on 1 September 1939. Nazi troops occupied the city on 6 September. Though Jewish leaders attempted to continue their activities, the Nazi occupation made their task increasingly difficult. The first *Aktion* occurred in

December 1939. In April 1940 the Nazis ordered the Jews to evacuate the city within four months. While some 35,000 fled, 15,000 remained. The ghetto in Cracow was located in the city's Podgórze neighbourhood in March of 1941. Deportations to the Bełżec death camp, near Lublin, began in the summer of 1942 and continued throughout the autumn. Starting in November 1942, teams of workers were taken from the ghetto to a nearby site on which two Jewish cemeteries were located. With the help of labour from the ghetto, the Nazis turned this site into the Płaszów labour camp. The Nazis liquidated the ghetto in mid-March 1943, transferring the last workers in the ghetto to Płaszów, itself very close to the ghetto. At least a thousand people were killed within several hours on the second day of the liquidation. While 4,000 were transferred to Płaszów, 2,000 were taken directly to Auschwitz, most of whom were sent immediately to the gas chambers.

In 1940, two groups of youth formed resistance groups that eventually joined the ŻOB, the Jewish Fighting Organization. Laban and Szymon Draenger and Adolf (Dolek) Liebeskind led the Zionist youth in the Akiba group, while H. Bauminger and Benjamin Halbrajch led a group of leftist youth. The most notable incident of the resistance during the war was the attack on German officers at Cracow's 'Cyganeria' club in December 1942. The resistance fighters succeeded in assassinating seven German officers during this attack. Though other resistance actions followed the 'Cyganeria' club attack, the Gestapo liquidated the resistance group in Cracow in early 1943.

An overview of Cracow's wartime experiences would not be complete without mention of the important efforts of two non-Jews to aid the Jews in the ghetto. The actions of Oskar Schindler are well known and the telling of this man's heroic story in novel and film has served to educate many about the conditions of life in the Cracow ghetto. A German businessman with an enamel factory in Cracow, Schindler managed to save 1,300 Jews by employing them in his factory and, in 1944, obtaining permission to relocate his enterprise from Cracow to Czechoslovakia. The bravery of another non-Jew also contributed to the education of future generations. The Pole Tadeusz Pankiewicz found himself in a unique situation when the ghetto was created. As the owner of a pharmacy, Pankiewicz received permission from the Germans to remain in the ghetto, thus making him a witness to the daily life of Jews during the war. Pankiewicz also aided Jews in his capacity as a pharmacist. His book, *The Cracow Ghetto Pharmacy*, details his experiences during the war and provides an important perspective on the history of the ghetto.[4]

Without the contributions of Jews from Cracow living in Israel and in other countries after the war, this study would have been significantly more difficult to write. The efforts of the Union of Jews from Cracow in Israel resulted in the publication of several memoirs that have been indispensable to this study. These include recollections about the Hebrew gymnasium by former students and graduates, who gathered in Israel around the respected figure of Chaim Hilfstein, the gymnasium's former director. Young writers and journalists who had just begun their careers in the late 1930s continued after the war to write of Cracow and their connection to the city. These include David Lazer, Rafael Scharf, Michał Borwicz (Maksymilian Boruchowicz) and Henryk Vogler. Their writings, together with the diaries and memoirs of Natan Gross, Halina Nelken, Irena Bronner, Henryk Ritterman-Abir and Bruno Shatyn, provide the most detailed picture of Jewish life in inter-war Cracow and the wartime trials of Cracow Jewry. Like the organizations and institutions discussed in this essay, these authors are a diverse group. Their memoirs offer different views of the Jewish community but, taken collectively, they reveal a society strong enough to tolerate diversity and flexible enough to change.

The Jewish subcultures of inter-war Cracow – the intellectuals of *Nowy Dziennik*, the Orthodox of *Dos yidishe vort* and *Dos likht*, the Yiddishists of *Di post*, the reading rooms and sports teams of varying political orientations – coexisted with each other and with the majority community. They allowed Jews to be Jews at a time when Jewish identity was not threatened by genocide but rather by linguistic and cultural assimilation. Divided in their interests, social backgrounds and political ideologies, Jews founded private Jewish cultural organizations of all kinds, ensuring the maintenance of various versions of a separate ethnic and, for some, explicitly national identity. Living in Cracow, the Jews also embraced Polishness, accepting their minority status but working to improve the material, social and cultural conditions of their people. The Jewish cultural identity evident in Cracow before the outbreak of war made possible an affiliation with more than one nation.

Before he was murdered on the street not far from his home, Mordecai Gebirtig bade farewell to his city in the anthem, 'Blayb gezunt, mayn kroke' (literally, 'stay well, my Cracow'). Gebirtig's Cracow was not simply his home town but a Jewish community in the forefront of developing a fragile multicultural society. The Jews of Cracow were not a people apart, but a nation trying both to maintain its own sense of identity and enter into the larger Polish community. For a time, they succeeded.

NOTES

1. Celia Heller, *On the Edge of Destruction*, 215.
2. Thomas Keneally, *Schindler's List* (New York: Simon and Schuster, 1982).
3. In addition to the memoirs already mentioned throughout the text, see also Malvina Graf, *The Cracow Ghetto and the Plaszów Camp Remembered* (Tallahassee: Florida State University Press, 1989); M. M. Mariańscy, *Wśród przyjaciół i wrogów. Poza gettem w okupanym Krakowie* (Cracow: Wydawnictwo Literackie, 1988); Stella Muller-Madej, *A Girl from Schindler's List*, trans. William Brand (London: Polish Cultural Foundation, 1997); Henryk Zvi Zimmerman, *Przeżyłem, pamiętam, świadczę* (Cracow: Wydawnictwo Barań i Suszczyński, 1997); Aryeh Bauminger, *Lohame geto krakov* (Tel-Aviv: ha-Menorah, 1967); and Aleksander Bieberstein, *Zagłada Żydów w Krakowie* (Cracow: Wydawnictwo Literackie, 1985).
4. Tadeusz Pankiewicz, *Apteka w getcie krakowskim* (Cracow: Wydawnictwo Literackie, 1982). Published in English as *The Cracow Ghetto Pharmacy* (New York: Holocaust Library, 1987), trans. Henry Tilles.

Bibliography

ARCHIVAL SOURCES

Województwo Archiwum Państwowe w Krakowie, Cracow
Żydowski Instytut Historyczny, Warsaw
Uniwersytet Jagielloński, Cracow
YIVO Institute for Jewish Research, New York
Central Zionist Archives, Jerusalem
Archives for the History of the Jewish People, Jerusalem
Orthodox Jewish Archives, New York
Szkoła Podstawowa 9, Cracow
Szkoła Podstawowa 11, Cracow
Szkoła Podstawowa 16, Cracow
Muzeum Historyczne m. Krakowa, Stara Synagoga, Cracow
Tsentralnyi Derzhavnyi Istorychnyi Arkhiv (Central State Historical Archives), L'viv, Ukraine
Derzhavnyi Arkhiv Lvivskoi oblasti (State Archives of L'viv Oblast), L'viv, Ukraine

INTERVIEWS

Natan Gross, Tel Aviv
Felicia Haberfeld, Los Angeles
Bernhard Kempler, Atlanta
Emilja Leibel, Cracow
Ryszard Löw, Tel Aviv
Emanuel Melzer, Tel Aviv
Leopold Page, Los Angeles
Henryk Vogler, Cracow

CONTEMPORARY PRESS AND SERIALS

Achdut
Ceirim
Chwila
Cofim
Diwrej Akiba
Gazeta Gminna
Hamitzpeh
Hanoar haiwri akiba
Hejd haszomer hadati
Dos likht
Der morgenshtern
Nasz Przegląd
Nasza Opinja/Opinja
Nasza Walka
Di naye tsayt
Nowe Życie
Nowy Dziennik
Ogniwa
Okienko na Świat
Di post
Przegląd Kupiecki
Przegląd Żydowski
Der reflektor
Rękodzieło i Przemysł
Der ruf
Rzut
Samopomoc
Shavuon
Sprawy Narodowościowe
Sztuka i Życie Współczesne
Trybuna Narodowa
Walka
Dos yidishe vort
Z Naszego Życia

PUBLISHED DOCUMENTS AND MEMOIRS

Akavia, Miriam, *Moja Winnica*, Warsaw: Państwowy Instytut Wydawniczy, 1990.

— *Jesien młodości*, Cracow: Wydawnictwo Literackie, 1989.

Aleksandrowicz, Julian, *Kartki z dziennika doktora Twardego*, Cracow: Wydawnictwo Literackie, 1983.

Almanach gmin żydowskich w Polsce, Warsaw, 1937.

Almanach ilustrowany gmin żydowskich w Polsce, Warsaw, 1934.

Almanach szkolnictwa żydowskiego w Polsce, t. 1–3. Warsaw: Wydawnictwo 'Renesans', 1937.

Almanach szkolnictwa żydowskiego w Polsce, Warsaw: Wydawnictwo 'Renesans', 1938.

Bader, Gershom, *Mayne zikhroynes*, Buenos Aires: Tsentralfarband fun poylishe yidn in argentine, 1953.

Bałaban, Majer, *Przewodnik po żydowskich zabytkach Krakowa*, Cracow: Nakładem Stowarzyszenia 'Solidarność – B'nei B'rith', 1935.

Bau, Joseph, *Dear God, Have You Ever Gone Hungry?* trans. Shlomo 'Sam' Yurman, New York: Arcade Publishing, 1990.

Bauminger, Aryeh, *Sefer Kroke*, Jerusalem: Mosad ha-Rav Kuk, 1958.

Begley, Louis, *Wartime Lies*, New York: Knopf, 1991.

Bidakowski, Kazimierz, ed., *Cyganeria i Polityka: Wspomnienia Krakowskie, 1919–1939*, Warsaw: Czytelnik, 1964.

Borwicz, Michał, *Ludzie, Książki, Spory*, Paris: Księgarnia Polska, 1980.

Bosak, Meir, *Bin tsilele 'ir*, Tel Aviv: Ekked, 1986.

Bronner, Irena, *Cykady nad Wisłą i Jordanem*, Cracow: Wydawnictwo Literackie, 1991.

Bursa Rękodzielnicza Sierót Żydowskich, Cracow: Stow. Rękodzielników Żyd. 'Szomer Umonim'.

Conrad, Joseph, *My Return to Cracow*, London, 1919.

Döblin, Alfred, *Journey to Poland*, trans. Joachim Neugroschel, New York: Paragon House Publishers, 1991.

Dorian, Emil, *The Quality of Witness: A Romanian Diary, 1937–1944*, trans. Mara Soceanu Vamos. Philadelphia: Jewish Publication Society of America, 1982.

Dos alte yidishe kroke, Cracow: Ferlag Makhziki Limud, 1939.

Drugi powszechny spis ludności z dn. 9 XII 1931 r. Miasto Kraków, mieszkania i gospodarstwa domowe ludności, Stosunki zawodowe, Warsaw: Główny Urząd Statystyczny, 1937.

Freudenheim, Mieczysław, 'Recollections about Two Cracow Bookstores', *Biuletyn Żydowskiego Instytutu Historycznego*, 1981, 1, 117, 83–95.

Gebirtig, Mordecai, *Mayne lider*, 4th edn, Tel Aviv: I. L. Peretz Ferlag, 1986.

— *Mayn Fayfele*, ed. and introduction by Natan Gross. Tel Aviv: Farlag 'Isroel-Bukh', 1997.

Gintel, Jan, ed., *Kopiec Wspomnień*, Cracow: Wydawnictwo Literackie, 1964.

Graf, Malvina, *The Cracow Ghetto and the Płaszów Camp Remembered*, Tallahassee: Florida State University Press, 1989.

Gross, Natan, *Co nam zostało z tych lat?* Tel Aviv: Nakładem Związku Wychowanków Hebrajskiego Gimnazjum w Krakowie, 1971.

—- *Okruszyny młodości*, Tel Aviv: Nakładem Irgun Yotzey Krakov, 1976.

— *Zeh hayah bet-ha-sefer ha-ivri*, Tel Aviv: Wydawnictwo Ekked, 1989.

— *Kim pan jest, panie Grymek?* Cracow: Wydawnictwo Literackie, 1991.

Hartglas, Apolinary, *Na pograniczu dwóch światów*, ed. and introduced by Jolanta Żyndul, Warsaw: Rytm, 1996.

Infeld, Leopold, *Quest: An Autobiography*, New York: Chelsea Publishing, 1980.

— *Szkice z przeszłości*, Warsaw: Państwowy Instytut Wydawniczy, 1964.

— *Why I Left Canada: Reflections on Science and Politics*, ed. Lewis Pyerson and trans. Helen Infeld, Montreal: McGill-Queen's University Press, 1978.

Jewish Life in Cracow, produced by Sektor Films, Shaul and Yitzhak Goskind, 1939, videocassette, restored by National Center for Jewish Film, 1991.

Krieger, Ignacy, *Album fotografii dawnego Krakowa*, Cracow: Krajowa Agencja Wydawnictwa, 1989.

Kronika Uniwersytetu Jagiellońskiego za lata akademickie 1926/27, 1927/28, 1928/29, i 1929/30, Cracow: Jagiellonian University, 1934.

Kronika Uniwersytetu Jagiellońskiego za lata akademickie 1930/31, 1931/32, i 1932/33, Cracow: Jagiellonian University, 1933.

Kronika Uniwersytetu Jagiellońskiego za rok akademicki 1933/34, Cracow: Jagiellonian University, 1935.

Krygowski, Władysław, *W moim Krakowie nad wczorajszą Wisłą*, Cracow: Wydawnictwo Literackie, 1989.

Książka adresowa członków Związku Żyd. Stowarzyszeń Humanitarnych 'B'nei B'rith' w Rzeczypospolitej Polskiej w Krakowie, Cracow, 1937.

Księga adresowa miasta Krakowa i województwa krakowskiego z informatorem miasta stołecznego Warszawy województwa kieleckiego i śląskiego Rocznik 1933–1934, Cracow, 1933–34.

Kudliński, Tadeusz, *Młodości mej stolica: Wspomnienia Krakowianina z okresu między wojnami*, 2nd edn, Cracow: Wydawnictwo Literackie, 1984.

Kurek, Jalu, *Mój Kraków*, Cracow: Wydawnictwo Literackie, 1970.

Kwiatkowski, T., *Niedyskretny urok pamięci*, Cracow: Wydawnictwo Literackie, 1982.

— *Płaci się każdego dnia*, Cracow: Wydawnictwo Literackie, 1986.

Łaszewski, Bolesław T., *Kraków: Karta z dziejów dwudziestolecia*, New York: Bicentennial Publishing, 1985.

Lazer, David, *Frezje, mimoza, i róże: szkice polskie z lat 1933–1974 (wybór)*, Tel Aviv, 1994.

Leśnodorski, Zygmunt, *Wspomnienia i zapiski*, Cracow: Wydawnictwo Literackie, 1959.

— *Wśród ludzi mojego miasta*, Cracow: Wydawnictwo Literackie, 1963.

Löw, Ryszard, *Pod znakiem starych foliantów, cztery szkice o sprawach żydowskich i książkowych*, Cracow: Universitas, 1993.

Mariańscy, M. M., *Wśród przyjaciół i wrogów. Poza gettem w okupanym Krakowie*, Cracow: Wydawnictwo Literackie, 1988.

Markiewicz, Henryk, ed., *Tadeusz Boy Żeleński o Krakowie*, Cracow: Wydawnictwo Literackie, 1968.

Mayzel, Nakhman, *Geven amol a lebn: dos yidishe kultur-lebn in poyln tsvishn beyde velt-milkhomes*, Buenos Aires: Tsentral farband fun poylishe yidn, 1951.

Muller-Madej, Stella, *A Girl from Schindler's List*, trans. William Brand, London: Polish Cultural Foundation, 1997.

Na progu nowego życia. Wspomnienia i refleksje uczennic klasy VIIIA Państwowego Gimnaszjum Żeńskiego im. Adama Mickiewicza w Krakowie, Cracow, 1937.

Nelken, Halina, *Pamiętnik z getta w Krakowie*, Toronto: Polski Fundusz Wydawniczy w Kanadzie, 1987, published in English as *And Yet, I am Here!* Amherst: University of Massachusetts Press, 1999.

Nowakowski, Zygmunt, *Mój Kraków*, New York: Biblioteka Polska, 1946.

Ogólne wyniki spisu ludności, domów, budynków, mieszkań i zwierząt domowych w Krakowie z 30 września 1921 r., Cracow: Biuro Statystyczne miasta Krakowa-Polska.

Otwinowski, Stefan, *Niedyskrecje i wspomnienia*, Cracow: Wydawnictwo Literackie, 1957.

Pankiewicz, Tadeusz, *Apteka w getcie krakowskim*, Cracow: Wydawnictwo Literackie, 1982.

Polański, Roman, *Roman*, London: Pan Books, 1985.

Ritterman-Abir, Henryk, *Nie od razu Kraków zapomniano*, Tel Aviv: Związek Żydów Krakowian w Izraelu, 1984.

Rocznik Statystyki Miast Polski, Warsaw: Nakładem Głównego Urzędu Statystycznego, 1928.

Rost, Nella Thon, *Ozjasz Thon (Wspomnienia córki)*, Lwów: Cofim, 1937.

Rubin, Devora, ed., *Daughters of Destiny: Women who Revolutionized Jewish Life and Torah Education*, Brooklyn: Mesorah, 1988.

Scharf, Rafael F., *Co mnie i tobie Polsko … Eseje bez uprzedzeń*, Cracow: Fundacja Judaica, 1996, published in English as *Poland, What Have I to Do with Thee … Essays without Prejudice*, London: Valentine Mitchell, 1998.

Schlang, Fabian, *… I pozostała tylko legenda. Wspomnienia z żydowskiego Krakowa*, Tel Aviv: Wydawnictwo 'Ekked', 1986.

Schneider, Artur, *Młode lata: 1920–1939, Wspomnienia, refleksja*, unpublished, YIVO, Institute for Jewish Research.

Segalovitch, Zusman, *Tlomatske 13*, Buenos Aires: Tsentralfarband fun poylishe yidn in Argentine, 1946.

Sprawozdanie dyrekcji prywatnego gimnazjum koedukacyjnego im. dra Chaima Hilfsteina, Liceum Ogólnokształcącego o Wydz. Humanistycznym, Przyrodniczym i Matematyczno-fizycznym, Szkoły powszechnej i męskiej szkoły rzemiósł Żydowskiego

Towarzystwa Szkoły Ludowej i Średniej w Krakowie za rok szkolny 1937–1938, Cracow, 1938.

Sprawozdanie dyrekcji prywatnego gimnazjum koedukacyjnego szkoły powszechnej i szkoły rzemiosł żydowskiego Towarzystwa Szkoły Ludowej i Średniej w Krakowie za rok szkolny, 1934–1935, Cracow, 1935.

Sprawozdanie z działalności zachodnio-małopolskiego Związku towarzystw opieki nad sierotami żydowskiemi w Krakowie, Cracow, June 1933.

Sprawozdanie z 10-lecia istnienia Bursy Rękodzielniczej sierót żydowskich 1927–1937, Cracow: Nakładem Bursy Rękodzielniczej Sierót Żyd., 1938.

Sprawozdanie Jubileuszowe 1906–1926, Cracow: 'Nadzieja' Towarzystwo ku wspieraniu chorej młodzieży żydowskiej szkół średnich i wyższych w Krakowie, 1927.

Sprawozdanie kierownictwa żyd. gimnazjum koedukacyjnego typu humanistycznego Tow. Żydowskiej Szkoły Ludowej i Średniej w Krakowie za rok szkolny 1928/29, Cracow, 1929.

Sprawozdanie kierownictwa gimnazjum koed. typu humanistycznego i czteroklasowej szkoły powszechnej żydowsk. Towarzystwa Szkoły Ludowej i Średniej w Krakowie za rok szkolny 1931–32, Cracow, 1932.

Sprawozdanie kierownictwa żyd. gimnazjum koedukacyjnego typu humanistycznego, Szkoły powszechnej i męskiej szkoły rzemiosł Żydowskiego Towarzystwa Szkoły Ludowej i Średniej w Krakowie za rok szkolny 1933–34, Cracow, 1934.

Sprawozdanie Stow, Domu Sierót Żydowskich w Krakowie. 1935/6, 1936/7, Cracow: Nakładem Stowarzyszenia Domu Sierót Żydowskich w Krakowie, 1937.

Sprawozdanie za lata szkolne 1936/37, 1937/38, Prywatna Żydowska Koedukacyjna Średnia Szkoła Handlowa Stowarzyszenia Żydowskich Absolwentów Wyższego Studium Handlowego w Krakowie, Cracow, 1938.

Sprawozdanie sekretarjatu naczelnego Agudat hanoar haiwri 'Akiba', Cracow: 23 February 1936.

Sprawozdanie Wydziału Stowarzyszenia Humanitarnego 'Solidarność" B'nei B'rith w Krakowie za rok 1937, Cracow, 1938.

Sprawozdanie Zarządu Głównego Towarzystwa za rok 1927, Cracow: 'Nadzieja' Towarzystwo ku wspieraniu chorej młodzieży żydowskiej szkół średnich i wyższych w Krakowie, 1927.

Sprawozdanie Zarządu Głównego Towarzystwa za rok 1929, Cracow: 'Nadzieja' Towarzystwo ku wspieraniu chorej młodzieży żydowskiej szkół średnich i wyższych w Krakowie, 1930.

Szatyn, Bronisław, *Na aryjskich papierach*, Cracow: Wydawnictwo Literackie, 1983.

Tshvartsbart, Yitzhak, *Tsvishn beyde velt-milkhomes*, Buenos Aires: Tsentral-farband fun poylishe yidn in argentine, 1958.

Tsveyter idiszer szul-tsuzamenfor, Warsaw: Wydawnictwo Idisze Szul, 1925.

Turkow, Zygmunt, *Di ibergerufene tekufe*, Buenos Aires: Tsentral-Farband fun poylishe yidn in argentine, 1961.

Vogler, Henryk, *Autoportret z pamięci*, 3 vols, Cracow: Wydawnictwo Literackie, 1978–81.

— *Przechadzki ze śmiercia. Wiersze z obozu Gross-Rosen-Gorlitz 1944–1945*, Cracow: Biblioteka Pisma Literacko-artystycznego, 1989.

— *Wyznanie mojżeszowe*, Warsaw: Państwowy Instytut Wydawniczy, 1994.

Wydawnictwo Jubileuszowe K. S. 'Cracovia' 50-lecie K. S. 'Cracovia', Cracow, 1956.

Zimmerman, Henryk Zvi, *Przeżyłem, pamiętam, świadczę*, Cracow: Wydawnictwo Barań i Suszczynski, 1997.

SECONDARY SOURCES

Adamczewski, Jan, *Mała Encyclopedia Krakowska*, Cracow: Wydawnictwo 'Wanda', 1996.

Allerhand, Markus, 'Wybory do Rad i zarządów gmin wyznaniowych żydowskich 1928', *Biuletyn Żydowskiego Instytuty Historycznego*, 2–3 (1987).

Banac, Ivo and Katharine Verdery, *National Character and National Ideology in Interwar Eastern Europe*, New Haven: Yale Center for Area and International Studies, 1995.

Bartal, Israel and Magdalena Opalski, *Poles and Jews: A Failed Brotherhood*, Hanover, NH: University of New England Press, 1992.

Barth, Frederik, *Ethnic Groups and Boundaries: The Social Organization of Cultural Difference*, Boston: Little, Brown, 1969.

Bartoszewski, Władysław and Antony Polonsky, eds, *The Jews in Warsaw: A History*, Cambridge, MA: Blackwell, 1991.

Bauman, Zygmunt, 'Exit Visas and Entry Tickets: Paradoxes of Jewish Assimilation', *Telos*, 77 (1988): 45–79.

Bauminger, Aryeh, *Lohame geto krakov*, Tel Aviv: ha-Menorah, 1967.

Bieberstein, Aleksander, *Zagłada Żydów w Krakowie*, Cracow: Wydawnictwo Literackie, 1985.

Bieniarzówna, Janina, *Kraków: Stary i Nowy*, Cracow: Państwowe Wydawnictwo Naukowe, 1968.

— and Jan M. Małecki, eds, *Dzieje Krakowa: Kraków w latach 1918–1939*, Cracow: Wydawnictwo Literackie, 1997.

Bieńkowska, Teresa, *Kraków: Przegląd wybranych opracowań z lat 1900–1939*, Cracow: Wojewódzka Biblioteka Publiczna, 1993.

Birnbaum, Pierre and Ira Katznelson, 'Emancipation and the Liberal Offer', in *Paths of Emancipation: Jews, States, and Citizenship*, eds, Birnbaum and Katznelson, Princeton, NJ: Princeton University Press, 1995.

Blum, Helena, *Jonasz Stern*, Cracow: Wydawnictwo Literackie, 1978.

Bornstein, Izaak, *Budżety gmin wyznaniowych w Polsce*, Warsaw, 1931.

Bradley, Joseph, 'Subjects into Citizens: Societies, Civil Society, and Autocracy in Tsarist Russia', *American Historical Review*, 107 (4): 1094–123.

Brass, Paul R., 'Ethnic Groups and Nationalities', in *Ethnic Diversity and Conflict in Eastern Europe*, ed. Peter Sugar, Santa Barbara, CA: ABC-CLIO, 1980.

Brenner, Michael, *The Renaissance of Jewish Culture in Weimar Germany*, New Haven, CT: Yale University Press, 1996.

— and Derek Penslar, eds, *In Search of Jewish Community: Jewish Identities in Germany and Austria, 1918–1933*, Bloomington, IN: Indiana University Press, 1998.

Bronsztejn, Szyja, *Ludność żydowska w Polsce w okresie międzywojennym*, Wrocław: Zakład Narodowy im. Ossolińskich, 1963.

Brzoza, Czesław, *Polityczna prasa Krakowska 1918–1939*, Cracow: Uniwersytet Jagielloński, Rozprawy habilitacyjne Nr 205, 1990.

— 'The Jewish Press in Cracow (1918–1939)', *Polin*, 7 (1992): 133–46.

— 'Jewish Periodicals in Cracow (1918–1939)', in *Bibliographies of Polish Judaica. International Symposium Cracow 5th–7th July 1988 (Proceedings)*, Cracow: Research Center of Jewish History and Culture in Poland, 1993.

— *Żydowskie partie polityczne w Polsce: 1918–1927 (wybór dokumentów)*, Cracow, 1994.

Bułat, Mirosława, 'Kraków – żydowska mozaika teatralna', in *Teatr Żydowski w Krakowie*, eds Jan Michalik and Eugenia Prokop-Janiec, Cracow: Międzywydziałowy Zakład Historii i Kultury Żydów w Polsce, 1995.

— 'Historia teatru żydowskiego w Krakowie: rekonesans badawczy', in *Żydzi i Judaizm we współczesnych badaniach polskich*, ed. Krzysztof Pilarczyk, Cracow: Księgarnia Akademicka, 1997.

Buszko, Józef, 'The Consequences of Galician Autonomy after 1867', in *Polin, Focusing on Galicia; Jews, Poles, and Ukrainians 1772–1918*, 12 (1999), 86–99.

Carter, Francis W., 'Ethnic Groups in Cracow', in *Ethnic Identity in Urban Europe*, ed. Max Engman, New York: New York University Press, 1992.

— *Trade and Urban Development in Poland*, Cambridge: Cambridge University Press, 1994.

Chmielowski, S., *Stan szkolnictwa wśród Żydów w Polsce*, Warsaw: Instytut Badań Narodowościowych, 1937.

Cohen, Israel, *Vilna*, Philadelphia: Jewish Publication Society of America, 1943.

Corrsin, Stephen D., *Warsaw Before the First World War: Poles and Jews in the Third City of the Russian Empire, 1880–1914*, Boulder, CO: East European Monographs, 1989.

Cygielman, A., 'Cracow', *Encyclopedia Judaica*.

Czajecka, Bogusława, *'Z domu w szeroki świat': Droga kobiet do niezależności w zaborze austriackim w latach 1890–1914*, Cracow: Universitas, 1990.

Deutsch, Karl, *Nationalism and Social Communication: An Inquiry into the Foundations of Nationality*, Cambridge, MA: M.I.T. Press, 1966.

Domańska, Hanna, *Żydzi znad Gdańskiej Zatoki*, Warsaw: Agencja Wydawnicza TU, 1997.

Dubin, Lois, *The Port Jews of Habsburg Trieste: Absolutist Politics and Enlightenment Culture*, Stanford, CA: Stanford University Press, 1999.

Duda, Eugeniusz, *Krakowskie judaica*, Warsaw: Wydawnictwo PTTK 'Kraj', 1991.

Eck, N., 'The Educational Institutions of Polish Jewry (1921–1939)', *Jewish Social Studies*, 9 (1947): 3–32.

Eisenbach, Artur, *The Emancipation of the Jews of Poland, 1780–1870*, trans. Janina Dorosz, Oxford: Blackwell, 1991.

Eisenstein, Miriam, *Jewish Schools in Poland*, New York: King's Crown Press, 1950.

Endelman, Todd M., *The Jews of Georgian England, 1714–1830: Tradition and Change in a Liberal Society*, Philadelphia, PA: Jewish Publication Society of America, 1979.

Engman, Max, ed., *Ethnic Identity in Urban Europe. Comparative Studies on Governments and Non-Dominant Ethnic Groups in Europe, 1850–1940*, Vol. 8, New York: New York University Press, 1992.

Erna Rosenstein, Stowarzyszenie Artystyczne Grupa Krakowska, Cracow, 1992.

Estreicher, Karol, *Kraków: Przewodnik dla zwiedzających miasto i jego okolice*, Cracow, 1938.

Fishman, Joshua, ed., *Studies on Polish Jewry: The Interplay of Social, Economic and Political Factors in the Struggle of a Minority for its Existence*, New York: YIVO Institute for Jewish Research, 1974.

— ed., *Never Say Die*, The Hague: Mouton, 1981.

— 'Ethnicity as Being, Doing, and Living', in *Ethnicity*, eds John Hutchinson and Anthony D. Smith, Oxford: Oxford University Press, 1996.

Frankel, Jonathan, *Prophecy and Politics: Socialism, Nationalism, and the Russian Jews, 1862–1917*, Cambridge: Cambridge University Press, 1981.

Freidenreich, Harriet Pass, *Jewish Politics in Vienna, 1918–1938*, Bloomington: Indiana University Press, 1991.

Frenkel, Jeremjasz, *Ozjasz Thon: Zarys biograficzny*, Cracow: Nowa Drukarnia, 1930.

Frost, Shimon, *Schooling as a Socio-political Expression*, Jerusalem: Magnes Press, 1998.

Gans, Herbert, 'Symbolic Ethnicity and Symbolic Religiosity: Towards a Comparison of Ethnic and Religious Acculturation',

Ethnic and Racial Studies, 17, no. 4 (1994), 577–92.

Gąsowski, Tomasz, *Między gettem a światem*, Cracow: Instytut Historii, Uniwersytet Jagielloński, 1996.

Gassowski, Szczepan, ed., *Państwowy Teatr Żydowski im. Ester Rachel Kaminskiej. Przeszłość i teraźniejszość*, Warsaw: Państwowe Wydawnictwo Naukowe, 1995.

Geller, Jakub, *Zagadnienie zapadalności i umieralności u ludności żydowskiej Krakowa w 1932 roku*, Cracow, 1937.

Gellner, Ernest, *Nations and Nationalism*, Oxford: Basil Blackwell, 1983.

— 'The Dramatis Personae of History', *East European Politics and Societies*, 4, no. 1 (Winter 1990): 117–33.

General Information Concerning the State of Elementary Schools in Poland in the School Year 1925–1926, Warsaw: Ministerstwo Wyznań Religijnych i Oświecenie Publicznego, 1928.

Gitelman, Zvi, 'The Decline of the Diaspora Jewish Nation: Boundaries, Content, and Jewish Identity', *Jewish Social Studies*, 4 (2): 112–31.

Glickson, Paul, *Preliminary Inventory of the Jewish Daily and Periodical Press Published in the Polish Langauge 1823–1982*, Jerusalem: Magnes Press, 1983.

Goldscheider, Calvin and Alan Zuckerman, eds, *The Transformation of the Jews*, Chicago, IL: University of Chicago Press, 1984.

Gordon, Milton, *Assimilation in American Life: The Role of Race, Religion, and National Origins*, New York: Oxford University Press, 1964.

Greenfeld, Liah, *Nationalism: Five Roads to Modernity*, Cambridge, MA: Harvard University Press, 1992.

Gross, Feliks, 'Comments on Ethnic Identity in a Polish-Jewish Context', *The Polish Review*, 35, no. 2 (1990): 137–48.

— *World Politics and Tension Areas*, New York: New York University Press, 1966.

Gross, Natan, *Cracow – Paintings and Sculptures*, Tel Aviv: Z.O.A. House, 1984.

Groth, Alexander J., 'Dmowski, Piłsudski and Ethnic Conflict in Pre-1939 Poland', *Canadian Slavic Studies*, III, no. 1 (1969): 69–91.

Grupa Krakowska, Warsaw: Galeria Sztuki Współczesnej Zachęta, 1996.

Guterman, Alexander, *Kehilat varshah ben shete milhamot ha-'olam: otonomyah le'umit be-khivle ha-hok veha-metsi'ut, 1917–1939,* Tel Aviv: Universitat Tel Aviv, 1997.

Gutman, Yisrael, et al., eds, *The Jews of Poland Between the Two World Wars,* Hanover, NH: University of New England Press, 1989.

Hałkowski, Henryk, 'Cracow – City and Mother of Israel', in *Cracow: The Dialogue of Traditions,* ed. Zbigniew Baran and trans. William Brand, Cracow: Znak, 1991.

Hedley, R. Alan, 'Identity: Sense of Self and Nation', *Canadian Review of Sociology and Anthropology,* 31, no. 2 (May 1994): 200–15.

Heller, Celia, 'Assimilation: A Deviant Pattern Among the Jews of Interwar Poland', *Jewish Journal of Sociology,* XV, no. 2 (1973): 221–39.

— *On the Edge of Destruction: The Jews of Poland Between the Two World Wars,* New York: Schocken Books, 1980.

Hoffman, Z., 'Prywatne Żydowskie Gimnazjum Koedukacyjne w Krakowie (1918–1939)', *Biuletyn Żydowskiego Instytutu Historycznego,* 3–4 (1988): 147–8.

Hollander, Nella Thon Rost, *Jehoshua Thon: Preacher, Thinker, Politician,* Montevideo: 1966.

Hyman, Paula, *The Emancipation of the Jews of Alsace: Acculturation and Tradition in the Nineteenth Century,* New Haven, CT: Yale University Press, 1991.

Isajiw, Vsevolod, 'Definitions of Ethnicity', *Ethnicity,* 1 (1974): 111–24.

Jaworski, Wojciech, *Struktura i wpływy syjonistycznych organizacji politycznych w Polsce w latach 1918–1939,* Warsaw: Oficyna Wydawnicza Rytm, 1996.

— *Ludność żydowska w województwie śląskim w latach 1922–1939,* Katowice: Oficyna 'Śląsk', 1997.

Kappeler, Andreas, ed., *The Formation of National Elites.* Comparative Studies on Governments and Non-dominant Ethnic Groups in Europe, 1850–1940, vol. VI, New York: New York University Press, 1992.

Katalog zabytków sztuki w Polsce, T. IV Miasto Kraków; Część VI, Kazimierz i Stradom, Judaica, Warsaw: Instytut Sztuki Polskiej Akademii Nauk, 1995.

Katz, Jacob, ed., *Toward Modernity: The European Jewish Model,*

New Brunswick, NJ: Transaction Books, 1987.

Kazhdan, Ch., *Di geshikhte fun yidishe shulvesen in umophengikn poyln*, Meksike D.P.: Gezelshaft 'Kultur un Hilf', 1947.

Keane, John, *Civil Society and the State: New European Perspectives*, London: Verso, 1988.

Keneally, Thomas, *Schindler's Ark*, New York: Simon and Schuster, 1982.

Kielkowski, Roman, *Zlikwidować na miejscu, Z dziejów okupacji hitlerowskiej w Krakowie*, Cracow: Wydawnictwo Literackie, 1981.

Klepfisz, Irena, '*Di mames, dos loshn* / The mothers, the language: Feminism, Yidishkayt, and the Politics of Memory', *Bridges*, 4, no. 1 (Winter / Spring 1993): 12–47.

Knoll, Paul N., 'The Urban Development of Medieval Poland, with Particular Reference to Cracow', in *Urban Society of Eastern Europe in Premodern Times*, ed. Barisa Krekic, Berkeley: University of California, 1987.

Kohlbauer-Fritz, Gabriele, 'Yiddish as an Expression of Jewish Cultural Identity in Galicia and Vienna', in *Polin: Studies in Polish Jewry, Focusing on Galicia: Jews, Poles, and Ukrainians 1772–1918*, 12 (1999): 164–76.

Korzec, Paweł, 'Antisemitism in Poland as an Intellectual, Social, and Political Movement', in *Studies on Polish Jewry, 1919–1939*, ed. Joshua Fishman, 12–104.

Krajewski, Stanisław, 'The "Jewish Problem" as a Polish Problem', *Więź, Under One Heaven: Poles and Jews*, 1988: 60–82.

'Krakov', *Pinkas Hakehillot*, Poland, Vol. III, Western Galicia and Silesia, Jerusalem: Yad Vashem, 1984.

Krasnowolski, Bogusław, *Ulice i Place Krakowskiego Kazimierza z dziejów Chrześcijan i Żydów w Polsce*, Cracow: Universitas, 1992.

Krzysztofory, Zeszyty Naukowe Muzeum Historycznego Miasta Krakowa, Vol. 15, Cracow, 1988.

Kułczykowski, Mariusz, *Żydzi – Studenci – UJ w dobie autonomicznej Galicji (1867–1918)*, Cracow: Instytut Historii Uniwersytetu Jagiellońskiego, 1995.

Lederer, Ivo and Peter Sugar, eds, *Nationalism in Eastern Europe*, Seattle: University of Washington Press, 1969.

Leopold Lewicki i Grupa Krakowska (w latach 1932–1937), Cracow: Stowarzyszenie Artystyczne, Grupa Krakowska, 1991.

Leser, Shlomo, ed., *Ha-yehudim b'krakov*, Haifa: Vaadat Hahantsakha shel yotsey Krakov b'haifa, 1981.

— *The Hebrew School in Cracow, 1908–1939. A Historical Study of a Bilingual Polish Hebrew School*, Haifa: Vaadat Hahantsakha shel yotsey Krakov b'haifa, 1990.

— *The Polish–Jewish Relations in Cracow and Vicinity, on the background of the events and the frictions in the area, in the years 1918–1925. Part I, The Anti-Jewish Events, the Jewish Self-Defense, the Frictions and the Attempts at Reaching Understanding in 1918–1920*, Haifa; preliminary edn, Vaadat Hahantsacha shel Yotsey Krakov b' khayfa, 1992.

Lestchinsky, J., 'Di shtotishe bafelkerung in poyln 1921–1931', *YIVO bleter*, XX, no. 1 (September–October 1942): 1–28.

— 'Yidn in di gresere shtet fun poyln 1921–1931', *YIVO bleter*, XXI, no. 1 (January–February 1943): 20–47.

— 'Di shprakhn bay yidn in umophengikn poyln: an analiz loyt der folkstseylung fun 1931', *YIVO bleter*, XXII, no. 2 (November–December 1943): 147–63.

Livezeanu, Irina, *Cultural Politics in Greater Romania: Regionalism, Nation Building, and Ethnic Struggle, 1918–1930*, Ithaca, NY: Cornell University Press, 1995.

— 'Inter-war Poland and Romania: The Nationalization of Elites, the Vanishing Middle, and the Problem of Intellectuals', in *Cultures and Nations of Central and Eastern Europe: Essays in Honour of Roman Szporluk*, ed. Zvi Gitelman, Lubomyr Hajda, John-Paul Himka, and Roman Solchanyk, Cambridge, MA: Ukrainian Research Institute, Harvard University, 2000.

Mahler, Raphael, 'Jews in Public Service and the Liberal Professions in Poland, 1918–1939', *Jewish Social Studies*, VI, no. 4 (October 1944): 291–351.

Małecka, Barbara, 'Ludność żydowska w Krakowie w latach, 1918–1939', Ph.D. dissertation, University of Warsaw, 1993.

Małecki, Jan M., 'Cracow Jews in the 19th Century: Leaving the Ghetto', *Acta Poloniae Historica*, LXXVI (1997): 85–97.

— ed. *Kraków międzywojenny*, Cracow: Towarzystwo miłośnikow historii i zabytków Krakowa, 1988.

Marcus, Joseph, *Social and Political History of the Jews in Poland, 1919–1939*, The Hague: Mouton, 1983.

Markiewicz, Henryk, ed., *Żydzi w Polsce: Antologia literacka*, Cracow: Universitas, 1997.

Mauersberg, Stanisław, *Komu służyła szkoła w drugiej Rzeczypospolitej? Społeczne uwarunkowanie dostępu do oświaty*, Wrocław: Ossolineum, 1988.

— 'The Educational System and Democratization of Society in Poland, 1918–1939', *Acta Poloniae Historica*, No. 55 (1987): 133–57.

McConachie, Bruce, 'Theatre History and the Nation-State'. *Theater Research International*, 2 (1995): 141–8.

Melzer, Emanuel, *No Way Out: The Politics of Polish Jewry, 1935–1939*, Cincinnati: Hebrew Union College Press, 1997.

Mendelsohn, Ezra, *Zionism in Poland: The Formative Years, 1915–1926*, New Haven, CT: Yale University Press, 1981.

— *The Jews of East Central Europe Between the Wars*, Bloomington: Indiana University Press, 1983.

— 'Interwar Poland: Good for the Jews, or Bad for the Jews', in *The Jews in Poland*, eds Chimen Abramsky, Maciej Jachimczyk and Antony Polonsky, Oxford: Blackwell, 1986.

— *On Modern Jewish Politics*, New York: Oxford University Press, 1993.

— ed. *People of the City: Jews and the Urban Challenge*, New York: Oxford University Press, 1999.

Michajłów, A. and W. Pacławski, eds, *Literary Galicia From Post-War to Post-Modern*, Cracow: Oficyna Literacka, 1991.

Michalik, Jan and Eugenia Prokop-Janiec, eds, *Teatr Żydowski w Krakowie*, Cracow: Międzywydziałowy Zakład Historii i Kultury Żydów w Polsce, 1995.

Mikułowski-Pomorski, Jerzy, *Kraków w naszej pamięci*, Cracow: Secesja, 1991.

Nath, Holger, 'Yiddish as the Emerging National Language of East European Jewry', *Sociolinguistica*, 6 (1992): 52–65.

Nathans, Benjamin, *Beyond the Pale: The Jewish Encounter with Late Imperial Russia*, Berkeley: University of California Press, 2002.

Nowa szkoła żydowska i jej położenie w państwie polskim, Warsaw: Wydawnictwo 'Szkoła i Życie', 1923.

Orton, Lawrence D., 'The Formation of Modern Cracow (1866–1914)', *Austrian History Yearbook*, XIX–XX (1983–84): 105–19.

Pajewski, Janusz, *Budowa Drugiej Rzeczypospolitej 1918–1926*, Cracow: Polska Akademia Umiejętności, 1995.

Pakentreger, Alesander, *Żydzi w Kaliszu w latach 1918–1939*, Warsaw: Państwowe Wydawnictwo Naukowe, 1988.

Paluch, Andrzej, ed., *The Jews in Poland*, Vol. 1, Cracow: Jagiellonian University, Research Center on Jewish History and Culture in Poland, 1992.

Pamiętnik Teatralny, Teatr Żydowski w Polsce do 1939, Rok XLI, Zeszyt 1–4 (161–4), Warsaw, 1992.

Patai, Raphael, *Apprentice in Budapest: Memories of a World that is No More*, Salt Lake City: University of Utah Press, 1988.

Pięćdziesiąt lat Związku Krakowian w Izraelu, 1936–1986, Tel Aviv: Związek Krakowia w Izraelu, 1986.

Piech, Stanisław, *W cieniu kościołów i synagog: Życie religijne międzywojennego Krakowa 1918–1939*, Cracow: Wydawnictwo i Drukarnia 'Secesja', 1999.

Polonsky, Antony, ed., et al., *Jews in Independent Poland, 1918–1939*, Vol. 8 of *Polin: A Journal of Polish-Jewish Studies*, London: Littman Library of Jewish Civilization, 1994.

Popieł, Jacek, *Dramat i teatr Polski dwudziestolecia międzywojennego*, Cracow: Universitas, 1995.

Prager, Leonard, 'On the Way to Modern Galician-Jewish Cultural and Political History: The Cases of Mordechai Gebirtig, Ignacy Shiper, and Dov Sadan'. International Conference, Galicja i jej Dziedzictwo, Rzeszów, 14–18 September 1992, unpublished.

Prof. Mojżesz Schorr. Materiały z sesji naukowej, Cracow 16 X 1993, Cracow: Polska Akademia Umiejętności, 1995.

Prokop-Janiec (Prokopówna), Eugenia, 'In Quest of Cultural Identity: Polish-Jewish Literature in the Inter-war Period', *Polish Review*, XXXII, no. 4 (1987): 415–39.

— *Międzywojenna literatura polsko-żydowska jako zjawisko kulturowe i artystyczne*, Cracow: Universitas, 1992.

Purchla, Jacek, *Jak powstał nowoczesny Kraków*, Cracow: Wydawnictwo Literackie, 1990.

Reiner, Elhanan, ed., *Kroka–Kaz'imiyez'-Krakov: mekharim be-toldot Yehude Krakov*. Tel-Aviv: ha-Merkaz le-heker toldot ha-Yehudim be-Polin u-morashtam, ha-Makhon le-heker ha-tefutsot, Universitat Tel-Aviv, 2001.

Rozenblit, Marsha, *The Jews of Vienna, 1867–1914: Assimilation and Identity*, Albany: State University of New York Press, 1983.

— *Reconstructing National Identity: The Jews of Habsburg Austria During World War I*, Oxford: Oxford University Press, 2001.

Rudnicki, Adolf, *Teatr zawsze grany*, Warsaw: Czytelnik, 1987.

Ruta, Zygmunt, *Szkolnictwo powszechne w okręgu szkolnym krakowskim w latach 1918–1939*, Wrocław: Ossolineum, 1980.

— *Prywatne szkoły średnie ogólnokształcące w Krakowie i województwie krakowskim w latach 1932–1939*, Cracow, 1990.

Sakowska, Ruta, 'Z dziejów gminy warszawskiej 1918–1939', in *Warszawa II Rzeczpospolita, 1918–1939*, Warsaw, 1972.

Salzmann, Ignacy, ed., *Krakowski informator kieszonkowy oraz przewodnik dla przejezdnych na rok 1925/26*, Cracow, 1925.

Samsonowska, Krystyna, 'Zarys Funkcjonowana Żydowskiej Gminy Wyznaniowej w Krakowie w latach 1918–1939', Master's thesis, Jagiellonian University, 1991.

— 'Wybory do władz żydowskiej gminy wyznaniowej w Krakowie: Z dziejów nieznanej samorządności Krakowa', *Historia, Pismo Młodych Historyków*, 2 (1994): 47–66.

Sandrow, Nahma, *Vagabond Stars: A World History of Yiddish Theater*, New York: Harper and Row, 1977.

Sherwin, Byron, *Sparks Amidst the Ashes: The Spiritual Legacy of Polish Jewry*, New York: Oxford University Press, 1997.

Shmeruk, Chone, 'Hebrew-Yiddish-Polish: A Trilingual Jewish Culture', in *The Jews of Poland Between the Two World Wars*, ed. Yisrael Gutman, et al., Hanover, NH: University of New England Press, 1989.

Shtayn, Kalman, 'Di yidn in krokover shtotrat tsvishn di tsvey velt-milkhomes', *Yorbukh*, Buenos Aires: World Federation of Polish Jews, 1970.

Silver Anniversary 1965–1990, New York: New Cracow Friendship Society, 1990.

Śnił mi się Artur Sandauer, ed. Józef Baran, Cracow: Centrum Kultury Żydowskiej na Kazimierzu, 1992.

Spiegel, Natan, *Złoty środek*, Cracow: Centrum Kultury Żydowskiej na Kazimierzu, 1992.

Spinner, Jeff, *The Boundaries of Citizenship: Race, Ethnicity, and Nationality in the Liberal State*, Baltimore, MD: Johns Hopkins University Press, 1994.

Stan i potrzeby szkolnictwa powszechnego w Krakowie, Cracow: Rada Szkolna Miejska w Krakowie, 1939.

Stanley, Alessandra, 'The Stones of Poland's Soul', *New York*

Times, 19 September 1999, 42–53.

Stauter-Halsted, Keely, *The Nation in the Village: The Genesis of Polish National Identity in Austrian Poland, 1848–1918*, Ithaca, NY: Cornell University Press, 2001.

Steinlauf, Michael, 'Polish-Jewish Daily Press', *Polin*, 2 (1987): 219–45.

Stendig, S., *Odrodzenie hebraizmu w fazie dzisiejszej*, Cracow, 1933.

Stola, Dariusz, *Nadzieja i Zagłada: Ignacy Schwartzbart żydowski przedstawiciel w Radzie Narodowej RP 1940–1945*, Warsaw: Oficyna Naukowa, 1995.

Świszczowski, Stefan, *Miasto Kazimierz pod Krakowem*, Cracow: Wydawnictwo Literackie, 1981.

Szeintuch, Yechiel, *Preliminary Inventory of Yiddish Dailies and Periodicals Published in Poland Between the Two World Wars*, Jerusalem: Magnes Press, 1986.

Szporluk, Roman, 'In Search of the Drama of History', *East European Politics and Societies*, 4, no. 1 (Winter 1990): 134–50.

Taubenschlag, Stanisław, *Wspomnienie z lat wojny*, Cracow: Wydawnictwo Parol, 1996.

Teatr Szkolny w Krakowie, Cracow: Kuratorium Okręg Szkolny Krakowskie, 1936.

Tomaszewski, Jerzy, *Mniejszości narodowe w Polsce w XX wieku*, Warsaw: Editions Spotkania, 1991.

Tomiak, Janusz, ed., et al., *Schooling, Educational Policy, and Ethnic Identity*, Comparative Studies on Governments and Non-Dominant Ethnic Groups in Europe, 1850–1940, vol. 1, New York: New York University Press, 1991.

Trzebiatowski, K., *Szkolnictwo powszechne w Polsce w latach 1918–1932*, Wrocław: Zakład Narodowy im. Ossolińskich, 1970.

Turkow-Grundberg, Icchak, *Idisze teatr in pojln*, Warsaw: Wydawnictwo Idisz Buch, 1951.

Urbach, J. K., *Udział Żydów w walce o niepodległość Polski*, Łódź: Związek Uczestników Walk o Niepodległość Polski, 1938.

Vital, David, *The Origins of Zionism*, Oxford: Clarendon Press, 1985.

Walicki, Andrzej, 'Intellectual Elites and the Vicissitudes of "Imagined Nation" in Poland', *East European Politics and Societies*, 11, no. 3 (1997): 227–54.

Weeks, Theodore R., 'Poles, Jews, and Russians, 1863–1914: The

Death of the Ideal of Assimilation in the Kingdom of Poland', in *Polin: Studies in Polish Jewry, Focusing on Galicia: Jews, Poles, and Ukrainians 1772–1918*, 12 (1999): 242–56.

Weissman, Deborah, 'Bais Yaakov: A Historical Model for Jewish Feminists', in *The Jewish Woman*, ed. Elizabeth Koltun, New York: Schocken Books, 1976.

— 'Bais Ya'akov as an Innovation in Jewish Women's Education: A Contribution to the Study of Education and Social Change', *Studies in Jewish Education*, VII (1995): 278–99.

Werses, Shmuel, 'The Hebrew Press and Its Readership in Interwar Poland', in *The Jews of Interwar Poland Between the Two World Wars*, eds, Yisrael Gutman et al., Hanover, NH: University of New England Press, 312–33.

Wierzbieniec, Wacław, *Społeczność żydowska Przemyśla w latach 1918–1939*, Rzeszów: Wydawnictwo Wyższej Szkoły Pedagogicznej, 1996.

Wordliczek, Zofia, 'Wystawa', unpublished material in the library of the Muzeum m. Krakowa, Stara Synagoga.

— 'Szkolnictwo żydowskie na terenie miasta Krakowa okresie II Rzeczypospolitej Polskiej', unpublished material in the library of the Muzeum m. Krakowa, Stara Synagoga.

Woźniak, Magdalena, 'Żydowskie szkoły w II rzeczypospolitej', in *Studia o szkolnictwie i oświacie mniejszości narodowych w XIX i XX wieku*, 91–104.

Wroński, T., *Kronika okupowanego Krakowa*, Cracow: Wydawnictwo Literackie, 1974.

Wynot, Jr, Edward D., *Polish Politics in Transition: The Camp of National Unity and the Struggle for Power, 1935–1939*, Athens: University of Georgia Press, 1974.

— 'Urban History in Poland: A Critical Appraisal', *Journal of Urban History*, 6, no. 1 (1979): 31–79.

— *Warsaw Between the World Wars: People of the Capital City in a Developing Land, 1918–1939*, Boulder, CO: East European Monographs, 1983.

— 'Polish–Jewish Relations, 1910–1939: An Overview', in *Religion and Nationalism in Eastern Europe and the Soviet Union*, ed. Dennis J. Dunn, Boulder, CO: Lynne Rienner Publishers, 1987.

Wyrozumska, Bożena, 'Did King Jan Olbracht Expel the Jews of Cracow in 1495?', in *The Jews in Poland*, Vol. 1, ed. Andrzej

Paluch, Cracow: Jagiellonian University, Research Center on Jewish History and Culture in Poland, 1992.

Wystawa Jonasza Sterna, Cracow: Galeria Krzysztofory, 1989.

Zalewska, Gabriela, *Ludność żydowska w Warszawie w okresie międzywojennym,* Warsaw: Państwowe Wydawnictwo Naukowe, 1996.

Żbikowski, Andrzej, *Żydzi krakowscy i ich gmina w latach 1869–1919,* Warsaw: Żydowski Instytut Historyczny, 1994.

Zgrzebnicki, Jacek, *Żydowski Kazimierz,* Cracow: Agencja Promocyjna Patchwork and Agencja Turystyczna Wiktor, 1994.

Zieliński, Konrad, *W cieniu synagogi: Obraz życia kulturalnego społeczności żydowskiej Lublina w latach okupacji austro-węgierskiej,* Lublin: Wydawnictwo Uniwersytetu Marii Curie-Skłodowskiej, 1998.

Zipperstein, Steven, *The Jews of Odessa: A Cultural History, 1794–1881,* Palo Alto, CA: Stanford University Press, 1985.

— *Imagining Russian Jewry: Memory, History, Identity,* Seattle: University of Washington Press, 1999.

Żydowski klub sportowy 'Makkabi' w Krakowie w dwudziestolecie swego istnienia 1909–1929, Cracow: Drukarnia Grafia, 1930.

Żydowskie gminy wyznaniowe, Vol. 1. Wrocław: Towarzystwo Przyjaciół Polonistyki Wrocławskiej, 1995.

Index